Realistic & Practical Firearms Training: 2017

ISBN: 978-0-9828099-7-6

Published 2017 by: Spring Morning Publishing

Edited by Sean Cooper

Printed in the United States of America

For training contact Sean Cooper at (662) 719-2840 (cell) or by email at coopersfirearmstraining@gmail.com Web: concealedweaponcarry.com

Realistic & Practical

Firearms Training

2017

**This book is dedicated to Jimmy Gresham of
Pine Grove Baptist Church in Hickory Flat, MS**

Jimmy has sponsored more classes than any other single person in the State of Mississippi. He became known as the person to go to if you wanted to attend an enhanced firearms course. He has been dedicated and worked hard for every class. The people are always there. Their fees have already been paid. The classroom is already set up. The food is always ready waiting for us to partake. While I am teaching he makes sure all the targets are already set up and while I am grading he always makes sure the targets are taken down. While I am awarding certificates, he is straightening up. He helps with monitoring the line on the range and anything else that comes up. We don't have to do anything but teach. We will always treasure our relationship with him.

Badges and Belt Carriers available at market price. Go to:

http://www.concealedweaponcarry.com

INTRODUCTION

This book called *Realistic and Practical Firearms Training (2017}* is actually an update for the book I previously wrote called *The Year of the Gun 2014.* Laws written in 2015 and 2016 made many positive changes but the book was never updated. This book contains all the new laws and all of the Attorney General Opinions written since 2011. Prior to then there were no significant new gun laws or opinions. But 2011 was a significant year because it was the first year we had Enhanced Carry Endorsements for our permits.

How we got here and the history of gun laws was discussed in the previous book but have been omitted from this one. If you are new to the material and would like to know those issues you can still purchase the old book.

State Representative Andy Gipson from Braxton has been credited with the passing of all the gun rights bills since 2013 and his four year streak of success has been helpful to all of us. However, in his fifth year he did not introduce any new gun legislation. Maybe he was just sitting this one out.

The only legislation introduced this year was introduced by a new Legislator from DeSoto County (Dana Criswell). It would have taken Stun Guns out of our Concealed Carry Law which never made any sense in the first place. It is not in the list of Deadly Weapons because it is not considered a deadly weapon, but rather a non-lethal or less than lethal weapon. It is also odd that no permit is required in MS to carry one but the permit is only good for pistols, revolvers and stun guns. It made perfect sense to take it out. I guess Dana has just not gotten the support he needs. He is a gun news editor and licensed gun dealer. But you know politics. Until he gets assigned a good committee that has to do with gun rights he will be less effective. Not his fault. He believes in our gun rights and will go far as long as he sticks with it.

TABLE OF CONTENTS

Chapters	Title	Page #

Chapter One
Gun Safety and Reality

I would be remiss if I wrote this book without addressing the issue of gun safety. I don't want anybody to think that I am against gun safety. I am not. But I think some people take safety a bit too far. You may say you can never take safety too far. If that's what you think, it may cost you your life.

The NRA trained instructors are usually the ones that I think go overboard with the issue. NRA drills it in their heads and I believe it is mostly to protect them, not the person teaching. For instance, some love to do things like jump on the floor and act like an idiot if you waive a gun across them knowing darn well the gun is unloaded, the slide is locked back and there is no magazine in it. I was criticized for doing the same thing when I awarded a gun to Representative Andy Gipson at an appreciation dinner in Florence a few years ago (see photo next page). I had already shown the gun to the NRA host and her boss in its case with the slide back and the magazine out and also in the case. I knew it was unloaded and she knew it was unloaded. My mistake was not holding it up and showing everybody it was a safe weapon. I had even taken it out of the box and had it engraved for him. Would I have loaded it and fired it before giving it to him as a gift? But anybody that knows me would know I would not have endangered that crowd. Imagine going to Bass Pro on a busy night and asking to look at a handgun. There are numerous people behind the counter walking back and forth and people all around you. The times you could examine the gun without somebody crossing the muzzle are few and far between. What really kills me is these guys who do "how to" videos on Youtube. They are quick to show you the magazine is empty, the gun is unloaded and the slide is back. Give me a break; do they think they are going to shoot you through the TV screen? It is NRA mentality.

If you use the mentality that no matter what, you can never, ever have the barrel of a weapon pointed at you, then you should never have a desire to be a gunsmith or assistant. My NRA certified enhanced instructor handed out 7 guns to us students to examine and pass around while we were in a small semi-circle at a bar. You should never walk in front of a car with dark windows, somebody could be in it and punch the accelerator and run over you. Imagine all the police and military teams that run in groups where there is no way possible you could go through the day without a gun having been pointed at you. That person wouldn't want to get in an airplane without a parachute. I just think it can be carried too far

I believe NRA is more concerned about liability than they are safety. One reason I believe that is the news that they don't "require" shooters to wear eye protection or ear protection. They only "recommend" it because of legal issues according to their head trainer in Washington, DC. I had to e-mail him to verify that. I can't believe what a stupid approach that is. A person could easily lose an eye or have long term hearing damage. So it seems that sometimes they worry about things they shouldn't worry about yet they don't include requirements that they should be worried about. I am not an enemy of NRA. I just write about what I see and know to be a fact.

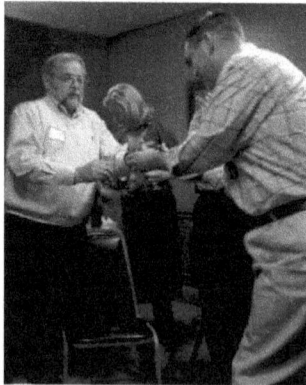

Pictured from left to right, Rick Ward presenting gun to Andy Gipson

John Howard 6/11/12

To: rickhoward7@hotmail.com

Actions

NRA does not "require" eye and ear protection. It is a recommendation.

There is a pre course assessment instructors can put potential students through to see if they possess the basic skills necessary to attend the Basic Personal Protection In The Home course. Another option would be to have potential students attend the Basic Pistol or FIRST Steps Pistol course first.

Sincerely,

John Howard

National Rifle Association of America

NRA National Instructor Trainer

11250 Waples Mill Road

Fairfax, VA 22030

703 267 1423

The next issue was not seen as a safety issue at all, rather a "political" issue on how they were founded. He said the instructors teaching their courses for these permits COULD NOT use silhouette targets. That is "off the record" because they were founded on hunting and marksmanship, not taking lives. Well, here's a news flash for you. The Second Amendment has absolutely nothing to do with hunting. Our State Constitution allows us to bear arms in defense of our homes, our property and our lives. Well tell me this, when is the last time either of them have ever been endangered by a bull's-eye or picture of a deer? I see not practicing on a silhouette target as a safety risk factor to you, the shooter. This is not a hunter safety education course, rather a self-defense course.

John Howard 1/27/14
To: nclhoward67@hotmail.com

Who is the POC for MS to notify? We only notify if we have the single point of contact issuing authority

Silhouettes are not authorized The actual targets to be used are in the appropriate lesson plans PPITH authorizes the D1, or AP1 action targets, the same target used for Bianchi Cup

We are evaluating this, but currently, the information you received is correct No silhouettes

Sincerely

John Howard
National Manager
NRA Training Department
11250 Waples Mill Road
Fairfax, VA 22030
703 267 1423

I also spoke to the NRA legislative liaison when we were trying to get statutory changes in the legislature to allow a portion of the enhanced carry classes done via video/internet. She told me NRA didn't allow that because of liability issues. I deducted from that conversation that NRA would not back a law in Mississippi that allowed it. I explained to her that the Game and Fish Commission already had the classroom portion of the Hunter Safety Course online and I had discussed it with Representative Andy Gipson whose own son had taken it online. Why could we not put the enhanced classroom portion online? She said NRA would not allow it. So, I took it to the Mississippi Highway Patrol, met with their lawyer Tim Smith and the Commissioner of Public Safety. We came to an agreement that those who desired to teach on video would be allowed to by DPS. Tim put the notice of change on the Secretary of State Administrative Procedures Act site in December 2013 and it was approved effective March 25, 2014. I am not sure the current leadership is in favor of it so I made some personal choices afterwards. I have never submitted my videos for approval. But now you can go online and take a Virginia course that lasts about four hours with no shooting and get a Virginia permit. Mississippi accepts Virginia permits. I do not teach under the NRA hat, not certified under them and I don't use their targets or training materials. I love what they do for us legislatively. But I have to seriously question some of their training issues including not accepting video training along with live fire and testing.

I have people ask me sometimes about teaching gun safety in the home. I don't teach that. People tell me they are worried about their kids with guns in the home. My response to that is that it is your responsibility to teach your kids what they should and should not do.

If I were a stove salesman, I wouldn't come into your home and try to teach your kids not to touch the hot eye. If I were an electrician installing a new outlet in your home, I wouldn't teach you or your kids not to stick paper clips in it. I wouldn't tell you that you shouldn't play with fire extinguishers either. We had a man a few years ago that was killed by picking up an old one not far from my house and it blew up killing him.

There are inherent dangers around your house that you as an adult know you shouldn't mess with. You either learned that the hard way, from your parents or simply by common sense.

I teach people to be safe on the range and I demand it. I go out of my way to make sure it happens and is adhered to but I don't teach safety courses and have no desire to do so. I raised three kids and shared my house with my wife of over 38 years without once ever having to tell them not to touch guns. I came home after working on patrol and hung my gun on my bedpost where it would be immediately accessible to me, loaded and unsecured. It was never a problem in my home. If it is in yours, I suspect it is a disciplinary problem.

I teach classes that help you to defend your life. Contrary to popular belief, that is the same in your home or outside your home. You have to be aware of your surroundings, be vigilant and have your weapon immediately accessible to be able to defend against an attacker. If your weapon is in one place and your ammo is in another, you won't be able to save your life. If your gun has a trigger lock or is inside a lock box and a burglar breaks in, you will never have time to get access to your gun and your entire family may die. You have to decide what you want, safety or security and I guarantee you that if you give in on either, the other will suffer.

About three years ago I received a call from Representative Andy Gipson asking me if I had read an article that came out in the Clarion Ledger Newspaper that morning. He explained that they rated Mississippi second only to Louisiana in Gun Related Deaths. He suggested I read it.

I read the article and it didn't specify whether the deaths were a result of accidental/negligent discharges, suicide or murder. But the agency submitting the report was from The Violence Policy Center so you would assume they were talking about violent crimes. But when you go to the bottom of the article and read where the data came from, it came from a 2002 study that wasn't published until 2005. It was written in the journal for the American Association of Pediatrics. That leads me to believe the data had something to do with guns and kids gaining access to them.

You would think this kind of information would have been gathered by a Criminal Justice Bureau, etc. You would also likely believe the data was retrieved for the specific purpose it was reported on. Lastly, you would think it was retrieved by statistics reported to the FBI by law enforcement agencies, wouldn't you? Well, here's a news flash for you. I went to their website and read the documentation for the study. Here is what I found:

Objectives. To examine the prevalence of household firearms and firearm-storage practices in the 50 states and the District of Columbia and estimate the number of children exposed to unsafe storage practices.

Methods. We analyzed data from the 2002 cross-sectional Behavioral Risk Factor Surveillance System survey of 240,735 adults from randomly selected households with telephones in the 50 states and the District of Columbia.

This 12 year old data should have been used for the purpose it was solicited. A report this old is HISTORY, not newsworthy and solicited in the name of safety, but sold in the name of deaths by guns, a violence issue. I want to make another point about gun safety. Plastic guns come to mind. Toy handguns and assault rifles are made to look so realistic now. In years past they weren't and one thing that commonly set a toy gun apart from a real gun was the color. Most toy guns were made of plastic and colored orange or blue or whatever but clearly looked like toy guns. Now most toy guns are so realistic (including air soft and pellet) guns that you have to really look close to tell the difference and it is very unlikely that a child could tell the difference. I think that alone poses a threat for people who have both real guns and toy guns in their home unless the real guns are properly guarded.

On the flip side of the coin though, now we see real guns that are made or colored to look like toy guns. I remember the first .22 rifle I saw at a gun show that was short like a toy, but it was also pink like a toy and I thought it was a toy. Now they are commonly sold at Wal-Mart for under $100.

It is not uncommon at all now to see real handguns that resemble toys if for no other reason, the color itself. I have seen pink, purple, rainbow, green, you name it and I have even seen guns painted like the American flag. What would a child think about that?

Another point I would like to make is that a criminal may approach you to rob you or whatever and you are able to draw your gun on him. He may not be aware of multi-colored guns because he is probably a convicted felon anyway and doesn't shop for handguns on the open market. He may look at that little pink gun of yours and laugh thinking it isn't real. The fact that he thinks that, might make him continue his aggression toward you and you will be forced into a shooting that might have been avoided if you would have had a real looking gun that commands respect on site.

Remember the Crocodile Dundee movie when the thug on the street pulled a small knife on him and Dundee whipped out that very scary, big old Bouie knife saying, "That's not a knife, this is a knife."

I think having a gun in your house that you use for self-protection is a necessity. But I also feel that instant access to it is a necessity.

So what does that mean for safety and the ability to protect yourself and your family? I think that clearly paints a picture that you cannot have both. I am not talking about a gun collection or your hunting guns. I am talking about the gun you choose to grab at the last second to save your life.

I don't think in most cases safety can be a physical fix. It has to be a learned fix and we are responsible for knowing that our children know the difference between toy guns and real guns. They must know the difference in what they can do and can't do with real guns, even if they are inadvertently left out. Otherwise you may as well let your kids play with snakes and not insure that they know the difference between the poisonous ones or the non-venomous. Most of us would just tell our kids not to touch any of them and to know that even getting close to them could be dangerous just like guns.

Some people recommend a shotgun for home protection. While it is certainly effective, it may not be the best choice for people other than the breadwinner. If you want "scatter power" and don't feel you could maneuver a long gun, you might want to consider one of the handguns that shoot shot shells or cartridges.

Taurus has made them for a while. Smith and Wesson makes one with a larger price tag. They usually have court names like, Judge, Prosecutor, etc.

The next couple of pages will depict the rules I have about guns in general and how they must be handled on my range.

SAFETY ISSUES I PRESCRIBE

Most important thing about handling a firearm is SAFETY
Always assume a gun is loaded before you pick it up
Maintain that assumption until you know otherwise
Never point the muzzle of the gun at anybody (loaded or not)
Never look down the barrel unless cleaning, inspecting (or repairing)
Always hand a gun to somebody else open and empty
Never put your finger in the trigger guard until you are ready to shoot
In the event of a jam in a semi-auto, use slap, rack or slap, rack, rack, procedures
(if live round tries to feed into one in the barrel, drop magazine first)
Always try to clear your jam or misfire yourself first without assistance
If unable to clear a mechanical problem on range, raise your non-firing hand
& keep the muzzle pointed down range; don't turn around
Move down range only as a group after told to do so, move back the same way
Anyone can yell "cease fire" for safety issue and everybody freezes
Always wear hearing and eye protection on the range
Listen and obey every command from the instructor
Never take any mind-altering drugs before going to range
Never draw your gun on the range unless you are on the shooting line
Once drawn, the muzzle will never go anywhere other than the holster/target
No horseplay on the range of any kind/no use of cell phones/no smoking
When the instructor speaks....nobody else does without raising a hand
Never consume alcohol prior to picking up a gun/no smoking on range
Always make sure your gun is in good operable order/allow inspection

No reloads allowed on my range (have had lead lodged in barrels twice)
Should provide emergency contact name/numbers prior to shooting
Should advise us of any allergies to drugs used for emergency treatment
You must sign a waiver for injuries before going onto the range
Never, ever turn around on the line with your gun turning also
Recommend electronic hearing protectors so you can hear all commands
If you are on the line and feel dizzy or overheated, tell the instructor NOW

If you enjoyed the course and would like to see others become more able to save their lives or the lives of their families, please advise your friends, family, neighbors, co-workers, club members, church members and anyone else you can think of.

Chapter Two
Guns, Bells and Whistles

This chapter will have what I consider good information but with limited detail. People often ask me what kind of gun, caliber, ammo, holster, sights, laser, lights and so on they should buy. I don't recommend brands as a rule but I suggest comfort and feel more than anything. Let's go down the list and I will give my recommendation.

Gun - What kind of gun should I buy? Everybody knows that's a loaded question...no pun intended. However, my answer is very simple. That is to buy a gun that you will carry all the time. If it isso big or cumbersome that you leave it at home or in your vehicle, "Murphy's Law" will pop up one day and you won't have it. Then it's like a parachute. If you don't have it when you really need it, you will probably never need it again.

I was at a Gun Show in Pascagoula about two years or so ago and a young man and woman in their mid-20's approached my table. He was limping badly and she was in a wheel chair. They said they had been at a lounge on the coast sitting at a table by the door. His gun was in the truck just outside the door. A guy got rowdy and was kicked out, but showed back up in the door with a .45 caliber 1911 in his hand pointing downward. He was not holding it in a threatening manner but was looking around for the person that threw him out. Noticing him getting nervous, the young man got up to cover his wife and the person in the doorway shot him in the back and then in the back of his left leg. As he fell, the guy shot his wife in a downward trajectory in her collar bone. The bullet lodged in her spine permanently paralyzing her. I don't think I have to tell you that he now understands the need to carry your gun ALL the time.

Sights - Should I get the three point white sights or the Tritium green night sights? My answer is NEITHER (for a "self-defense" weapon). In fact if I were you I would take the sights off the gun you carry for self-defense. The likelihood of you getting into a shooting at 21 feet or more is highly unlikely. If you have to take time to aim, you will probably die. I have found that a lot of people are actually distracted by the sights. This is interesting to most; I prove that to them when I tape the top of the barrel with Gorilla tape from the front ramp to the rear blade. They always have a better score. Another problem with sights is the potential for snagging on your clothing. You will likely never get into a shooting more than arm's length away.

Lasers - Should I get a red one or green? Neither. People that I have observed using them refuse to pull the trigger until they get the dot right on the X Ring. Sometimes that takes up to three seconds as they move it around. Unless they have practiced a lot and developed "muscle memory" the red dot could appear anywhere on the target or even off the target. They move it back to the middle section but they still won't pull the trigger until they have the red dot right on the X ring.

Holsters - What kind of holster should I get? Get anything but a high retention holster. It depends on the finish on your gun, whether or not you like inside the pants or outside the pants. Depends on whether or not you want a magazine pocket on it. It depends on the type gun. Depends on what angle you want to carry it. Depends on whether or not you are a male or female. If you are a female, it depends if you dress plainly or fashionably "lady like." Don't ever put it in your purse not designed for that purpose. The most prominent property crime committed against women is purse snatching. Take your gun to a gun show and find one you like. If you go to a local store, you will get everything a cop would recommend and only the two or three brands that the store has. You will find a much larger variety at a gun show.

That is also true for any of the other items listed here. Stores only carry certain brands that they have dealership wholesale contracts with.

Lights - What kind of light should I get? Unless you are a street cop/SWAT, get a small but very bright light with adjustable beam and strobe that will easily fit in your pocket. It could be very valuable to cause a distraction. The brightness is determined by the number of "lumens" and a good one will be several hundred lumens. You can get those that use regular batteries or those that have a charger unit. You should be able to get a good one for under $100 and they seem to be getting cheaper as they get brighter, some very bright for $20 or $30 but they may not be durable enough.

Ammo - For target shooting or practice, anything you can get your hands on that's cheap. Be particular and follow the rules when shooting metal targets. Comply with the ammo types allowed and comply with the distance required from the metal plates. For self-defense, a lot of ammo now is labeled as such. You should learn how to make ballistic gel by watching a Youtube video. Fire a slug into it from about six feet and if it doesn't penetrate at least 12 inches, it isn't powerful enough. Use 1/4"plywood to simulate bone. You want a large bullet cavity that will push fluid and tissue in an omni-directional pattern so as to cause trauma to vital organs that you may not even hit. The bullet will need to expand a lot within an inch after entering the body. It should not travel more than 18 inches through the gel. If so and you shoot somebody with it, you may very well shoot an innocent bystander after your round passes through the intended target. There are tons of options with regard to projectile makeup, weight of projectile, grains or grams of powder, jacketed bullet or not. Do not use full metal jacket or ball ammo for carry ammo. It could pass through more than one person.

Targets - What kind of target should I get? Whatever you like in a silhouette, but try the different shapes and colors, for skills building. Don't buy the hostage type targets. Unless you are a police officer you most likely won't be saving hostages. If you really feel like doing something like that though, have some target company make you a target with innocent bystanders in the background like maybe a child on a tricycle or an old man with a cane.

Caliber - What caliber should I get to really get the knock down power I want? Well you can watch Hickock 45 on Youtube and see his (or others) demos at shooting different calibers into metal plates starting with .22 and going up to .44 magnums. You can certainly see how far back the round makes the metal target go but I am not sure what that tells you about its ability to knock a person down not made of metal. Some people may say, "Well you told us earlier to get a gun we will carry all the time. If that is true, I would have to get a .22 and that will just make somebody mad. I don't recommend .22 calibers for carry weapons but if you will carry it all the time as opposed to a larger gun, it is better to have it than no gun at all. The first rule of a gunfight is "bring a gun." Nobody ever said what caliber it had to be. The second rule is to get the first shot off (on target) and you will be more likely to win. I used to shoot big hogs (several hundred pounds) we raised as a kid with a .22 short in a single shot bolt action rifle. I hit them between the eyes and they fell over instantly. One year I missed the dead center head shot and hit the old sow slightly to the right as I jerked the trigger. She went wild and tore the pen down with me on it, ran into the woods behind our house and started running into trees. My neighbor had to shoot her seven times with his .45 caliber 1911 pistol to finally bring her down. Shot placement is more important than caliber or so-called "knock down power". The only way you are going to be good at shot placement is practice, practice, practice and practice more.

We have only had one major hit type murder solved in MS in the last quarter century. The weapon of choice for the hit man in the 1987 Sherry murder case in Biloxi was a .22 Ruger pistol. It was very effective.

Over time you will develop good grip and trigger pull. There are other factors in taking the right shot and work good if you have plenty of time to aim at the target. One of those includes breathing. Most instructors will tell you to take three deep breaths holding half of the last breath and shoot just before exhaling the last half of that breath. That is great for target practice or snipers but you will never have enough time in a real shooting situation.

Chapter Three
The Course: Practical and Realistic

I n order to obtain a concealed Firearms Permit in Mississippi you must be 21 or older (unless in military, guard or reserves); must be at least that old. Military ages are waived if you fit into one of the above categories. However, you can take the course early. You just won't be able to be certified for enhanced carry until you are 21 and receive your basic permit.

You need to understand that there are all types of instructors in our "pool" of over 500. Some may be 23 years old with no experience and just paid NRA for their instructor certificate. Some may be over 60 and have a great deal of varying experiences. Some may be competition shooters. Some may be a local cop in their 30's needing a part-time job on their off days. Some may be retired military. Some are just gun enthusiasts. Some are male, some are female. Most of them will use their backgrounds to pass on the same information they are familiar with to you. That could be a good thing or it could be a bad thing.

When I used to sit at gun show tables and sign people up for classes, I would often have a person walk by and listen as I explained how I do this course. Then inevitably one bystander would speak up and say, "That's not how my instructor did it" or "We didn't learn all that" or "We learned to do house clearing and it was awesome, just like a SWAT team" or "I already have my enhanced sticker but I would like to sign up for one of your classes."

When the Mississippi Highway Patrol was handed the requirements of House Bill 506 in 2011 to implement the enhanced program, they had no notice. They weren't prepared for the course and met with other law enforcement officers who had varying ideas of the type training you should receive and the number of hours, days and even weeks the course should be. Nobody could agree.

The end result was 8 hours of training given by anybody the Highway Patrol approved of based on experience, training and/or their subjective judgment. In one sense I like that because I am not an NRA instructor, never have been one, never want to be one. That is because they were founded on principals of the 2nd Amendment but are politically guided. They don't want their instructors to use silhouette targets. Ear and Eye protection is suggested but not mandated. They have too many different types of classes that seem to solicit money more so than experienced shooters and place little emphasis on "self-defense." If they had chosen one cookie cutter, NRA would have been it. And if you are an NRA instructor you are expected to use their training materials, etc. which again have little to no emphasis on self-defense. I didn't want to be tied to those requirements (that many NRA instructors ignore). You could lose your certification for ignoring though.

Not by law, but an agreement between the instructor and Highway Patrol is that you teach at least one hour of Mississippi Law from two or three statutes. That might have been okay in 2011 when it was decided, but since then we have had multiple changes in the various gun statutes and one hour is not enough. I fear that people will go to jail that have enhanced endorsements on their permits because they didn't know the law. I hate to say this but I have had a number of active and former police officers take this class and don't know enough about the law to fill a page in large script with double spacing. Sadly, those instructors that haven't been in law enforcement know less than that.

But let's look at how the backgrounds of people affect the training you receive. If you go to enhanced training and the instructor stands over you with a beeping timer, his primary background and interest is in competition shooting. But he and his friends shoot all the time. They are fanatics at it. They want nothing more than to get faster and more accurate on shooting targets that they often engage but running towards them and shooting as fast and as accurately as they can. There is nothing wrong with their field. But from what I have seen, the average person who comes to the Enhanced Carry Classes, will never practice enough to be that proficient. Good on them if they do! But I would guess that 99 of 100 will not.

You only have eight hours to teach a class and you have to eat in between, often travel to a range from the classroom, set up targets, grade and record them afterwards, sometimes deal with inclement weather. You have to listen to an hour or so on gun laws and another hour or two on gun nomenclature, gun safety and safety on the range along with the other topics you need to know. At the range you are going to have dud ammo, guns that jam, students unfamiliar with their guns, elderly people, many with bent arthritic fingers and so on. As far as I am concerned, you should keep that timer in your car for another day. These people are not ready for speed drawing and shooting yet. It is certainly a wonderful trait to have but it will take much practice. You don't have time for that in that eight hour day. I have no doubt that some of my competition friends (and enemies) will disagree. That's fine, but use common sense. Speed and accuracy will come with practice. You need to learn all the basics you can in that eight hours, both classroom and range material.

Another problem I see from instructors with competition backgrounds is that they like to have you run forward engaging a target. This is also a problem with instructors who have law enforcement backgrounds. Always train the way you are going to act in a real situation and act the way you were trained when that time comes. If you start running towards a suspect as a private citizen in my mind, you have lost yours. You carry a gun for DEFENSE only. You do not close the distance between you and the suspect. You do not run after somebody as if to arrest them. In almost every situation, your best reaction to a man trying to kill you is to take cover while drawing your weapon or put as much distance between you and him as possible. You don't have the authority to shoot a fleeing felon. You only have the authority to use deadly force when you feel and can articulate (at least to your lawyer) why you chose that option. This is a subject I could write an entire book on. If you shoot somebody for any reason other than self-defense, such as stealing your motorcycle and you pop a cap on him before he gets out of the driveway, your life was in no danger. You are shooting him to punish him and if that is what you are doing, you will likely end up in jail. There are times when people get away with killing somebody over a property crime but they are few and far between. They also have special circumstances that posed some doubt in the jury's mind. The best I can say is DON'T DO IT! Call your insurance company and get another motorcycle. The money you will spend on a civil suit and maybe criminal charges could buy you a truck load of motorcycles. That is not legal advice. I am not an attorney and can't give it but I bet if you confronted your attorney with the same or similar circumstances he would tell you the same thing. I got shot in front of six other police officers but I wrestled the gun out of the suspect's hand and he no longer posed a threat. All six of them wanted to shoot him but the threat no longer existed. He did sustain some serious injuries as he resisted arrest from those officers while one of them took me to the hospital emergency room. I will leave that story at that.

I would be remiss if didn't explain my concerns with another instructor who happened to be a law enforcement officer. One of his students told me he taught them room and building clearing and they loved it because it was just like what they had seen on TV. That was based on the assumption that you might come home one night and your headlights illuminate a figure behind the door glass curtain. He said you may have to go in and conduct a room search. Again, that is police mentality. DON'T DO THAT. Put your car in reverse; get out your cell phone and call 911. That is what the cops get the "big bucks" for. It is their job. They are trained, have the authority to pursue somebody and hopefully have help only minutes away when called. It is very dangerous for one person to conduct a home search. As you are in the hallway with your back to one door as you enter another, you may very well get shot in the back. It should only be done with multiple officers (and hopefully and aggressive patrol dog) and preferably with more protective gear. Don't be stupid. I don't care how fun it is. Go home later and do that with your buddies in an old empty house using paint guns. It doesn't hurt to spill that "blood."

So you listen to all of this knowing there are no standards required by the Highway Patrol and no set curriculum. You realize that many of these instructors have the mentality that matches their experience and you know it is hard for them to walk away from that. So, how do you do it?

I have a BS in Criminal Justice and a Master's in Adult Education. So I use the techniques I learned from that and my many years of civilian and military law enforcement experience and training drawing from each one, something that would benefit you. So how do I arrive at the curriculum? If you have ever been in a management position especially at the federal level and created a new job that didn't already exist, you have to ask yourself a number of questions to decide what you expect of this person and you take it from there. For instance, you manage a business that is climbing to the top of their ladder with new technology and you are turning out a brand new "widget." You don't have the ability to hire a bunch of experts because they don't exist yet. You have to look for somebody with a certain set of skills. You have to send him to specialized training and he must be able to come back and teach others who had similar skill sets and supervise their activity and maybe do quality assurance inspections on the product sampling the output from time to time. He must be able to work inside for a minimum of eight hours inside a warehouse. These widgets weigh 60 pounds each and the person must be able to assist in the loading and unloading from time to time and be physically able. So this person either has to already know or be trained in making the part from raw materials, training others to do so, have supervisory skills, in good physical condition and be able to stay inside for a long period of time often using his skills as an inspector. Now that you know what he has to do and know a little about him, you have to know what type training you will have to give him to make him successful at doing his job. You will need to verify his ability to communicate his understanding of that job on paper and he must demonstrate his skills in doing so under your managerial authority.

That is the same approach I took here with this class and I don't know of any other instructor who has done so. They are either following the scripts from competition shooting, law enforcement, NRA (which uses a test that is made for nationwide use) and they don't even cover Mississippi law on the tests.

So here is my approach after having said all that. I posed these questions.

Q.   Is this student going to be experienced or a layman with a handgun?

A.   I found that they come from all walks of life which tells me I am going to have to be flexible with my teaching and expectations to best fit.

Q.   Will the person need to know how to shoot from long distances?

A.   I use FBI and other statistics that show most shootings happen within a few feet and those are law enforcement officers who are trained to stay more than an arm's reach from the suspect. (Arm is about three feet, slightly more might be two or three more feet). That happens to be the distance that most are killed. We civilians are more likely to be killed with a suspect sticking his gun in our gut or against the side of our head and we won't be able to clear that distance that police who have control of the scene use.

Q. Will the person need to be able to shoot fast?

A. I concluded that the answer to that was no, at least not at the end of this day. This is the first time some of these people have ever shot a pistol. Given the classroom time, lunch, travel, set up, take down, grading, recording, water breaks, etc. there simply is not enough time to learn advanced skills and no time to practice. A person not willing to practice to hone his skills to become faster and more accurate is not really thinking that he will ever have to use those skills perfected to save his life. It always happens to somebody else.

Q. Will the person need to draw fast?

A. Again, the faster the better but later! You wouldn't go out as a youngster with a bicycle and intentions of being a stunt driver and start doing stunts the first day. You first have to learn to ride the bicycle before jumping of cliffs, spinning around in the air, landing on ramps and so on. This is another very in depth subject because of all the many different kinds of holsters that are out there and the clothing, especially worn in the winter that hinders drawing. A lot of men especially like the greatest thing available that the cops use like retention holsters of varying degrees that require special practice to make one to three movements just to get the gun out.

Q. You train a person to face criminals so how do you expose him them to it?

A. Classroom demonstrations and dashboard/body videos of real scenes. They are all over the internet on Youtube at no cost. Some are surveillance videos from a homeowner during a break in and attack.

Q. Aren't a lot of people unaware of where to even look for laws, etc.?

Y. Yes, that's why they need ready references that contain the laws they will most likely need to know and Attorney General Opinions as well as other jurisdictional (Federal) laws. That's why I update them in this book yearly.

Q. Will you supply guns or will they bring their own and be familiar with them?

A. All guns are the responsibility of the student. They should be very familiar with it when they come to class. But that rarely happens in an entire group so you have to be ready to stop and provide individual training. Some of the instruction should include Nomenclature so they will know they have a magazine and not a clip; know that they hold it by the grip (not a handle) and so on.

Q. If students come from all walks of life do they all know about safety?

A. No, there must be instructions on safety in the beginning and additional instruction on safety at the range. You have to keep in mind that some are novices and some are beginners that never touched a weapon while others are experienced, but you can never get enough GOOD training on safety.

Q. Will they need to clean their guns before they leave?

A. I don't think there is enough time and students will be tired after 8 hours. If anything you can find cleaning, disassembly and assembly on most guns just by searching it on Youtube. Recommend they do that. But when I buy a new pistol, I often shoot it regularly for months without cleaning it at all, just so I know it can take rough treatment and continue to function properly. I don't carry that particular one until I am sure of it because my life depends on it. That is a matter of choice and not a suggestion but some people clean them too often, which may not hurt but is unnecessary and the time could be better spent with the gun empty, practicing drawing in the mirror. It is easy, can be done in your own bedroom, doesn't cost anything and as long as you unload it there is no danger present. The worst thing you could do is get holster wear on the sides of the weapon depending on the finish.

So, I arrived at this decision. I would teach a class that starts with Nomenclature and bells/whistles, and Safety with maybe a slide or two, or a chart on the wall. I often spend the last 10 minutes of the class reviewing the most important items covered in the last lecture. That will kill an hour.

Then I think it is important to spend a little time on the mentality of concealed carry permit holders and their adversaries with a little background by way of statistics and studies. I may pose questions about their abilities to react and ask them to think about the outside influences. I will make sure they know about the need to carry a weapon compared to the likelihood of a police responding in time to help them and just cover a little about crime and criminals. There goes another hour.

I will spend another hour showing them through charts, slides and classroom demonstration how to draw, where and how to hold a weapon, using a plastic training gun. I will demonstrate different stances taught by most instructors but they leave out the most important positions. (The ones you might be in at the time, not the one you are in on the average range fire training). I will also cover the different type jams and how to clear them and how to seek help on the range when they are unsuccessful at clearing them. There's another hour.

My fourth hour will help the students understand factors that minimize hitting the target and how unsuccessful most law enforcement officers are at hitting the target during a shootout. I will provide FBI and New York Police statistics and charts that will make a believer out of the students. I will explain in great detail four factors that prevent shooters from hitting the target when it is a real man shooting back. They are: (1) The target is shooting back, forcing your head and eyes down hopefully behind cover (2) The target is most often moving and if not is (3) behind cover and lastly (4) most shootings occur at night (77%) and it is hard to see the target (or do anything with soiled pants).

After a short lunch break or during (while they eat and listen) depending on time lost or large classes, I will begin with the law in hour five, maybe longer. I will primarily use the book for that instruction following highlights in the law verbatim.

Hour six will touch on Attorney General Opinions and a general cleanup of missed items, questions and concerns.

Hour seven will begin on the range and will most likely last another hour with grading and recording grades, etc. As you can see, there is no time for practice and there is nothing covered in this 8 hour lecture I have developed that wouldn't be needed by a person new at defending his own life or that of others. I used exactly the same techniques that a manager would use after creating a new position. You are now a new employee in a job of defending your life. What I have explained in this chapter is the basics of what you need to know in order to defend your life and hopefully stay out of jail and free of lawsuits.

I do think you should leave the class and practice drawing with an empty weapon. Do so with a t-shirt on, then a button up, then a sweater, then a jacket, then a large coat. Turn the lights on and off while doing so and don't look at your holster. Time yourself if possible.

Then go to the range and practice a technique that you will be briefed on using various size, shape and color targets, doing so close up and farther back with somebody else calling out either a number, a shape or a color so you will have to find that particular target on the backboard. It will help you develop shooting skills.

Later work with a partner using training guns or paint guns, etc while wearing proper protective gear and you will become more proficient at dealing with an actual suspect. Switch good guy and bad guy roles often for a different perspective.

Lastly if you can find one, go to a place where they have an electronic firearms simulator with pre-recorded scenarios that will let you put your skills to work while using your mind to determine whether or not to shoot given the instructions and what you see on the screen. Most simulators measure Speed, Accuracy and Judgment with the later being most important at this phase. I owned a system at one time but sold it later. I trained police officers all over the state with it and we learned a lot more just using it. I learned that there are three factors that impact a shooter in all situations. They are:

1. Time Distortion (may see things in slow motion).
2. Audio Blocking (may think you heard three shots when you fired six).
3. Tunnel Vision (can't see through peripheral vision other suspects off to the side of you because you are focused on the guy in front of you).

Another interesting phenomenon I figured out was how fatigue (or alcohol and drugs) reduce your response time, alters your judgmental decisions and makes you less accurate. Police officers working 12 hour shifts and/or second jobs are often victims of fatigue, especially if they have wives and/or girlfriends and children who wake them up after a night shift to go to their school events. This is an issue that affects our Circadian Rhythm or sleep patterns and many major accidents around the world happen all the time based on this issue. I can run a person through the scenarios when he is fresh and again after a long work schedule in his speed, accuracy and judgment will drop all the time plagued also by the Time Distortion, Audio Blocking and Tunnel Vision. When you add the fact that somebody is shooting back at him at night while moving and taking cover, you can understand why he can't hit the target.

One final thing I learned from the electronic simulator was that when a shooter is faced with a scenario where the suspect quickly draws a weapon requiring a very quick response, it changes the whole outlook. Here is why; your hands follow your eyes. If somebody asked you where the bathroom is, you might look down a hall and then point to show the person. The pointer finger on your hand is following your eyes that are already focused on the "target." In this case a bathroom. If the scenario requires a rapid response, you will very likely hit the bad guy's hand, gun or somewhere on the plane of the gun, but not up and halfway across the body to center mass. The reason for this is you see a gun come out and your brain tells you it is a threat and you draw and fire at the threat without time to re-focus your attention on the center mass of the target.

I may one day get another simulator but you can find one at one of the shooting schools in Jackson. If you attend, make sure you tell them you don't want any police scenarios but those more tailored to the private citizen in defense of his life. Have the system weapon on your body (not in your hand or on a table) so you can react realistically.

Chapter Four
Enhanced Training

Following the passing of House Bill 506, it took the Department of Public Safety a few months to decide on who would conduct the training, how much training would be required, and how the program would run. Meetings with attorneys, firearms instructors, academy staff, and other interested parties took place to iron out the final plan.

I joined the program in April 2012 as instructor number 53 and as of June 2014 that number was 300. Most instructors are part-timers and stay close to home. I am a full-timer (retiree) and travel the entire state. By the end of July 2014, I had taught over 160 classes with over 1,800 students.

The Highway Patrol does not mandate any particular instructor credentials or curriculum. They just require that the training be conducted in accordance with nationally accepted standards but improved upon whenever possible. That left the door wide-open for instructors to improvise and be creative.

Many law enforcement officers and veterans of law enforcement who teach the enhanced program allow their experiences to enter the program often teaching what they have been taught and such things as pursuit of criminals and house clearing as part of their program. That is a function that should be done by a trained tactical team. I think if you come home and see someone through your window, you should back away and call the police on your cell phone. Yes, I know I have said that already but I want to emphasize it. Let them do it.

Many nationally accepted organizations that offer firearms instruction are very restrictive in their methodologies. The National Rifle Association (NRA), for instance, prohibits their instructors from using silhouette targets in their sanctioned classes. Surprisingly, they don't "require" the use of eye or ear protection. Nor do they allow their training to be conducted in a video format. NRA instructors are expected to stick with the traditional simplistic (often static training) required "by the book." Instructors must order training packets from NRA to include tests that have no mention of Mississippi law which is a required part of the training. When I say something more than once, take note.

They also require costly annual recertification and prerequisite courses for different instructor certifications. I think recertification should be every three or five years. However, if you get that piece of paper on the wall and sit back on your buns without aggressively teaching classes, then you may need it more often. There is an old saying, "You Teach to Learn." An instructor who teaches three or more courses each month is far more capable at the end of the year with an estimated 35 classes behind him, than an instructor who subscribes to every NRA class in their book, but only teaches a class once or twice a month (or less). Having an instructor re-qualify every year who teaches a class every month is an insult to the instructor and nothing more than a money-making business with no real concern for quality of instruction or safety.

Since the return of many troops from Iraq and Afghanistan with tactical combat training experience, many young veterans certified as instructors are imposing lessons learned from the battlefield as a part of the program.

Surprisingly the 4-H program is accepted. But more surprisingly, anyone researching their program will find that the methodologies taught far exceed most safety requirements, gun knowledge, and range procedures. The program for young people includes their path to the Olympics. The program is very professional but leaves tactics to others.

Some competition shooters certified as instructors often influence their students with quick draw, run and chase the bad guy, and sometimes attempt to make students believe they can perform faster than a person who already has a gun pointed at them. I don't believe that, but I do believe those that shoot as much as many of them do become very proficient. They may impress their students but most students will never be that much of a shooter and will never practice to that level. Their proficiency will remain mediocre. If you want good competition shooter training, from good qualified people, I recommend Jimmy Callender in Vicksburg (601) 918-8255 or Scott Womack in Magee (601) 573-2006. Other programs offered by gun manufacturers like Glock, Smith and Wesson, Sig-Sauer and others are also accepted by DPS, allowing instructors to modify their programs as they see fit. Each has different recertification requirements or none at all.

Many former military instructors may have a broad range of training. Some teach basic "watch standers" (fixed post guards) who periodically carry a gun more in line with a security guard or duties on an infrequent basis. Others may teach military police officers who have the same duties as civilian police officers on bases around the world. Still others may be responsible for training rapid response forces that have the same duties of a civilian SWAT team. Lastly, there are Special Operations teams who may start with basics and regularly receive realistic type training associated with a wartime environment with "hit and run" covert tactics.

In the end, the student will receive what the instructors believe is best for them based on the influence from their experiences and training. Coupled with the requirements of DPS which include a minimum of 8 hours training, with at least one hour in the subject of law.

Many instructors do not comply with the mandated 8 hours of instruction which pleases many of the students who just want a ticket punched but displeases others who are there to learn and those who want to comply with the laws and regulations. No enforcement of that requirement is ever done due to lack of manpower and funding for DPS.

Whichever instructor you choose, whether it is me or one of the many others, try your best to find one with a broad range of many years experience in all aspects of shooting/training. If that person tries to impress you with how well or how fast he can shoot shinning the light on himself, find somebody else. The instructor should be focused on the program he intends to give you with confidence that you will leave the class with the most information you could have gotten in the time frame required.

I don't offer traditional classes or basic static courses taught by many instructors. I don't teach target practice or competition and don't try to impress you with my shooting ability. I know that you carry a gun for self-defense and I want to teach you the things you will need to know in order to defend your life. I won't be there to protect you when you need it. I want to give you the tools you will need, hoping that you will practice using them and be prepared if that time comes. There will be more classroom than range time. With a Masters Degree in Education and a Bachelor of Science in Criminal Justice coupled with my training, I bring you a program that I would best describe as a Practical Self-Defense Program. I admit there is an overtone of law enforcement, but not to just draw on my own background because I have more years in the military than law enforcement. The fact is, our training should be based on needs, determined through facts and statistics about shootings similar to those you might be involved in.

If for no other reason we can, and should use this type data to conduct training. Let's look at teaching anybody anything. Where should we start? We first need to look at the skills that person needs to do a particular job. Then we need to fashion a program that will teach that person everything they need to know to do that particular job. It may include classroom instruction, practice, hands-on, field exercise, and testing (practical and written).

I don't believe there is a need to re-invent the wheel but many others have done this before. We need to find what best fits our needs and go with it. Let's stop for a moment and look at another issue before we go on. Since we now have the ability to open carry, will you do so? If you are like most people, the answer is probably NO. Let me ask you 3 questions. Please write down your answers (be specific on #3) before you continue to read.

1. Will you open carry?

2. Do you feel that if somebody was attacking you with a gun or knife that you could draw your gun and save your life?

3. What would another person have to do to you, a member of your family, your home, or occupied vehicle before you would be willing to cross that line and draw your weapon and kill them?

So if you are like most people in the enhanced classes, your response to whether or not you would open carry is "no". If you are also like the average person responding to the second question as to whether or not you could defend your life against somebody attacking you with a gun or knife, by killing that person with your gun, your answer is unequivocally "yes". Then when asked what another person would have to do to you in order for you to respond by taking their life, you most likely responded by saying threatening yourself or your family with a weapon or other object likely to produce death or serious bodily harm. While I don't argue with any of those responses, let's examine them with a practical and realistic view.

First, if you aren't going to open carry, you are going to conceal carry or in the case of your home, business or car, may store it, and your gun may not be readily or quickly accessible. Your draw may not be instinctive. It may require thought, practice, and manipulation of different types of clothing from day to day or even different holsters from time to time. If that person already has the draw on you, it is doubtful that you will be able to respond in order to save your life or the lives of others around you.

So let's look at other shooters starting with soldiers on the battlefield. If you were one, your job may have been to chase down the enemy and kill them before they killed you.

If you were a police officer, your job may be to chase down the bad guy hoping to capture him, but it may be necessary for you to kill him.

If you were a hunter in a tree stand watching that deer coming down the trail, you would slowly and cautiously raise the rifle and shoot before the animal ever knew you were there.

If you were a competition shooter, you may be required to run through different positions shooting the targets as they appear in front of you.

In all those cases, you would be the aggressor in an offensive mode. If you are carrying a gun to defend yourself, the word "defend" should tell you something. You are on the defensive. All those advantages you had in the previously mentioned scenarios are down the tube. A person may jump out of the dark or out of a crowd, or appear at your door or sales counter or show up standing by your car when you start to get out. In any of those cases they may have a gun already pulled on you before you even know they are there. You are now behind the eight-ball. You have to figure how you are going to get out of this situation without losing your life. Please don't get lulled into the idea from a hot-shot competition shooter full of testosterone to think you will be able to draw and shoot that person with his finger on the trigger and barrel in your gut. It is not possible and you could die.

Unless you just intend to give in to the person's demands and hope he goes away, your best opportunity will be to distract that person in some way as you duck out of the way and/or attack aggressively during total surprise. Let's face it, he got the best of you by surprising you. The best defense, if you are going to act, is surprising him. You may have a cup of coffee in your hand you can throw on him, be standing next to a potted plant with soil you can throw in his face, you may spit in his face or shine a small bright light in his eyes to make him cover them, turn away or night blind him.

My favorite video to show in class to make the point but keep the students attention and make them laugh is the old Trinity movie clips. Quick draw Trinity stands at the bar facing his opponent, looks him deeply in the eyes and quickly uses his right hand to slap the crap out of his opponent. As his opponent's head turns to the right, Trinity draws his gun and by the time the opponent turns back around, he is facing the gun. It is funny but effective showing people how they need to think of something to distract their assailant. You may just keep glancing over the person's shoulder making him suspicious of what's behind him, or yell out, "look out, he's got a gun." When he turns around, you have the advantage.

https://www.youtube.com/watch?v=Yd8TpzioY6k

I have had male students say they would kiss the guy on the lips to totally distract them. I have had female students say they would pull up their shirts and show the assailant their breasts to distract them. I have had martial arts trained students who said they would jump into an imposing position while yelling out a certain scream to distract the person. Whatever works. A small flashlight could blind them. At that point, you don't have much to lose.

So now let's look at our ability to respond to an attack. First, we must be always vigilant and aware of our surroundings. When we leave a building to go to our car, we can't have blinders on with our car in tunnel vision ahead of us. We need to show a would-be attacker that we are on guard.

But here's our problem. We aren't like the military or police. We can't just arrive on the scene with our guns drawn. We have to first be placed in fear of our lives or in fear for the lives of people around us before we can even draw our guns. To do so otherwise, could be considered a violation of the law by exhibiting a weapon in a rude, angry, or threatening manner. For instance, you drive to your office and somebody is sitting in their car occupying your marked parking space. That doesn't give you the right to draw a gun on the person. However, if during a confrontation, he drew one on you, it would put you in fear of your life and you would then be justified in drawing yours, but probably unable to, without getting shot.

So how fast do we need to be? Studies show that the average person, not under the influence of alcohol, drugs or fatigue, has eight tenths of a second perception time and another eight tenths of a second reaction time (75-80 hundredths of a second usually) or about three quarters of a second. Perception time is when your eyes send a signal to your brain and your brain perceives it as a threat. Reaction time is the time it takes for you to begin to react as a result of your brain telling you to do so. Most of the studies show that females have a slower reaction time than men but that men begin to lose their ability to react quickly after they pass the age of 35 and it consistently drops with older age. Your reaction time may slow your ability to apply your car brakes or draw your gun in self-defense. Combined perception time and the time it takes you to react, at least 1.6 seconds has already passed before drawing.

Let's compare drawing and shooting with hitting our brakes and stopping before hitting a deer on the roadway. If you are driving 55 miles per hour down the road and a deer jumps out in front of you 100 feet ahead. At that speed, we cover 80 feet per second. Other factors come into play like road, tire and brake conditions, and perception time, but most of all, reaction time. Given the best case scenario with perfect conditions and normal reaction time, you would be able to stop in 128 feet. However, we don't live in a perfect world. But add to the fact that this encounter may be after work when you are fatigued, or over 35 with slower reaction time, now what?

Hitting our brakes and stopping when we see danger in the road is instinctive. Drawing our weapon and stopping the threat must also be instinctive. That brings another issue to the forefront. Are you familiar with the so-called high level retention holsters? You may even have one. They come in varying degrees of protection designed to make it difficult for someone to steal your gun when you are not looking or when you are engaged in a scuffle with that person. We see the police with these add-ons and feel like we need the same thing. Some of them require as many as three moves to draw their weapon. They may have to move the weapon a certain way, release a snap or shroud and push a button below the trigger guard. That may be okay for police officers regularly engaged in scuffles to protect their guns but those extra measures will have to be practiced and rehearsed during mock attacks in order for the officer to become proficient with it.

Let's go back and compare this deer in the road with a potential shooting situation using level 3 holsters that require 3 movements to release the gun. What if you saw that deer in the road suddenly and had to react by (1) moving a lever across the dash, then (2) pulling out a knob on the console, then (3) hitting the brake? Would those 3 movements confuse you, slow you down, make you hit the deer? All of those things would take place and I submit to you that the same thing happens with officers and high retention level holsters. A few holsters even have a button under the trigger guard that you push as you are quickly drawing with your trigger finger continuing upward.

Type this link on your computer and view this video so you can see:

http://www.youtube.com/watch?v=zYvAxLX6OzE&sns=em

Go to this link to see how an officer under stress handles the holster:

https://www.youtube.com/watch?v=8pgNUFGmz3U

A police officer is wrestling with a bad guy, who has been beating him with his own baton next to a van. At some point the baton falls to the ground as the officer is trying to keep his weapon against the vehicle and away from the bad guy. The cop finally breaks loose and runs to the side trying to draw his firearm. He is unable to do so but jerks upward on it for what appears to be almost four seconds. When he broke loose the bad guy ran to the back of his van, but seeing the police officer unable to get his gun out, he gets brave enough to run back to the front of the van and retrieve the baton from the ground in hopes of re-attacking the officer. Finally the officer gets the gun out and shoots the bad guy from about six feet and the guy doesn't stay down. He has taken multiple rounds center mass from the officer's weapon close range.

Go here: https://www.youtube.com/watch?v=Cym8vOgb3qU (draw/shooting) You will see TBDEAUX (YouTube name) fire three shots on target, fired in .75 seconds from the time he heard the buzzer on a shot timer. That is, if you remember from reading earlier about the same amount of time we have on average as reaction time which is only the time when your eyes see something, your brain processes it, then tells you to draw. That does not include actual draw time, target acquisition or trigger time. He is in a ready stance with his hand close to the gun, ready for the threat. Go here for a look at a fast shooter.

https://www.youtube.com/watch?v=giSaNiQ-Wb4

I only have a few comments about this law. First, if you want to know how many places you CANNOT carry a gun even with a basic permit, just read paragraph (13). But pay attention to the "NO GUN" signs authorized near the end of paragraph (13) and decide if they apply to people with Enhanced Permits or people who choose to open carry with no permit at all. Also a person with an enhanced permit who goes into one of the locations with a sign prohibiting it would not be violating the gun law, but rather the trespassing law (only after receiving actual notice and refusing to leave).

in a size readable in book format so if you have further interest, I recommend you go to the link.

Going back to the issue of retention holsters, I would like you to read these statistics and ask yourself the cause of failing to draw. I can reason only about two causes. One might be fatigue but I think the other is high retention level holsters that cannot result in instinctive draws without many, many hours of practice that most people won't do or have time to do. Therefore, some try to get the weapon out (small percentage) while most show no sign of ever trying to get the weapon out. You might conclude that the officers must have been ambushed but that is only true in a small percentage of the time.

According to the FBI latest figures, there were 41 officers feloniously killed in 2015. Only six of them (14.6%) were able to return fire against their assailant, firing on average 1.7 rounds each. Of those firing, on average only seven tenths of those firing even struck their target. No information is available on how many of those rounds killed the offenders. Six others showed signs of trying (14.6%) but were unable to return fire, and 25 (60.9%) showed no attempt to return fire. So only about 75.5 percent of the slain officers were able to return fire. Of those 41 officers killed, only four (9.75%) were ambushed. The rest were killed during various calls for service.

Of the 41 officers feloniously killed, 38 were killed with firearms. Twenty-nine were killed with handguns; seven were killed with rifles and one with a shotgun. One agency did not report the type of gun used. Of those 38 killed with firearms, 12 (31.6%) officers were within 0-5 feet. Five (13.2%) were killed within 6-10 feet. Six (15.8%) were killed within 11-20 feet. Two were killed within 21-50 feet. Two were killed at a distance in excess of 50 feet. Twelve agencies did not report the distance of the officer from the assailant. A rounded average of 61 percent of the officers killed, died in 20 feet or less. Had the agencies reported on the distances in the other 12 officers who died, each percentage could have risen significantly, most likely highest in the 0-5 foot category. The 2016 statistics are being assembled an analyzed now but not ready for print. The 2015 statistics have no anomalies but rather compare similarly to past years which show an increase leading me to suspect the main problem is that more high level retention holsters appear on the street.

The only two reasons I could explain these numbers is either fatigue or retention holsters. Fatigue has long been a factor in police shootings. Most have always worked two jobs to survive and their circadian rhythm upsets due to rotating shifts often cause sleep deprivation. Sometimes their deprived sleep is due to family issues with school age children waking them up to go to school events, ball games, etc. They aren't able to react quickly enough to save their lives much less save ours. This points to the real need for us to be able to protect ourselves rather than rely on the police.

Add that to the fact that the average response time for a 911 call in this country is 12 minutes, but most incidents are over in less than three minutes. That too tells us, we had better be able to protect ourselves. Remember the saying, "A gun in your hand is better than a cop on the phone?" How about, "When seconds count, cops are only minutes away?" While those issues are true, it is not their fault. Our government agencies will only hire so many and they often have large areas of responsibility to cover. At peak times they are often behind on calls for service and can only get to you as soon as they can. Remember, the officers were most likely responding to calls where they should have been prepared for the worst or they implemented the call themselves through a vehicle stop or whatever, again they should have been ready. The problem though is just like the problem with us. Things get routine and we always think it will never happen to us. We don't recognize a threat quickly enough and we don't have sufficient time to react. We become complacent and we get shot.

Anything that slows our response, whether it is clothing over our gun, a retention holster, lack of practice drawing or shooting, fatigue, alcohol, drugs (prescription or otherwise) or anything else that slows us down or detracts from our ability to initiate fire or return fire will potentially cost us our lives. I recommend open carry even if you have a permit, for the sole reason of being able to draw rapidly. I don't recommend retention holsters (especially for civilians) for obvious reasons. I do recommend practice in both drawing and shooting from different positions as much as you possibly can.

Now to make sure the 2015 FBI numbers were not unique from the Table 18 link, let's look at Table 36 from the FBI reports of law enforcement officers killed over several years. It was small enough to copy and actually place the table on the page without having to link to it. It deals with the distance between the officer and the offender as well as offender's gun caliber.

FBI: UCR

Law Enforcement Officers Feloniously Killed with Firearms
Type of Firearm and Size of Ammunition by Distance Between Victim Officer and Offender, 2006–2015

Download Excel

Type of firearm	Size of ammunition	Total	0-5 feet	6-10 feet	11-20 feet	21-50 feet	Over 50 feet	Distance not reported
Number of victim officers killed with firearms	Total	458	190	77	69	36	27	55
Handgun	Total	330	173	58	41	14	5	39
	.22 Caliber	11	5	1	1	1	0	3
	.22 Magnum	1	1	0	0	0	0	0
	.25 Caliber	6	5	0	0	0	0	1
	.32 Caliber	4	4	0	0	0	0	0
	.357 Caliber	12	6	2	2	0	0	2
	.357 Magnum	9	2	2	1	2	0	2
	.38 Caliber	33	24	5	3	0	0	1
	.380 Caliber	25	12	4	6	2	0	1
	.40 Caliber	77	41	11	12	5	1	6
	.44 Caliber	5	4	0	1	0	0	0
	.44 Magnum	2	1	0	0	1	0	0
	.45 Caliber	35	11	13	4	1	1	5
	5.7x28 Millimeter	1	0	0	0	0	0	1
	9 Millimeter	92	48	17	11	4	3	9
	10 Millimeter	2	2	0	0	0	0	0
	Not reported	15	7	3	0	0	0	5
Rifle	Total	88	6	10	19	20	21	12

Notice above in the 2006-2015 column at the top you will see that 454 police officers were feloniously killed with firearms during those years. Of those 454 that were killed, 55 agencies did not report the distance leaving 399 left to analyze. 190 (48 percent) were killed within 5 feet of their assailant. If you move over one category to view the number of officers killed between 6 and 10 feet, there were only 77 which accounts for 19 percent of the officers dying at that distance. Move over one more category to 11-20 feet and you see there were 69 officers killed accounting for only 17 percent of the total deaths. However if you look at the highest rate of deaths and use 20 feet or less as a rule, you find that 48 percent were killed at 5 feet or less but 86 percent of all police officers are killed in less than 21 feet. To me, that tells us where and how we should train but most people are not doing it.

A police officer is trained to arrive on a scene or approach a suspect, driver, etc. at slightly more than arm's reach, with his gun side turned away from the person he is approaching. Well, our arms average about 3 feet long, so add a couple of more feet to be outside arm's reach and you find yourself at about 5 feet. Where are they getting killed most often? Five feet or less.

A police officer usually arrives on a call after the fact. Even when he is there, unless it is at the time of a violent situation, he generally responds with little to no emotion because he doesn't have a "dog in that fight." He is simply doing his job and he responds the way he was trained.

However, people are killed over the dumbest things. Unless it is a robbery gone bad or an intentional pre-meditated murder, most killings begin as very minor things. The first murder I went to was a man who shot his girlfriend for only fixing him two eggs for breakfast instead of three. Another one involved kids shooting fireworks and a homeowner cursing them while the mother listened and told him she would have her husband kill him when he got home. The husband went over, broke into the house and was killed himself. Another was killed for stepping on the white tennis shoes of another, making a black mark on it which led to a stabbing death. During Hurricane Katrina there was a man in Hattiesburg who killed his sister over a bag of ice. Friends, family, and neighbors often kill each other. The key to all of these though is that there is a great deal of hostility between each other unlike the cool, calm police officer that arrives on the scene. These people are hostile and lose track of what is really going on, often taking the lives of a friend or loved one. The real commonality though is these incidents are "in your face" type incidents where people are so close they could spit on each other or smell each other's breath.

So you say, "I see all that now about police officers, but what does that have to do with me?" It has everything to do with you if you expect to get trained properly. It tells you how far away you should practice most of your shooting. It tells you the greatest distance you should try to maintain your proficiency and it tells you what methodology you should use in holding your gun since you are most likely going to be well within arm's reach whether you are in an argument with a neighbor or facing a robber who has a gun in your gut or a carjacker with a gun in your ear. This is where I differ greatly with my law enforcement friends who train in full-arm extensions from 9 to 25 yards. I insist they are not learning from these statistics.

Unfortunately there are few statistics to speak of between civilians so we have to rely on the shooting facts from law enforcement against civilian. As in the 2001 New York study on number of rounds fired by officers versus number of hits on the perpetrator, most studies of this type are few and far between, with few compatible studies on a regular and recent basis.

Claude Werner conducted a limited study under Firearms Safety Training, LLC with an analysis of statistics over a five-year period between1997- 2001. A total of 482 incidents where citizens successfully defended themselves in armed confrontations were taken from the "Armed Citizen Column" of the NRA Journals.

Some interesting points found in the study included:

LOCATION:
52% of the incidents took place in the home.
32% of the incidents took place in businesses.
 9% of the incidents took place in public places.
 7% of the incidents took place in and around vehicles.

TYPE INCIDENT:
48% of the incidents involved home invasion/burglary.
32% of the incidents involved armed robbery.

CIRCUMSTANCES:
72% of the incidents involved shots fired by the defender.
53% of incidents involved at least one intruder killed by the defender.
29% of incidents involved at least one intruder wounded by the defenders.

FIREARMS USAGE
Average number of shots fired by defenders was two.
Reloading was only required in three incidents.
Most shooting incidents occurred just outside "touching distance."

We should look at all of these statistics and use them to design our training programs but most people don't. For example, the Mississippi Board on Law Enforcement Officers Standards and Training sets the training standards for law enforcement. They also approve the course of fire "recommended" for officers to sustain annually with qualifications tests using seven stages of timed fire.

Police officers typically use two types of stances in training. The first one is called Isosceles. The characteristics are: feet about shoulder width apart, knees slightly bent, both hands on the weapon, both arms fully extended and leaning forward slightly. The other stance is referred to as the Weaver Stance which is actually just a modification of the first one. It allows the shooter to move the strong leg (usually right leg) back, with the strong arm fully extended and the weak arm bent in a support mode under the weapon. They aim the weapon by focusing on the front sight.

Let's examine that for a moment. If the officer is about five feet from the suspect as they usually are, their arms are about three feet long, their gun is almost a foot long and they lean into it. That puts the gun almost in the suspect's chest where he could easily grab it and may overpower the officer. As if to do his own data study, Reporter Jerry Mitchell published a story in the Jackson Clarion Ledger April 2013 that indicated 60 percent of all police officers killed in Mississippi were killed with their own weapons. What does that say for these stances? Also notice on the chart that they don't even start training until they are at nine feet (three yards).

The course in the table is taken directly from their manual. I would like to point out a few things about it. (Course follows on next page)

Why would you start your training four feet further away than you are most likely to be shot? Why would you extend your arms to put your gun even closer to the suspect? Why would you need to aim if you are only nine feet away from the target and your barrel is only six feet at the most away?

Let's look at another issue. You probably think most police officers are good at shooting, get a lot of practice and so on. Let me remind you this is an annual "recommendation" (not a requirement). Add the times from each stage of fire and you will see that the actual shooting time they get is 110 seconds per year.

STAGE 1 3 Yard Line, on command, draw and fire 2 rounds, weapon hand only in 3 seconds. On completion of time, scan and holster. Repeat two additional times. A total of 6 rounds are to be fired.
Note: After Stage 1, the weapon will be loaded with 6 rounds only. For Stage II only semi-autos will be loaded with 5 rounds in the magazine.

STAGE 2 5 Yard Line, on command, draw and fire 6 rounds, weapon hand only and reload in 14 seconds. (Mandatory speed reload). On completion of time, scan and holster. A total of 6 rounds are to be fired.

STAGE 3 5 Yard Line, on command, the shooter will draw and transfer the handgun to his/her support hand and remain at the ready position for the next string of fire. On command, fire 6 rounds with the support hand only in 6 seconds. On completion of time, scan and holster. A total of 6 rounds are to be fired.

STAGE 4 5 Yard Line, on command, draw and fire 2 rounds center of mass and 1 round within the head in 4 seconds. On completion of time, scan and holster. Repeat one additional time. A total of 6 rounds are to be fired.

STAGE 5 7 Yard Line, on command, draw and fire 2 rounds in 3 seconds. On completion of time, scan and holster. Repeat two additional times. A total of 6 rounds are to be fired.

STAGE 6 15 Yard Line, on command, draw and fire 3 rounds standing, drop to a kneeling position and fire 3 additional rounds in 12 seconds. On completion of time, scan, stand, scan and holster. Repeat one additional time. A total of 12 rounds are to be fired.

STAGE 7 25 Yard Line, if range has barricades, they will be used as simulated cover for this stage. Barricades may not be used for support. On command, draw and fire 4 rounds standing and 4 rounds kneeling in 45 seconds. On completion of time, scan and holster. A total of 8 rounds are to be fired.

I had a Dentist in one of my classes recently and I asked the rest of the group if they knew he only had 110 seconds of training per year in the use of a needle or a drill, and only used it once in a career, would they go to him. Of course all of them said, "No" and he even agreed. You might say, "Well the cops get a lot more training and use of their weapon than that". Really? Some might, but most work two jobs and raise families or go to school on the side. They don't have time for additional training in drawing or shooting their weapons. They can't even afford extra ammo or targets. The ones that do practice more are the exception and certainly not the rule. In addition, the average police officer only fires his weapon in the line of duty once in an entire career. If you are an avid shooter or lover of guns, you probably are more proficient than they are. It is a heavy weight attached to their side that they rarely use unlike pens, papers, ticket books, radios, cell phones, computers, and cars.

What about a citizen's use of judgment against armed criminals as opposed to the judgment used by police officers?

Dr. Gary Kleck pointed out in his book _Point Blank: Guns and Violence inAmerica_ that citizens shoot and kill at least twice as many criminals every year as do police (1,527 to 606). In a related article titled, "Are We a Nation of Cowards'?" in the November 15, 1993 issue of Newsweek Magazine, George Will reported that police are over 5 times more likely than a civilian to shoot an innocent person by mistake. But, when you consider that citizens shoot and kill at least twice as many criminals as do police every year, it means that, per capita, you are more than 11 times more likely to be accidentally shot by a policeman than by an armed citizen.

We use our weapons 2.5 million times a year to defend ourselves. However, only about eight percent of those uses result in somebody being shot. The rest are due to telling or showing of a weapon resulting in deterrence.

Again, more reasons you should consider carrying a gun to defend yourself without relying on a police officer.

So what does deterrence do for us? Well let's go back to the attack on Pearl Harbor. Discussions were well underway in Japan between top leaders with the Emperor himself wanting to attack the US mainland. According to many reports, Japanese Admiral Isoroku Yamamoto said, "We cannot attack the mainland of the US. There will be a rifle behind every blade of grass."

Fast forward to post World War II and Korea during the years of the so-called "Cold War" with Russia. Why did we never go to war with them? Because they knew we had big guns, many of them and the ability to deploy missiles to every major Russian city simultaneously and a man willing to stand his ground, so we backed them down.

What does that say for open carry? "Nothing," you might say. Try this example. Like it or not, right or wrong, enhanced carriers can carry guns into bars. Like this or not, but there is no law that prohibits a person in possession of a gun from consuming alcohol in Mississippi. However, we know that some will. So here's a guy with a few drinks. He is now "10 feet tall and bullet proof," not completely inebriated and somewhat in control of his senses. At any rate, he sees some guy at the end of the bar with a smirk on his face and he's a pretty big old boy. But our guy decides he can pick up a pool cue and take him. He grabs it off the pool table and heads in that direction. Just before he gets there, he sees the guy sporting a big old hog leg on his side. He suddenly sobers up enough to know he is not that stupid. The altercation is avoided because of open carry.

Now, let's rewind that scenario and this time that big old boy has a jacket on concealing his weapon. Our "10 feet tall, bullet proof man" sees no weapon, makes his attack and the old boy draws his weapon and kills the idiot who used a weapon likely to produce death or serious bodily harm on him, putting him in fear of his life. Had the pistol been exposed, that would never have happened, even though the assailant was at fault.

If we had kept quiet with Russia during the Cold War and appeared weak, the same thing would have happened.

Let's go back to the cops and look at another issue and examine their ability to use their firearms if need be and handle a situation. If they arrive and a shoot-out is in progress, will they be able to direct fire at the right person with success? To make that determination, we need to look at the police officers' ability to hit the target most often and hit in a kill zone if need be.

One day I listened to a police officer brag about shooting a score of 99 percent and so on. While that is impressive, it is no representation of how well that officer would have fired in a real situation being fired back at. I got into a huge disagreement after mentioning that. Obviously that person had never been in a real fire fight where many rounds are often fired with only a few hits or no hits at all. The cop may even freeze or run. They are human just like us.

I usually tell my students that I predict they will shoot a score of about 85 percent or better on the range because some are avid shooters and others are not. However, I ask them what they think their scores would be or how much they would drop (if any), if they were involved in a real fire fight that could be scored the next day.

Some say due to the recent training, they would be better the next day. Some say it would drop somewhat and others say their scores would be about 50% as opposed to 85. Very few students ever say their new score would be in the 20% range. Low twenties are about the national average. What they don't realize is there are at least four factors that cause police officer's scores in real shooting situations to drop drastically.

1. They are being shot back at and you cannot simulate that fear factor.
2. The target is most likely moving (you can simulate).
3. The bad guy is most likely taking cover (you can simulate).
4. About 77% of all shootings take place in low light (you can simulate).

The first one is what many competition shooters often won't concede to.

The chart you will see next is from New York Police Department. I wanted to use the latest year but when this report was done, 2001 was incomplete so I have encapsulated the results from the year 2000. Notice the number of shots fired. Their hit ratio was 15.8%. Also of those 58 hits, only nine resulted in death.

YEAR	TOTAL SHOTS FIRED BY OFFICERS AT PERP.	TOTAL HITS BY OFFICERS AT PERP.
1988	540	100
1989	823	157
1990	965	220
1991	846	175
1992	875	193
1993	928	173
1994	689	138
1995	1245	255
1996	892	201
1997	708	121
1998	529	302
1999	389	88
2000	367	58
2001†	103	22
TOTALS	9899	2203

Nobody can do their job while being shot at but police have to try.

What about the ability to hit the target during actual shooting situations as you increase your distance from the target? Here is a study done by New York Police Department that shows 69 percent of their shootings took place within two yards (six feet) of the suspect. The next chart also has interesting facts.

Notice that when the officers were involved in actual shootings, their hit ratio at six feet was 38 percent. However when they moved back just one category not exceeding 21 feet, their ability to hit the target drops to 17 percent (less than half of what it was at six feet). When they moved back to 25 yards plus (which is the distance most law enforcement agencies use), their ability to hit the target dropped to only four percent.

It is very difficult to get this information through the heads of those so proud of their scores on the target range. They think they will be as good in a real shooting as they are in competition or target shooting. NO WAY.

Now as you see, those are older figures because this type study, especially officer hit ratio, isn't done very often, usually years apartOnly about four large departments conduct them.

Distances In Which NYPD Officers Were Involved In Shooting Incidents 1994-2000		
0-2 Yards	1188	69%
3-7 Yards	332	19%
8-15 Yards	109	6%
16-25 Yards	41	2%
25+ Yards	24	1%
Unknown	31	2%
TOTALS*	**1719**	**99%**
*Percentages rounded		

1994-2000 NYPD Hit Ratios By Distance Gunfights, Other Shootings vs. Perpetrator, and Against Dogs						
DISTANCE (Yards)	0-2	3-7	8-15	16-25	25+	Unknown
HIT RATIO	38%	17%	9%	8%	4%	2%

So if that doesn't make you understand that you need to protect yourself, maybe this will. Most people see the language on police cars that say, "Protect and Serve." They see the badge as a symbol of authority worn by somebody that will protect them. A north Mississippi newspaper article where the Cleveland Police Chief was opposing open carry quoted him as saying the people didn't need to carry guns into stores, etc., that it was the police department's job to protect the people.

Well, get ready for a news flash sports fans. Go to your Google browser and key in "Warren v. District of Columbia". You will learn that the United States Supreme Court has ruled that the police have no duty, obligation or responsibility to protect you. They have a duty overall to protect society at large. The only way they would have a duty to protect you would be if they had established a special relationship with you. That means they put you in harm's way. For instance they send you into a drug dealer's house that you know and wire you up to buy drugs from him while they conduct surveillance outside. If the dispatcher tries to send them on a call of a barking dog down the street, they can't leave because they have a duty to protect you. It is not just stated in the Warren case but many others as you will see quoted in the Warren case as a reason for their decision. It makes no difference how badly the police botched the cases listed, the court still ruled in favor of the police.

Ninety-nine percent of the people I have talked to about this issue either didn't believe me or were completely shocked that this was indeed true. If you read that case and one referenced that occurred in Colorado, you won't believe how much a police response could be botched and them still not held liable.

Don't take my word for it, look it up. You can Google "do the police have a responsibility to protect us." I just did and the results are shown opposite this page from a captured screen shot.

Go**gle**   do the police have a responsibility to protect us

Web   News   Shopping   Videos   Images   More ▾   Search tools

About 28,400,000 results (0.45 seconds)

Justices Rule Police Do Not Have a Constitutional Duty to ...
www.nytimes.com/2005/06/28/.../28scotus.html ▾   The New York Times ▾
Jun 28, 2005 - WASHINGTON, June 27 - The Supreme Court ruled on Monday that
the police did not have a constitutional duty to protect a person from harm, ...

Police have no responsibility to protect individuals (referen...
www.freerepublic.com/focus/news/1976377/posts ▾   Free Republic ▾
That was the essence of a U.S. Supreme Court decision in the early 1980's when they
ruled that the police do not have a duty to protect you as an individual, but ...

Police Have No Duty to Protect Individuals
www.firearmsandliberty.com/kasler-protection.html ▾
Self-Reliance For Self-Defense -- Police Protection Isn't Enough! ... And we've also
seen that even if they did have a duty to protect us, practically- speaking they ...

"The Police Have No Obligation To Protect You. Yes, Really ...
overlawyered.com/.../the-police-have-no-obligation-to-pro... ▾   Overlawyered ▾
Dec 28, 2011   And doesn't that mean we do not have to obey the police when we ...
Rock say is that the police have no constitutional duty to protect you.

NRA President James Porter on the job of police: No duty to ...
dailycaller.com/.../nra-president-james-porter-on-the-job... ▾   The Daily Caller ▾

So in summary let's look at the police:

1. They are often fatigued/un-responsive suffering from sleep deprivation.
2. They get very little firearms training and often not the right kind.
3. They are not likely to arrive on the scene until after the fact.
4. They aren't likely able to get their gun out to fire at a suspect.
5. Even if they do fire they have less than a 20% chance of hitting him.
6. Even if they hit the live target only about 13% of those hit are killed.
7. They are more likely to shoot your child who is in the line of fire by mistake.
8. They have no obligation to protect you or your family and can botch it resulting in your death or the death of others and walk away from it.

You may fire a couple of shots and feel the need to evaluate the target (suspect) to see if you need to continue to fire, or if the threat no longer exists. All of those issues are what I have built my firearms course on and you will experience it if you go to one.

I see these basic firearms courses or so-called personal protection courses, and protection in the home, versus protection outside the home and they make me sick. I personally think that due to the issues I have raised in this chapter, along with questions, discussions and coverage of the law, we need to spend more time in the classroom than on the range. I think you should show the students what to do on the range after covering safety with them in great detail. But the things they learn are things they will have to go back and practice to be proficient. I don't agree with timing students in these classes because many of them are not well versed upon arrival and some are very nervous, elderly or frail. Practice after training improves speed (and accuracy).

I believe speed will come with practice, and accuracy will follow the practice. Here's an example I often use. I could give you the keys to my car in an abandoned K-Mart parking lot and tell you to drive through the cones I set up at five miles per hour. You will come back happy with 100 percent precision. Then I tell you to go back and try again at 55 miles per hour. You will likely hit all but one or two cones by mistake. But somewhere between those speed ranges, with practice, you will be able to excel. That is where you have found your balance between speed and accuracy. I provide a course and special target for you to go back and practice that will help you find that balance and learn how often you must practice using colors, numbers and shapes.

Before I show you my course, I would like to show you the course required by the State of Louisiana for permits.

i.   Live range fire shall include 12 rounds each at 6 feet, 10 feet and 15 feet for a total of 36 rounds;

ii.   Each applicant or permittee must perform at least one safe reload of the handgun at each distance;

iii. Each applicant or permittee must score 100 percent hits within the silhouette portion of a N.R.A. B-27 type silhouette target with at least 36 rounds.

There is no left hand/right hand shooting, no sitting, no kneeling, no lying, no limited light, no target evaluation and only 36 rounds fired. Everything is fired from a standing position with both arms fully extended towards the target. Please look next to see my course of fire.

3 Feet	5 rounds (from the hip or side underarm)
7 Feet	5 rounds with both arms extended (Isosceles or Weaver)
14 Feet	6 rounds (load, shoot, and move back with dark goggles)
21 Feet	6 rounds (double tap) to evaluate target for more shots
14 Feet	5 rounds strong hand only
14 Feet	5 rounds weak hand only
14 Feet	6 rounds (kneeling on strong knee) both arms extended
7 Feet	6 rounds (3 straight on sitting on bucket/3 spin to side)
3 Feet	6 rounds drop to ground fire strong hand fully extended while lying on weak side

----

Students will fire a total of 50 rounds experiencing all phases unless they have hip, back, or knee issues that might cause injury. Minimum score is 70 percent. Most do much better. They always shoot silhouette targets.

I think this course is much more practical and realistic than any I have seen and it puts the person into almost every possible position he might be in when required to shoot. These are not just static dummy, unrealistic positions. If you are in bed and a bad guy breaks into your house, he is not going to give you time to jump up and assume the Weaver stance to shoot him.

I trained the nurses at Forrest General Hospital who attended to five victims shot at Cucco's Mexican Restaurant in Hattiesburg a few years ago. I would also like to point out that two police officers were killed in Las Vegas a few years ago while sitting and eating Pizza at the mall. More have been killed around the country while sitting in their cars. Too much full arm extension.

A good skill building course using the same mentality as on video games, once mastered, is a little harder and/or faster than the one before.

The targets involve shapes, colors, and numbers. You might take 3 paper plates and leave one of them round but color it orange and put the number 6 in the middle with a black magic marker. You might cut one of them into a triangle, leave it white and put the number 3 in it. Lastly, you might cut one of the plates into a square, color it blue and put the number 9 in it. Then tape or staple all three plates onto your target board.

At first you stand only a few feet away (five feet or less) and shoot from the hip as your buddy calls out the target. He could call a color, shape, or number and it is up to your brain to find the threat. Initially, you shoot at your normal rate of speed. In the beginning, you won't hit every target every time. But when you do get to that point, you have mastered that level and can go to the next.

The next level (2) maintains the same distance, but factors in speed. You should set a high goal for yourself on time and have your buddy call out the target. When you are able to hit the target every time at the speed you have chosen, you have mastered that level.

Then for level 3, move back to about 10 feet or so and start over without speed, but this time using full arm extension. When you master that level, stay at that distance and try level 4 with speed as a factor. Keep practicing until you master that level.

After that, don't come back for a month. Find all the ammo you can and then come back, but next time, don't start at the beginning. Start where you left off because you know what skill level you attained. If you can reach that level quickly, you can go without practice for a month. If not, you will need to practice more often, but you can even do head shots now.

People often ask me about improving their shots with various gadgets like night sights. I ask these questions:

Q. What do the night sights light up?
A. Only themselves
Q. Do you need them in the daytime?
A. No
Q. Are you the type person to shoot into a rustling bush?
A. No
Q. Then you wouldn't shoot into the dark without seeing or ID the target?
A. No

OK, so let's review. The sights only light themselves up, not the target. You don't need them in the day time and you wouldn't shoot at a target you couldn't positively identify, so what good are they? They may be of some value about a half hour before sunset or sunrise.

What about lasers? It has been my experience watching people use lasers that they will not pull the trigger until the red (or green) dot is on the X ring. When they first draw, the dot may be over the shoulder they move it to the middle then down and fire when it rests on the X Ring. In a real shooting situation, they would have already gotten shot.

What about sights at all? If you are going to shoot 44 rounds at 14 feet or less and only six rounds at 21 feet, do you need to aim at all? NO, this training is all about instinctive, point-shoot tactics, with both eyes open so no concern for which eye is dominant and they are based on real life scenarios.

I have taken students who made poor scores trying to focus on the front sight and taped their sights up. I put Gorilla tape on the front sight and pull it back to cover the rear sight so they won't be distracted by the sights at all and in every case I have done that, they achieved a higher score than they did with the sights. I don't believe sights are needed for self-defense shooting. Remember over 50% of police officers between 2006 and 2015 were shot within 20 feet of the suspect and we (citizens) will be closer. Forget sights.

Look who else finally decided to heed their own statistics as of 2013. (I have been teaching this since April 21, 2012).

FBI focuses firearms training on close-quarters combat
Kevin Johnson, USA TODAY 11:35 p.m. EST January 7, 2013
Dramatic shift in emphasis follows a review that found that 75% of shootings over 17 years involved suspects who were within 3 yards of agents.

Story Highlights - Until last January, the pistol-qualification course required agents to participate in quarterly exercises in which they fired 50 rounds, more than half of them from between 15 and 25 yards. The new course involves 60 rounds, with 40 of those fired from between 3 and 7 yards.

QUANTICO, Va. — *The FBI has quietly broken with its long-standing firearms training regimen, putting a new emphasis on close-quarters combat to reflect the overwhelming number of incidents in which suspects are confronting their targets at point-blank range.*

The new training protocols were formally implemented last January after a review of nearly 200 shootings involving FBI agents during a 17-year period. The analysis found that 75% of the incidents involved suspects who were within 3 yards of agents when shots were exchanged.

The move represents a dramatic shift for the agency, which for more than three decades has relied on long-range marksmanship training.

Chapter Five
The Supreme Court, the Police, and Us

Most of us think nothing of the language on many police car doors that say "Protect and to Serve." We might think that if we were in a bad situation, it is the police officer's job to drop what he is doing and rush to our aid and that if he doesn't get to us in a timely manner, we can sue the department. That would be especially true if he screwed around getting there and stopped along the way or maybe failed to look in the window of the house when we didn't answer after a 911 call. That is the way it seems but that isn't the way it is. On the next few pages you will read examples of US Supreme Court decisions or articles about them that say the police have no duty or responsibility to protect us as individuals rather they have the responsibility to protect society at large or as a whole as mentioned previously in this book.

When you have the time, I recommend you Google this issue and read more about it. Then try to apply it to a sad case that happened in Jackson, MS in mid-July 2014. A lady called 911 and very calmly explained that there were prowlers around her house. The dispatcher asked for her name and address, then told her she would send a unit out. The unit arrived and the officers failed to get anybody to come to the door so they left. The next day neighbors found her dead in the back yard of her home. She had been severely beaten, her neck was broken, and she had been shot in the face.

The dispatcher violated protocol because she was supposed to keep her on the line until officers arrived. The officers violated police procedure and common sense by leaving without a look around knowing the lady had just called 911 and should have been home to answer the door.

http://www.msnewsnow.com/story/26036239/jpd-chief-says-911-callto-womans-house-was-not-handled-properly

The New York Times
June 28, 2005

Justices Rule Police Do Not Have a Constitutional Duty to Protect Someone
By LINDA GREENHOUSE

WASHINGTON, June 27 - The Supreme Court ruled on Monday that the police did not have a constitutional duty to protect a person from harm, even a woman who had obtained a court-issued protective order against a violent husband making an arrest mandatory for a violation.

The decision, with an opinion by Justice Antonin Scalia and dissents from Justices John Paul Stevens and Ruth Bader Ginsburg, overturned a ruling by a federal appeals court in Colorado. The appeals court had permitted a lawsuit to proceed against a Colorado town, Castle Rock, for the failure of the police to respond to a woman's pleas for help after her estranged husband violated a protective order by kidnapping their three young daughters, whom he eventually killed.

For hours on the night of June 22, 1999, Jessica Gonzales tried to get the Castle Rock police to find and arrest her estranged husband, Simon Gonzales, who was under a court order to stay 100 yards away from the house. He had taken the children, ages 7, 9 and 10, as they played outside, and he later called his wife to tell her that he had the girls at an amusement park in Denver.

Ms. Gonzales conveyed the information to the police, but they failed to act before Mr. Gonzales arrived at the police station hours later, firing a gun, with the bodies of the girls in the back of his truck. The police killed him at the scene.

Gun Owners of America
Monday, 29 September 2008 00:00
The Police: No Duty To Protect Individuals
(Warren v. D.C.)

The Court's Decision: Appellants Carolyn Warren, Miriam Douglas, and Joan Taliaferro in No. 79-6, and appellant Wilfred Nichol in No. 79-394 sued the District of Columbia and individual members of the Metropolitan Police Department for negligent failure to provide adequate police services. The respective trial judges held that the police were under no specific legal duty to provide protection to the individual appellants and dismissed the complaints for failure to state a claim upon which relief could be granted. Super.Ct.Civ.R. 12(b)(6). However, in a split decision a three-judge division of this court determined that appellants Warren, Taliaferro and Nichol were owed a special duty of care by the police department and reversed the trial court rulings.

The division unanimously concluded that appellant Douglas failed to fit within the class of persons to whom a special duty was owed, and affirmed the lower court's dismissal of her complaint. The court en banc, on petitions for rehearing, vacated the panel's decision. After re-arguments, notwithstanding our sympathy for appellants who were the tragic victims of despicable criminal acts, we affirm the judgments of dismissal.

So how do you think the courts will rule on the Jackson case? Will the lady's family have a leg to stand on? Was the police department responsible? Does it matter? Is it likely that the family will receive any financial compensation? Do you think they should? Do you think the officers should be disciplined? What about the dispatcher?

Appeal No. 79-6

The Gruesome Facts of the Case: In the early morning hours of March 16, 1975, appellants Carolyn Warren, Joan Taliaferro, and Miriam Douglas were asleep in their rooming house at 1112 Lamont Street, N.W. Warren and Taliaferro shared a room on the third floor of the house; Douglas shared a room on the second floor with her four-year-old daughter. The women were awakened by the sound of the back door being broken down by two men later identified as Marvin Kent and James Morse. The men entered Douglas' second floor room, where Kent forced Douglas to sodomize him and Morse raped her.

Warren and Taliaferro heard Douglas' screams from the floor below. Warren telephoned the police, told the officer on duty that the house was being burglarized, and requested immediate assistance. The department employee told her to remain quiet and assured her that police assistance would be dispatched promptly.

Warren's call was received at Metropolitan Police Department Headquarters at 6:23 a. m., and was recorded as a burglary in progress. At 6:26 a.m., a call was dispatched to officers on the street as a "Code 2" assignment, although calls of a crime in progress should be given priority and designated as "Code 1." Four police cruisers responded to the broadcast; three to the Lamont Street address and one to another address to investigate a possible suspect.

Meanwhile, Warren and Taliaferro crawled from their window onto an adjoining roof and waited for the police to arrive. While there, they saw one policeman drive through the alley behind their house and proceed to the front of the residence without stopping, leaning out the window, or getting out of the car to check the back entrance of the house. A second officer apparently knocked on the door in front of the residence, but left when he received no answer. The three officers departed the scene at 6:33 a.m., five minutes after they arrived.

Warren and Taliaferro crawled back inside their room. They again heard Douglas' continuing screams; again called the police; told the officer that the intruders had entered the home, and requested immediate assistance. Once again, a police officer assured them that help was on the way. This second call was received at 6:42 a. m. and recorded merely as "investigate the trouble" -- it was never dispatched to any police officers.

Believing the police might be in the house, Warren and Taliaferro called down to Douglas, thereby alerting Kent to their presence. Kent and Morse then forced all three women, at knifepoint, to accompany them to Kent's apartment. For the next fourteen hours the women were held captive, raped, robbed, beaten, forced to commit sexual acts upon each other, and made to submit to the sexual demands of Kent and Morse.

Appellants' claims of negligence included: the dispatcher's failure to forward the 6:23 a.m. call with the proper degree of urgency; the responding officers' failure to follow standard police investigative procedures, specifically their failure to check the rear entrance and position themselves properly near the doors and windows to ascertain whether there was any activity inside; and the dispatcher's failure to dispatch the 6:42 a. m. call.

Appeal No. 79-394

No Duty to Protect: On April 30, 1978, at approximately 11:30 p.m., appellant Nichol stopped his car for a red light at the intersection of Missouri Avenue and Sixteenth Street, N.W. Unknown occupants in a vehicle directly behind appellant struck his car in the rear several times, and then proceeded to beat appellant about the face and head breaking his jaw.

A Metropolitan Police Department officer arrived at the scene. In response to the officer's direction, appellant's companion ceased any further efforts to obtain identification information of the assailants. When the officer then failed to get the information, leaving Nichol unable to institute legal action against his assailants, Nichol brought a negligence action against the officer, the Metropolitan Police Department and the District of Columbia.

The trial judges correctly dismissed both complaints. In a carefully reasoned Memorandum Opinion, Judge Hannon based his decision in No. 79-6 on "the fundamental principle that a government and its agents are under no general duty to provide public services, such as police protection, to any particular individual citizen." See p. 4, infra. The duty to provide public services is owed to the public at large, and, absent a special relationship between the police and an individual, no specific legal duty exists. Holding that no special relationship existed between the police and appellants in No. 79-6, Judge Hannon concluded that no specific legal duty existed. We hold that Judge Hannon was correct and adopt the relevant portions of his opinion. Those portions appear in the following Appendix.[fn1]

Judge Pryor, then of the trial court, ruled likewise in No. 79-394 on the basis of Judge Hannon's opinion. In No. 79-394, a police officer directed Nichol's companion to cease efforts to identify the assailants and thus to break off the violent confrontation. The officer's duty to get that identification was one directly related to his official and general duty to investigate the offenses. His actions and failings were solely related to his duty to the public generally and possessed no additional element necessary to create an overriding special relationship and duty.[fn2]

Here the effort to separate the hostile assailants from the victims -- a necessary part of the on-scene responsibility of the police -- adds nothing to the general duty owed the public and fails to create a relationship which imposes a special legal duty such as that created when there is a course of conduct, special knowledge of possible harm, or the actual use of individuals in the investigation. See Falco v. City of New York, 34 A.D.2d 673, 310 N.Y.S.2d 524 (App. Div.

1970), aff'd, 29 N.Y.2d 918, 329 N.Y.S.2d 97, 279 N.E.2d 854 (1972) (police officer's Page 4 statement to injured motorcyclist that he would obtain name of motorist who struck the motorcycle was a gratuitous promise and did not create a special legal duty); Jackson v. Heyman, 126 N.J. Super. 281, 314 A.2d 82 (Super.Ct.Law Div. 1973) (police officers' investigation of vehicle accident where pedestrian was a minor child did not create a special legal duty to child's parents who were unsuccessful in their attempt to recover damages because police failed to identify drivers of vehicle). We hold that Judge Pryor did not err in dismissing No. 79-394 for failure to state a claim.

In either case, it is easy to condemn the failings of the police. However, the desire for condemnation cannot satisfy the need for a special relationship out of which a duty to specific persons arises. In neither of these cases has a relationship been alleged beyond that found in general police responses to crimes. Civil liability fails as a matter of law.

So how should the lower courts rule? By that I mean should they rule by using the "letter of the law" or the "spirit of the law?" The letter of the law can be defined as any formal code, rule, regulation, or principle that must be followed according to governmental mandates or policies. In short, it is the law as written. The spirit of the law is defined as a social and moral consensus of the interpretation of the letter of the law. A Circuit Court Judge friend of mine had this to say about it:

"Case law gives you guidance. Look for cases that are on "all fours" with the facts of your case. That means the facts are the same as in your case. If you find one, then you can be pretty confident that is how the court would rule in your case. However, more often than not, all the facts of your particular case are not like cases you can find that control particular areas of the law. That is when the lawyer/judge must anticipate, estimate, interpret, guess, (whatever word you may choose to use) how a court, trial court or appellate, will apply the law to

your particular case. There are instances where there are two conflicting lines of authority. In those cases each lawyer will argue the line of authority that supports his position and the court will rule."

AG Opinion on Letter v. Spirit. *In construing statutes, the chief desire of the courts is to reach the real intention of the Legislature, and knowing this to adopt that interpretation which will meet the real meaning, though such interpretation may be beyond or within, wider or narrower, than the mere letter of the statute. Un-thought of results must be avoided if possible, especially if injustice follows, and unwise purpose will not be imputed to the Legislature when a reasonable construction is possible.*

The primary rule of construction of statutes is to ascertain and declare the intention of the legislature. State v. Necaise, 228 Miss. 542, 87 So. 2d 922 (1956). Intent of the legislature is to be ascertained primarily from the language used in a statute and the apparent object of its enactment. Russell v. State, 231 Miss. 176, 94 So.2d 916 (1957)9. As to language, words in a statute will be taken in their usual and ordinary meaning. Brady v. John Hancock Mutual Life Insurance Company, 342 So.2d 295 (Miss. 1977).

Chapter Six
Deadly Weapons Law

I don't profess to be a lawyer, nor do I give legal advice. However, after enforcing one law or the other for all of my adult life, I became very familiar with those laws and learned how to read and interpret many others. If you asked me if something were against the law, I would most likely be able to point you in the direction of the specific law concerned and be able to reason from a few facts at hand as to whether or not a violation of the law had been committed. My opinion is simply that, my opinion, but I am not often wrong. That is not to say you should act on my opinion. If you need legal advice, you need to contact a lawyer.

I don't often recommend specific lawyers, but if I needed one on gun laws, I would contact Stephen Stamboulieh in Ridgeland. There is one thing unique about Stephen. Unlike most lawyers, he often takes cases on a flat rate fee. He is fairly young, very aggressive, believes in our rights, and will not back down. He is very involved with the National Rifle Association. He is not a free lawyer. Most any work he does will most likely result in charges but I have found him to be very reasonable. It has been my experience in the past when dealing with lawyers that they are very interested to hear from you the first time and take your case. However, when you need to talk to them later, they are in court, in a meeting, out of town, or taking a deposition. Stephen is certainly not like that and takes your call immediately unless he truly is not available. If he can't take your call, he will call you back as soon as possible.

He contacts you while working on your case and keeps you informed of all filings and responses. He is an Enhanced Concealed Carrier and has been successful both in and out of state in representing our best interests. Contact him at: (601) 260-3375 or by e-mail at stephen@sdslaw.us.

Before you read this law I would like to make some comments. Paragraph (1) attempts to describe every conceivable deadly weapon that an officer could use to charge you with carrying that weapon concealed. Of course we know that anything could be used as a deadly weapon and that item, be it a baseball bat, pool cue, sword, bow and arrow or golf club could also be included as a deadly weapon if it were used in that capacity or attempt.

I heard a statement made one time by somebody from the Game and Fish Commission who said there are more hunters in the woods on opening day of deer season in Mississippi than there are at all our collegiate ball games in a year. That sounds like an awfully high number and I don't know if it is true or not, but the bottom line is, there is a great number of people in our state who hunt. The legislature knows that and they also know that those people vote in addition to hunting. They believe our shotguns and rifles were made for hunting and unless they have been sawed off to have nothing other than a criminal purpose, they should not be considered deadly weapons (unless used as such). For that reason, I think a good lawyer could defend anybody who cut a slit across their truck seat, put their full length shotgun down in it and taped it up with duct tape, then sat on it. Because I don't believe that is a concealed weapon the way this statute is written. Does that mean a police officer couldn't arrest you for doing so and claim you are in possession of a concealed weapon unlawfully? It absolutely does not. Just like law suits, they can arrest you for just about anything if they want. That doesn't mean they will get a conviction if you demand a trial, especially if you get a good lawyer. Too many just don't know the law.

97-37-1. Deadly weapons; carrying while concealed; use or attempt to use; penalties; "concealed" defined

> The violation of law is "carrying." Not the Weapons.

(1) Except as otherwise provided in Section 45-9-101, any person who carries, concealed on or about one's person, any bowie knife, dirk knife, butcher knife, switchblade knife, metallic knuckles, blackjack, slingshot, pistol, revolver, or any rifle with a barrel of less than sixteen (16) inches in length, or any shotgun with a barrel of less than eighteen (18) inches in length, machine gun or any fully automatic firearm or deadly weapon, or any muffler or silencer for any firearm, whether or not it is accompanied by a firearm, or uses or attempts to use against another person any imitation firearm, shall, upon conviction, be punished as follows:

(a) By a fine of not less than One Hundred Dollars ($ 100.00) nor more than Five Hundred Dollars ($ 500.00), or by imprisonment in the county jail for not more than six (6) months, or both, in the discretion of the court, for the first conviction under this section.

(b) By a fine of not less than One Hundred Dollars ($ 100.00) nor more than Five Hundred Dollars ($ 500.00), and imprisonment in the county jail for not less than thirty (30) days nor more than six (6) months, for the second conviction under this section.

(c) By confinement in the custody of the Department of Corrections for not less than one (1) year nor more than five (5) years, for the third or subsequent conviction under this section.

(d) By confinement in the custody of the Department of Corrections for not less than one (1) year nor more than (10) years for any person previously convicted of any felony who is convicted under this section.

18 year old with gun, knucks, switchblade, etc., not breaking law if carried in his car, job, home.

(2) It shall not be a violation of this section for any person over the age of eighteen (18) years to carry a firearm or deadly weapon concealed within the confines of his own home or his place of business, or any real property associated with his home or business or within any motor vehicle.

(3) It shall not be a violation of this section for any person to carry a firearm or deadly weapon concealed if the possessor of the weapon is then engaged in a legitimate weapon-related sports activity or is going to or returning from such activity. For purposes of this subsection, "legitimate weapon-related sports activity" means hunting, fishing, target shooting or any other legal activity which normally involves the use of a firearm or other weapon.

(4) For the purposes of this section, "concealed" means hidden or obscured from common observation and shall not include any weapon listed in subsection (1) of this section, including, but not limited to, a loaded or unloaded pistol carried upon the person in a sheath, belt holster or shoulder holster that is wholly or partially visible, or carried upon the person in a scabbard or case for carrying the weapon that is wholly or partially visible.

Scenario: You are offered a high paying job in Jackson. You are concerned about carjacking and other crimes. You consider the offer, but you don't want to take your car. You believe in the escalation of force preferring to hit somebody with your fist to stop a crime. If that doesn't work, you would choose to stab them and if that didn't work, you would shoot them. You are offered a corporate apartment with a bus stop right outside your door to go to and from work. You agree to go, with the understanding that you will carry brass knuckles, a switchblade knife, and a gun on your person concealed on the bus. I then ask the rest of the group if that is possible. Almost all of them say, "No" for various reasons. I then ask them to read paragraph (2).

Most of the students read paragraph (2) and conclude it is permissible. However, some will say something along the lines that the short distance between the bus stop and the front door of the apartment could pose a problem since that is a gray area where you are not in your business, home or motor vehicle.

While that is a valid concern, I then ask them to read paragraph (3) which allows carrying of a gun concealed without a permit to a hunting, fishing or sports related shooting events.

I try to stimulate thought and discussion with these methods and rarely give a concrete answer. I allow them to arrive at their own conclusions and seek legal advice if they intend to pursue any of these issues.

I also ask my students how many of them have a Concealed Weapons Permit already. Many hands go up and then I tell them that none of them do. They all look puzzled. I usually ask one of them to take theirs' out and read the big red letters in the middle of their permit. It says, "Firearms Permit." Why does that matter? Well in this statute you can carry a firearm OR any deadly weapon WITHOUT a permit, but only in the places identified in the statute. However, a permit only authorizes you to carry a Pistol, Revolver or Stun Gun. I think the stun gun issue is in error because it is not even a deadly weapon. Yes, I know people HAVE been killed by them. More people are bludgeoned to death every year than are killed by assault rifles but we can't make every bludgeoning device a deadly weapon, especially if it was designed for another legal purpose.

Slingshot, originally "slungshot," replaced not by a revision in the law but a clerk or printer who thought the word was misspelled. A slungshot is a bludgeoning device constructed of woven balls with heavy weights inside and connected to woven line with a wrist loop on it. They were used in the 18th century by sailors who weaponized their monkey fists used to bring in heavy mooring lines.

I make sure my students know that paragraph (4) was revised in 2016 to allow non-permit carry as long as the weapon is carried in a holster, sheath, scabbard, or case. A person with a permit can even carry loose inside a pocket if desired.

Another issue that readers need to understand about this law is that the punishments are and always have been minor. The minimum fine is $100 and the maximum is $500 but a person found guilty COULD face the maximum fine and up to 6 months in jail. This statute doesn't mention it but the weapon will also be forfeited. A person facing the minimum fine would most likely pay it and give up the gun rather than take a chance of a larger fine and/or potential jail time.

The penalties described in the sub-paragraphs have nothing to do with how dangerous the particular weapon is that a person is found guilty of carrying concealed. It is based on the number of offenses, like DUI first offense, second offense and so on. The penalty increasing is based on multiple offenses. So if you had a slingshot or a sawed off shotgun, the state crime is the same. The feds COULD take the shotgun as an illegal weapon under federal law but rarely prosecute possession charges on arrest made by local officers. They want to prove manufacture or re-manufacture, unless they really want you for something else. It's kind of like prosecuting Al Capone on Income Tax violations. If they could have gotten him on anything else, they would have, but given the opportunity to lock him up, they jumped on it.

I also ask my students how many "illegal weapons" we have under Mississippi Law. The response is usually in the thousands. We have none. Our deadly weapons statutes allows prosecution for carrying any of those items concealed (except in certain places) but the weapons themselves are not illegal. A bag of heroin is illegal. You can't possess it, sell it, give it away or use it. But weapons are not in themselves a violation of the law. You can possess them, sell them, use them or give them away under most circumstances. It is illegal to possess a silencer that is not properly registered, but they are not weapons themselves. Silencers also have to be registered with the feds to get a tax stamp. Many people don't realize that our state statute that once required registering of firearms was repealed several years ago. People often mention the legal issues around Class 3 firearms. Most know that you can buy a tax stamp and own a short gun or a fully automatic firearm or even a silencer. However, what I point out to them is that the Federal Tax Stamp only allows them to "own" or "possess" the otherwise illegal device under federal law. Carrying of the same is something controlled by state law so you have to carry in accordance with state law.

SLUNGSHOT

GUNS ARE
WELCOME
ON PREMISES

PLEASE KEEP ALL WEAPONS
HOLSTERED UNLESS
NEED ARISES,
IN SUCH CASE,
JUDICIOUS MARKSMANSHIP
IS APPRECIATED.

Chapter Seven
Basic Permit Law

There is really only one permit (license) even though we refer to it as the "Basic Permit" (Enhancement is an "endorsement" to the permit).

45-9-101. License to carry stun gun, concealed pistol or revolver

(1) (a) Except as otherwise provided, the Department of Public Safety is authorized to issue licenses to carry stun guns, concealed pistols or revolvers to persons qualified as provided in this section. Such licenses shall be valid throughout the state for a period of five (5) years from the date of issuance. Any person possessing a valid license issued pursuant to this section may carry a stun gun, concealed pistol or concealed revolver.

Applies only to these.

(b) The licensee must carry the license, together with valid identification, at all times in which the licensee is carrying a stun gun, concealed pistol or revolver and must display both the license and proper identification upon demand by a law enforcement officer. A violation of the provisions of this paragraph (b) shall constitute a noncriminal violation with a penalty of Twenty-five Dollars ($ 25.00) and shall be enforceable by summons.

(2) The Department of Public Safety shall issue a license if the applicant:

(a) Is a resident of the state. However, this residency requirement may be waived if the applicant possesses a valid permit from another state, is active military personnel stationed in Mississippi, or is a retired law enforcement officer establishing residency in the state;

(b) (i) Is twenty-one (21) years of age or older; or

(ii) Is at least eighteen (18) years of age but not yet twenty-one (21) years of age and the applicant:

1. Is a member or veteran of the United States Armed Forces, including National Guard or Reserve; and

2. Holds a valid Mississippi driver's license or identification card issued by the Department of Public Safety;

(c) Does not suffer from a physical infirmity which prevents the safe handling of a stun gun, pistol or revolver;

(d) Is not ineligible to possess a firearm by virtue of having been convicted of a felony in a court of this state, of any other state, or of the United States without having been pardoned for same;

(e) Does not chronically or habitually abuse controlled substances to the extent that his normal faculties are impaired. It shall be presumed that an applicant chronically and habitually uses controlled substances to the extent that his faculties are impaired if the applicant has been voluntarily or involuntarily committed to a treatment facility for the abuse of a controlled substance or been found guilty of a crime under the provisions of the Uniform Controlled Substances Law or similar laws of any other state or the United States relating to controlled substances within a three-year period immediately preceding the date on which the application is submitted;

(f) Does not chronically and habitually use alcoholic beverages to the extent that his normal faculties are impaired. It shall be presumed that an applicant chronically and habitually uses alcoholic beverages to the extent that his normal faculties are impaired if the applicant has been voluntarily or involuntarily committed as an alcoholic to a treatment facility or has been convicted of two (2) or more offenses related to the use of alcohol under the laws of this state or similar laws of any other state or the United States within the three-year period immediately preceding the date on which the application is submitted;

(g) Desires a legal means to carry a stun gun, concealed pistol or revolver to defend himself;

(h) Has not been adjudicated mentally incompetent, or has waited five (5) years from the date of his restoration to capacity by court order;

(i) Has not been voluntarily or involuntarily committed to a mental institution or mental health treatment facility unless he possesses a certificate from a psychiatrist licensed in this state that he has not suffered from disability for a period of five (5) years;

(j) Has not had adjudication of guilt withheld or imposition of sentence suspended on any felony unless three (3) years have elapsed since probation or any other conditions set by the court have been fulfilled;

(k) Is not a fugitive from justice; and

(l) Is not disqualified to possess a weapon based on federal law.

(3) The Department of Public Safety may deny a license if the applicant has been found guilty of one or more crimes of violence constituting a misdemeanor unless three (3) years have elapsed since probation or any other conditions set by the court have been fulfilled or expunction has occurred prior to the date on which the application is submitted, or may revoke a license if the licensee has been found guilty of one or more crimes of violence within the preceding three (3) years. The department shall, upon notification by a law enforcement agency or a court and subsequent written verification, suspend a license or the processing of an application for a license if the licensee or applicant is arrested or formally charged with a crime which would disqualify such person from having a license under this section, until final disposition of the case. The provisions of subsection (7) of this section shall apply to any suspension or revocation of a license pursuant to the provisions of this section.

(4) The application shall be completed, under oath, on a form promulgated by the Department of Public Safety and shall include only:

(a) The name, address, place and date of birth, race, sex and occupation of the applicant;

(b) The driver's license number or social security number of applicant;

(c) Any previous address of the applicant for the two (2) years preceding the date of the application;

(d) A statement that the applicant is in compliance with criteria contained within subsections (2) and (3) of this section;

(e) A statement that the applicant has been furnished a copy of this section and is knowledgeable of its provisions;

(f) A conspicuous warning that the application is executed under oath and that a knowingly false answer to any question, or the knowing submission of any false document by the applicant, subjects the applicant to criminal prosecution; and

(g) A statement that the applicant desires a legal means to carry a stun gun, concealed pistol or revolver to defend himself.

(5) The applicant shall submit only the following to the Department of Public Safety:

(a) A completed application as described in subsection (4) of this section;

(b) A full-face photograph of the applicant taken within the preceding thirty (30) days in which the head, including hair, in a size as determined by the Department of Public Safety, except that an applicant who is younger than twenty-one (21) years of age must submit a photograph in profile of the applicant;

(c) A nonrefundable license fee of Eighty Dollars ($ 80.00). Costs for processing the set of fingerprints as required in paragraph (d) of this subsection shall be borne by the applicant. Honorably retired law enforcement officers, disabled veterans and active duty members of the Armed Forces of the United States shall be exempt from the payment of the license fee;

(d) A full set of fingerprints of the applicant administered by the Department of Public Safety; an

(e) A waiver authorizing the Department of Public Safety access to any records concerning commitments of the applicant to any of the treatment facilities or

institutions referred to in subsection (2) and permitting access to all the applicant's criminal records.

(6) (a) The Department of Public Safety, upon receipt of the items listed in subsection (5) of this section, shall forward the full set of fingerprints of the applicant to the appropriate agencies for state and federal processing.

(b) The Department of Public Safety shall forward a copy of the applicant's application to the sheriff of the applicant's county of residence and, if applicable, the police chief of the applicant's municipality of residence. The sheriff of the applicant's county of residence and, if applicable, the police chief of the applicant's municipality of residence may, at his discretion, participate in the process by submitting a voluntary report to the Department of Public Safety containing any readily discoverable prior information that he feels may be pertinent to the licensing of any applicant. The reporting shall be made within thirty (30) days after the date he receives the copy of the application. Upon receipt of a response from a sheriff or police chief, such sheriff or police chief shall be reimbursed at a rate set by the department.

(c) The Department of Public Safety shall, within forty-five (45) days after the date of receipt of the items listed in subsection (5) of this section:

(i) Issue the license;

(ii) Deny the application based solely on the ground that the applicant fails to qualify under the criteria listed in subsections (2) and (3) of this section. If the Department of Public Safety denies the application, it shall notify the applicant in writing, stating the ground for denial, and the denial shall be subject to the appeal process set forth in subsection (7); or

(iii) Notify the applicant that the department is unable to make a determination regarding the issuance or denial of a license within the forty-five-day period prescribed by this subsection, and provide an estimate of the amount of time the department will need to make the determination.

(d) In the event a legible set of fingerprints, as determined by the Department of Public Safety and the Federal Bureau of Investigation, cannot be obtained after a minimum of two (2) attempts, the Department of Public Safety shall determine eligibility based upon a name check by the Mississippi Highway Safety Patrol and a Federal Bureau of Investigation name check conducted by the Mississippi Highway Safety Patrol at the request of the Department of Public Safety.

(7) (a) If the Department of Public Safety denies the issuance of a license, or suspends or revokes a license, the party aggrieved may appeal such denial, suspension or revocation to the Commissioner of Public Safety, or his authorized agent, within thirty (30) days after the aggrieved party receives written notice of such denial, suspension or revocation. The Commissioner of Public Safety, or his duly authorized agent, shall rule upon such appeal within thirty (30) days after the appeal is filed and failure to rule within this thirty-day period shall constitute sustaining such denial, suspension or revocation. Such review shall be conducted pursuant to such reasonable rules and regulations as the Commissioner of Public Safety may adopt.

(b) If the revocation, suspension or denial of issuance is sustained by the Commissioner of Public Safety, or his duly authorized agent pursuant to paragraph (a) of this subsection, the 0 party may file within ten (10) days after the rendition of such decision a petition in the circuit or county court of his residence for review of such decision. A hearing for review shall be held and shall proceed before the court without a jury upon the record made at the hearing before the Commissioner of Public Safety or his duly authorized agent. No such

party shall be allowed to carry a stun gun, concealed pistol or revolver pursuant to the provisions of this section while any such appeal is pending.

(8) The Department of Public Safety shall maintain an automated listing of license holders and such information shall be available online, upon request, at all times, to all law enforcement agencies through the Mississippi Crime Information Center. However, the records of the department relating to applications for licenses to carry stun guns, concealed pistols or revolvers and records relating to license holders shall be exempt from the provisions of the Mississippi Public Records Act of 1983, and shall be released only upon order of a court having proper jurisdiction over a petition for release of the record or records.

(9) Within thirty (30) days after the changing of a permanent address, or within thirty (30) days after having a license lost or destroyed, the licensee shall notify the Department of Public Safety in writing of such change or loss. Failure to notify the Department of Public Safety pursuant to the provisions of this subsection shall constitute a noncriminal violation with a penalty of Twenty-five Dollars ($ 25.00) and shall be enforceable by a summons.

(10) In the event that a stun gun, concealed pistol or revolver license is lost or destroyed, the person to whom the license was issued shall comply with the provisions of subsection (9) of this section and may obtain a duplicate, or substitute thereof, upon payment of Fifteen Dollars ($ 15.00) to the Department of Public Safety, and furnishing a notarized statement to department that such license has been lost or destroyed.

(11) A license issued under this section shall be revoked if the licensee becomes ineligible under the criteria set forth in subsection (2) of this section.

(12) (a) No less than ninety (90) days prior to the expiration date of the license, the Department of Public Safety shall mail to each licensee a written notice of the expiration and a renewal form prescribed by the department. The licensee must renew his license on or before the expiration date by filing with the department the renewal form, a notarized affidavit stating that the licensee remains qualified pursuant to the criteria specified in subsections (2) and (3) of this section, and a full set of fingerprints administered by the Department of Public Safety or the sheriff of the county of residence of the licensee. The first renewal may be processed by mail and the subsequent renewal must be made in person. Thereafter every other renewal may be processed by mail to assure that the applicant must appear in person every ten (10) years for the purpose of obtaining a new photograph.

(i) Except as provided in this subsection, a renewal fee of Forty Dollars ($ 40.00) shall also be submitted along with costs for processing the fingerprints;

(ii) Honorably retired law enforcement officers, disabled veterans and active duty members of the Armed Forces of the United States shall be exempt from the renewal fee; and

(iii) The renewal fee for a Mississippi resident aged sixty-five (65) years of age or older shall be Twenty Dollars ($ 20.00).

(b) The Department of Public Safety shall forward the full set of fingerprints of the applicant to the appropriate agencies for state and federal processing.

The license shall be renewed upon receipt of the completed renewal application and appropriate payment of fees.

(c) A licensee who fails to file a renewal application on or before its expiration date must renew his license by paying a late fee of Fifteen Dollars ($ 15.00). No license shall be renewed six (6) months or more after its expiration date, and such license shall be deemed to be permanently expired. A person whose license has been permanently expired may reapply for licensure; however, an application for licensure and fees pursuant to subsection (5) of this section must be submitted, and a background investigation shall be conducted pursuant to the provisions of this section.

(13) No license issued pursuant to this section shall authorize any person to carry a stun gun, concealed pistol or revolver into any place of nuisance as defined in Section 95-3-1, Mississippi Code of 1972; any police, sheriff or highway patrol station; any detention facility, prison or jail; any courthouse; any courtroom, except that nothing in this section shall preclude a judge from carrying a concealed weapon or determining who will carry a concealed weapon in his courtroom; any polling place; any meeting place of the governing body of any governmental entity; any meeting of the Legislature or a committee thereof; any school, college or professional athletic event not related to firearms; any portion of an establishment, licensed to dispense alcoholic beverages for consumption on the premises, that is primarily devoted to dispensing alcoholic beverages; any portion of an establishment in which beer or light wine is consumed on the premises, that is primarily devoted to such purpose; any elementary or secondary school facility; any junior college, community college, college or university facility unless for the purpose of participating in any authorized firearms-related activity; inside the passenger terminal of any airport, except that no person shall be prohibited from carrying any legal firearm into the terminal if the firearm is encased for shipment, for purposes of checking such firearm as baggage to be lawfully transported on any aircraft; any church or other place of worship, except as provided in Section 45-9-171; or any place where the carrying of firearms is prohibited by federal law. In addition to the

places enumerated in this subsection, the carrying of a stun gun, concealed pistol or revolver may be disallowed in any place in the discretion of the person or entity exercising control over the physical location of such place by the placing of a written notice clearly readable at a distance of not less than ten (10) feet that the "carrying of a pistol or revolver is prohibited." No license issued pursuant to this section shall authorize the participants in a parade or demonstration for which a permit is required to carry a stun gun, concealed pistol or revolver.

NOTE: A person with a basic permit or no permit at all would violate the law for entering these locations while armed but enhanced permit holders do not.

(14) A law enforcement officer as defined in Section 45-6-3, chiefs of police, sheriffs and persons licensed as professional bondsmen pursuant to Chapter 39, Title 83, Mississippi Code of 1972, shall be exempt from the licensing requirements of this section. The licensing requirements of this section do not apply to the carrying by any person of a stun gun, pistol or revolver, knife, or other deadly weapon that is not concealed as defined in Section 97-37-1.

(15) Any person who knowingly submits a false answer to any question on an application for a license issued pursuant to this section, or who knowingly submits a false document when applying for a license issued pursuant to this section, shall, upon conviction, be guilty of a misdemeanor and shall be punished as provided in Section 99-19-31, Mississippi Code of 1972.

(16) All fees collected by the Department of Public Safety pursuant to this section shall be deposited into a special fund hereby created in the State Treasury and shall be used for implementation and administration of this section. After the close of each fiscal year, the balance in this fund shall be certified to the Legislature and then may be used by the Department of Public

Safety as directed by the Legislature.

(17) All funds received by a sheriff or police chief pursuant to the provisions of this section shall be deposited into the general fund of the county or municipality, as appropriate, and shall be budgeted to the sheriff's office or police department as appropriate.

(18) Nothing in this section shall be construed to require or allow the registration, documentation or providing of serial numbers with regard to any stun gun or firearm.

(19) Any person holding a valid unrevoked and unexpired license to carry stun guns, concealed pistols or revolvers issued in another state shall have such license recognized by this state to carry stun guns, concealed pistols or revolvers. The Department of Public Safety is authorized to enter into a reciprocal agreement with another state if that state requires a written agreement in order to recognize licenses to carry stun guns, concealed pistols or revolvers issued by this state.

(20) The provisions of this section shall be under the supervision of the Commissioner of Public Safety. The commissioner is authorized to promulgate reasonable rules and regulations to carry out the provisions of this section.

(21) For the purposes of this section, the term "stun gun" means a portable device or weapon from which an electric current, impulse, wave or beam may be directed, which current, impulse, wave or beam is designed to incapacitate temporarily, injure, momentarily stun, knock out, cause mental disorientation or paralyze.

(22) (a) From and after January 1, 2016, the Commissioner of Public Safety shall promulgate rules and regulations which provide that licenses authorized by this section for honorably retired law enforcement officers and honorably retired correctional officers from the Mississippi Department of Corrections shall (i) include the words "retired law enforcement officer" on the front of the license, and (ii) that the license itself have a red background to distinguish it from other licenses issued under this section.

(b) An honorably retired law enforcement officer and honorably retired correctional officer shall provide the following information to receive the license described in this section: (i) a letter, with the official letterhead of the agency or department from which such officer is retiring, which explains that such officer is honorably retired, and (ii) a letter with the official letterhead of the agency or department, which explains that such officer has completed a certified law enforcement training academy.

(23) A disabled veteran who seeks to qualify for an exemption under this section shall be required to provide, as proof of service-connected disability, verification from the United States Department of Veterans Affairs.

(24) A license under this section is not required for a loaded or unloaded pistol or revolver to be carried upon the person in a sheath, belt holster or shoulder holster or in a purse, handbag, satchel, other similar bag or briefcase or fully enclosed case if the person is not engaged in criminal activity other than a misdemeanor traffic offense, is not otherwise prohibited from possessing a pistol or revolver under state or federal law, and is not in a location prohibited under subsection (13) of this section.

I only have a few comments about this law. First, if you want to know how many places you CANNOT carry a gun even with a basic permit, just read paragraph (13). But pay attention to the "NO GUN" signs authorized near the end of paragraph (13) and decide if they apply to people with Enhanced Permits or people who choose to open carry with no permit at all. Also a person with an enhanced permit who goes into one of the locations with a sign prohibiting it would not be violating the gun law, but rather the trespassing law (only after receiving actual notice and refusing to leave).

Chapter Eight
Enhanced Carry Law

Mississippi issues Basic Firearms Permits (licenses) without any training. However, Mississippi Code Annotated (MCA) 45-9-101, which is the licensing statute, lists approximately 20 places in paragraph (13) that you cannot carry a gun even with that permit or carry without a permit.

In the 2011 term of the Mississippi Legislature, House Bill 506 introduced by Representative Brandon Jones (D) was passed and signed by the Governor effective July 1, 2011. However, the bill's opposition was already surfacing before the law even became effective. It allowed people with permits who received training from an instructor approved by the Department of Public Safety (DPS) to access most of the 20 places previously off limits without training. The bill has been referred to as the Enhanced Carry Bill which was codified into MCA Section 97-37-7. Since that time those with Enhanced Endorsements/Instructor Certified (IC Stickers) have been able to access any location under state control except law enforcement facilities, courtrooms during judicial proceedings, and places of nuisance (loosely defined by statute as houses of prostitution and drug dealers' houses).

97-37-7. Deadly weapons; persons permitted to carry weapons; bond; permit to carry weapon; grounds for denying application for permit; required weapons training course; reciprocal agreements

    (1)   (a) It shall not be a violation of Section 97-37-1 or any other statute for pistols, firearms or other suitable and appropriate weapons to be carried by duly constituted bank guards, company guards, watchmen, railroad special agents or duly authorized representatives who are not

sworn law enforcement officers, agents or employees of a patrol service, guard service, or a company engaged in the business of transporting money, securities or other valuables, while actually engaged in the performance of their duties as such, provided that such persons have made a written application and paid a nonrefundable permit fee of One Hundred Dollars ($ 100.00) to the Department of Public Safety.

(b) No permit shall be issued to any person who has ever been convicted of a felony under the laws of this or any other state or of the United States. To determine an applicant's eligibility for a permit, the person shall be fingerprinted. If no disqualifying record is identified at the state level, the fingerprints shall be forwarded by the Department of Public Safety to the Federal Bureau of Investigation for a national criminal history record check. The department shall charge a fee which includes the amounts required by the Federal Bureau of Investigation and the department for the national and state criminal history record checks and any necessary costs incurred by the department for the handling and administration of the criminal history background checks. In the event a legible set of fingerprints, as determined by the Department of Public Safety and the Federal Bureau of Investigation, cannot be obtained after a minimum of three (3) attempts, the Department of Public Safety shall determine eligibility based upon a name check by the Mississippi Highway Safety Patrol and a Federal Bureau of Investigation name check conducted by the Mississippi Highway Safety Patrol at the request of the Department of Public Safety.

(c) A person may obtain a duplicate of a lost or destroyed permit upon payment of a Fifteen Dollar ($ 15.00) replacement fee to the Department of Public Safety, if he furnishes a notarized statement to the department that the permit has been lost or destroyed.

(d) (i) No less than ninety (90) days prior to the expiration date of a permit, the Department of Public Safety shall mail to the permit holder written notice of expiration together with the renewal form prescribed by the department. The permit holder shall renew the permit on or before the expiration date by filing with the department the renewal form, a notarized affidavit stating that the permit holder remains qualified, and the renewal fee of Fifty Dollars ($ 50.00); honorably retired law enforcement officers shall be exempt from payment of the renewal fee. A permit holder who fails to file a renewal application on or before its expiration date shall pay a late fee of Fifteen Dollars ($ 15.00).

(ii) Renewal of the permit shall be required every four (4) years. The permit of a qualified renewal applicant shall be renewed upon receipt of the completed renewal application and appropriate payment of fees.

(iii) A permit cannot be renewed six (6) months or more after its expiration date, and such permit shall be deemed to be permanently expired; the holder may reapply for an original permit as provided in this section.

(2) It shall not be a violation of this or any other statute for pistols, firearms or other suitable and appropriate weapons to be carried by Department of Wildlife, Fisheries and Parks law enforcement officers, railroad special agents who are sworn law enforcement officers, investigators employed by the Attorney General, criminal investigators employed by the district attorneys, all prosecutors, public defenders, investigators or probation officers employed by the Department of Corrections, employees of the State Auditor who are authorized by the State Auditor to perform investigative functions, or any deputy fire marshal or investigator employed by the State Fire Marshal, while engaged in the performance of their duties as such, or by fraud

investigators with the Department of Human Services, or by judges of the Mississippi Supreme Court, Court of Appeals, circuit, chancery, county, justice and municipal courts, or by coroners. Before any person shall be authorized under this subsection to carry a weapon, he shall complete a weapons training course approved by the Board of Law Enforcement Officer Standards and Training. Before any criminal investigator employed by a district attorney shall be authorized under this section to carry a pistol, firearm or other weapon, he shall have complied with Section 45-6-11 or any training program required for employment as an agent of the Federal Bureau of Investigation. A law enforcement officer, as defined in Section 45-6-3, shall be authorized to carry weapons in courthouses in performance of his official duties. A person licensed under Section 45-9-101 to carry a concealed pistol, who (a) has voluntarily completed an instructional course in the safe handling and use of firearms offered by an instructor certified by a nationally recognized organization that customarily offers firearms training, or by any other organization approved by the Department of Public Safety, (b) is a member or veteran of any active or reserve component branch of the United States of America Armed Forces having completed law enforcement or combat training with pistols or other handguns as recognized by such branch after submitting an affidavit attesting to have read, understand and agree to comply with all provisions of the , or (c) is an honorably retired law enforcement officer or honorably retired member or veteran of any active or reserve component branch of the United States of America Armed Forces having completed law enforcement or combat training with pistols or other handguns, after submitting an affidavit attesting to have read, understand and agree to comply with all provisions of Mississippi shall also be authorized to carry weapons in courthouses except in courtrooms during a judicial proceeding, and any location listed in subsection (13) of Section 45-9-101, except any place of nuisance as defined in Section 95-3-1, any police, sheriff or highway patrol station or any detention facility, prison or jail. For the purposes of this subsection (2), component branch of the United States Armed Forces includes the Army, Navy, Air Force, Coast Guard or Marine Corps, or the Army National Guard, the Army National Guard of the United States, the Air National Guard or the Air National Guard of the United States, as those terms are defined in Section 101, Title 10, United States Code, and any other reserve component of the United States Armed Forces enumerated in Section 10101, Title 10, United States Code. The department shall promulgate rules and regulations allowing concealed pistol permit holders to obtain an endorsement on their permit indicating that they have completed the aforementioned course and have the authority to carry in these locations. This section shall in no way interfere with the right of a trial judge to restrict the carrying of firearms in the courtroom.

(3) It shall not be a violation of this or any other statute for pistols, firearms or other suitable and appropriate weapons, to be carried by any out-of-state, full-time commissioned law enforcement officer who holds a valid commission card from the appropriate out-of-state law enforcement agency and a photo identification. The provisions of this subsection shall only apply if the state where the out-of-state officer is employed has entered into a reciprocity agreement with the state that allows full-time commissioned law enforcement officers in Mississippi to lawfully carry or possess a weapon in such other states. The Commissioner of Public Safety is authorized to enter into reciprocal agreements with other states to carry out the provisions of this subsection.

The primary changes made here are those changes that allow veterans to obtain an enhanced endorsement without completing the training. However, not all veterans qualify. Only those who have completed Law Enforcement or Combat Firearms Training and are willing to sign an affidavit attesting to that qualify for the training waiver. It is well known that not all veterans received "law enforcement or combat" pistol training while in the military. If a veteran has not, and signs the affidavit claiming he has, he could be charged with perjury in the event it comes to the attention of the Department of Public Safety.

Chapter Nine
Justifiable Homicide Law

Under certain circumstances homicide may be considered justifiable in the State of Mississippi. Generally speaking, in order for a person to take another's life and be justified in doing so, that person causing the other's death must be in fear of his life and be in imminent danger of serious, grievous bodily harm or death. In certain circumstances the person taking the other's life may be doing so in defense of another's life facing the same perils. In other cases such as facing a person attempting to break in their home, occupied vehicle or business, a person may be presumed to be facing death or bodily harm but that presumption may be overcome also depending on the facts. This is a very serious issue and should never be faced after the fact without a lawyer to properly advise them on what to say if it does happen.

Using a firearm against any other person is likely to cause death or serious bodily harm. **Under no circumstances** should you ever point a gun at anyone unless you intend to use it. That doesn't mean you have to use it because the individual placing you in fear of your life may comply and give up without having to use deadly force against him. Studies show that we use our guns 2.5 million times per year but only in about 8 percent involve injury or death.

Many of you may have heard the old saying, "If you kill somebody on your front porch, you had better drag their body inside the house, maybe even into the kitchen and put a steak knife in his hands swearing when the cops arrive that he broke into your house, grabbed a sharp knife and came at you with it."

That is a ludicrous statement and would imply that you have no right to protect or defend your life in other situations or places. That probably comes from people like you and I as laymen trying to interpret the constitution which allows us to bear arms in defense of our homes, property, and persons. However, we have the inherent right of self-defense anywhere in this country. Otherwise, if you got into a gun fight across town trying to defend your life and ended up killing the guy, you would have to drag him across town to your house and pretend he assaulted you there.

Still, you should not take my interpretation of the law, especially when it pertains to a life and death situation. I am not a lawyer and cannot give legal advice. Attorney Stephen Stamboulieh has an excellent understanding of this law. You should contact him directly to satisfy your mind on your actions.

Even then, if you find yourself in this unfortunate circumstance, the best any lawyer can do is argue your case in an attempt to raise reasonable doubt in the mind of a jury if you end up charged with murder.

An old lawyer, prosecutor, and Judge told a group of my students once that if you happen to kill somebody, you will most likely want to cooperate with the police. The police are not necessarily your enemy in this case and may not have an opinion either way. They may just be trying to get to the bottom of what happened. He said you may feel you are going to make the cop mad if you refuse to answer questions and you may do so. If you do so, most police officers have broad discretion and might arrest you just because you refused to cooperate. However, sometimes your words are turned around whether intentional or not by a law enforcement officer and those words may come back to haunt you. The old Judge said, you might make the cop mad and you might spend a night in jail, but you will most likely bond out the next day and spending one night in jail would be better than spending 30 years. He suggested just telling the officer you will be glad to cooperate and go down to the station as soon as you are able to speak to your lawyer and provide a statement if it is ok with him.

Some departments, especially larger ones often have a policy that take the discretion away from the officer on the scene of a homicide in the event of one person's word against another or no witnesses or physical evidence that truly tells the story. Those departments usually have the officer collect evidence, interview witnesses and present their information to a grand jury to decide whether or not to indict the shooter. In those cases, the gun is usually taken as evidence but returned in the event the grand jury fails to indict.

Review this law but disregard paragraph 1 (a) thru (d) unless you are a public officer. Paragraphs 1 (e) and (f) apply to private citizens. Paragraph (g) applies to apprehensions and (h) applies to preserving the peace, both jobs normally performed by public officers.

Paragraph 1 (e) is written in what I would call "lawyerly language" and is hard for a layman to understand. I even had a seasoned prosecutor and retired member of the Attorney General's Office told me he couldn't tell for sure what it means. One thing that concerns me is where it says "any felony against you." That could mean somebody stealing your riding lawn mower if the value is sufficient. Does that mean you can kill the person for that?

In June 2013 a young black man broke into the Hinds County Sheriff's vehicle at his home in NE Jackson. He didn't find anything so he went a few doors down and broke into another vehicle. The homeowner came out and shot the young man five times through the windshield at 5:32 in the morning. He died on the scene. Four hours later, the Jackson Police spokesperson was quoted in the Clarion Ledger as saying the shooter would not be charged because under the Castle Doctrine he had a right to protect his PROPERTY. About a week or so later I requested a copy of the police report and it was denied. A few days later the shooter was in the news again claiming he was in fear of his life.

97-3-15. Homicide; justifiable homicide; use of defensive force; duty to retreat

(1) The killing of a human being by the act, procurement or omission of another shall be justifiable in the following cases:

(a) When committed by public officers, or those acting by their aid and assistance, in obedience to any judgment of a competent court;

(b) When necessarily committed by public officers, or those acting by their command in their aid and assistance, in overcoming actual resistance to the execution of some legal process, or to the discharge of any other legal duty;

(c) When necessarily committed by public officers, or those acting by their command in their aid and assistance, in retaking any felon who has been rescued or has escaped;

(d) When necessarily committed by public officers, or those acting by their command in their aid and assistance, in arresting any felon fleeing from justice;

(e) When committed by any person in resisting any attempt unlawfully to kill such person or to commit any felony upon him, or upon or in any dwelling, in any occupied vehicle, in any place of business, in any place of employment or the immediate premises thereof in which such person shall be.

(f) When committed in the lawful defense of one's own person or any other human being, where there shall be reasonable ground to apprehend a design to commit a felony or to do some great personal injury, and there shall be imminent danger of such design being accomplished;

(g) When necessarily committed in attempting by lawful ways and means to apprehend any person for any felony committed;

(h) When necessarily committed in lawfully suppressing any riot or in lawfully keeping and preserving the peace; and

(i) When necessarily committed in the performance of duty as a member of a church or place of worship security program as described in Sect. 45-9-171.

(2) (a) As used in subsection (1)(c) and (d) of this section, the term "when necessarily committed" means that a public officer or a person acting by or at the officer's command, aid or assistance is authorized to use such force as necessary in securing and detaining the felon offender, overcoming the offender's resistance, preventing the offender's escape, recapturing the offender if the offender escapes or in protecting himself or others from bodily harm; but such officer or person shall not be authorized to resort to deadly or dangerous means when to do so would be unreasonable under the circumstances. The public officer or person acting by or at the officer's command may act upon a reasonable apprehension of the surrounding circumstances; however, such officer or person shall not use excessive force or force that is greater than reasonably necessary in securing and detaining the offender, overcoming the offender's resistance, preventing the offender's escape, recapturing the offender if the offender escapes or in protecting himself or others from bodily harm.

(b) As used in subsection (1)(c) and (d) of this section the term "felon" shall include an offender who has been convicted of a felony and shall also include an offender who is in custody, or whose custody is being sought, on a charge or for an offense which is punishable, upon conviction, by death or confinement in the Penitentiary.

(c) As used in subsections (1)(e) and (3) of this section, "dwelling" means a building or conveyance of any kind that has a roof over it, whether the building or conveyance is temporary or permanent, mobile or immobile, including a tent, that is designed to be occupied by people lodging therein at night, including any attached porch.

(3) A person who uses defensive force shall be presumed to have reasonably feared imminent death or great bodily harm, or the commission of a felony upon him or another or upon his dwelling, or against a vehicle which he was occupying, or against his business or place of employment or the immediate premises of such business or place of employment, if the person against whom the defensive force was used, was in the process of unlawfully and forcibly entering, or had unlawfully and forcibly entered, a dwelling, occupied vehicle, business, place of employment or the immediate premises thereof or if that person had unlawfully removed or was attempting to unlawfully remove another against the other person's will from that dwelling, occupied vehicle, business, place of employment or the immediate premises thereof and the person who used defensive force knew or had reason to believe that the forcible entry or unlawful and forcible act was occurring or had occurred. This presumption shall not apply if the person against whom defensive force was used has a right to be in or is a lawful resident or owner of the dwelling, vehicle, business, place of employment or the immediate premises thereof or is the lawful resident or owner of the dwelling, vehicle, business, place of employment or the immediate premises thereof or if the person who uses defensive force is engaged in unlawful activity or if the person is a law enforcement officer engaged in the performance of his official duties.

(4) A person who is not the initial aggressor and is not engaged in unlawful activity shall have no duty to retreat before using deadly force under subsection (1)(e) or (f) of this section if the person is in a place where the person has a right

to be, and no finder of fact shall be permitted to consider the person's failure to retreat as evidence that the person's use of force was unnecessary, excessive or unreasonable.

(5) (a) The presumptions contained in subsection (3) of this section shall apply in civil cases in which self-defense or defense of another is claimed as a defense.

b) The court shall award reasonable attorney's fees, court costs, compensation for loss of income, and all expenses incurred by the defendant in defense of any civil action brought by a plaintiff if the court finds that the defendant acted in accordance with subsection (1)(e) or (f) of this section. A defendant who has previously been adjudicated "not guilty" of any crime by reason of subsection (1)(e) or (f) of this section shall be immune from any civil action for damages arising from the same conduct.

Although paragraph (3) starts out saying that you are PRESUMED to have feared death under certain circumstances, I urge you to read about this issue on Oxford, MS Attorney Reed Martz's website where it is explained that this is not absolute. One case may be when the police break in with a search warrant. Paragraph (4) is my favorite. I watched the Zimmerman-Martin murder case in Florida on TV every day. This paragraph mirrors that incident. Read it and you will understand why the prosecutors pushed so hard to try and make Zimmerman appear as the "aggressor." The way I read this statute and apply it to that Florida case, if he wasn't the initial aggressor (and I don't think he was), he had no duty to retreat and had the right to stand his ground. My question would be "Is a person who follows a suspect and reports his location to the police an aggressor or is a person who hides in the shadow of a building, jumps a man, knocks him down, bangs his head against concrete and punches him in the face the initial aggressor?" That is a no-brainer and the case was nothing more than a racial assault on our second amendment (and that is not a racial comment). The first part of 5(b) requires that a person bringing a suit against another for wrongful death but fails to prove the case must pay all costs to the individual. The second part of 5(b) says that a person found not guilty (of murder in this case) is immune from a future civil suit from the same conduct. I think we have some pretty good laws in this respect.

Chapter Ten

House Bill 314 of 2014/MCA 45-9-53

I am very thankful for this bill. However, it fell short of what we really needed. There are problems with it. Before I go into those issues I want to first tell you everything House Bill 314 does, then what it doesn't do.

Section 1 makes it clear that our guns and ammo cannot be confiscated by governmental agencies. If you don't think it happens you need to go to this link and look at the footage from New Orleans, LA during Hurricane Katrina:

https://www.youtube.com/watch?v=MLvZPcYDfKs

Section 2 spells it out that the Governor, even through Emergency Management cannot act in contravention with Section 1.

Section 3 prevents Public Housing Authorities from banning weapons.

Section 4 is what we have waited for. After the Chiefs of Police Association convinced all the businesses to post "NO GUN" signs, the city and county officials followed suit and began passing ordinances. The law already prohibited cities and counties from doing that since their ordinances were more restrictive than the state law. However, there were no teeth in the law that allowed the citizen to retaliate. Under this section since July 1, 2014, if signs still exist at county or city buildings banning weapons, the citizens can file complaints with the Attorney General's Office. They have 30 days to investigate. If the city or county is found in violation of the law, they will have 30 days to correct the ordinance/signs. If they don't, the citizen can sue with the board members paying legal costs, plus $1,000 each.

When the Speaker of the House came to Laurel in late 2013, I went to his town meeting and sat on the front row. I had a prepared statement for him and I had a copy of the Florida Preemption Law. It was a very strict takeover of the gun laws by the Florida Legislature and in my view would have been the best thing to pass here. I made the point to the Speaker that we needed relief for having to deal with public officials who continued to pass ordinances and/or refuse to do their jobs and our only recourse was to sue them. I explained to him that we the people did not have the funds or wherewithal to sue public officials to make them do their jobs and I felt like the Attorney General should assist us on these matters.

The fix came about in the 2014 session of the Legislature with the passage of House Bill 314, bill that only allowed us to go after the county and city board members. The bill also required the board members to pay the legal costs. In addition, the board members are required to pay us (the people) a fee of $1,000 if they voted Yea or abstained from voting. Lastly, the bill involves the Attorney General, requiring him to investigate it. I don't doubt that the Speaker included those things based on my presentation and it had an impact on other sections.

But here are the problems with House Bill 314. It only addresses city and counties who post signs in violation of the law. There are a number of state agencies that keep violating the law. The parks that are operated by the Harrison County Waterway's District were the worst with "NO GUN" signs everywhere. I raised enough hell last year that encouraged them to take the signs down and change their policy. The law only prohibits guns for Enhanced Carriers at police facilities, courtrooms (during judicial proceedings) and places of nuisance. No authority is granted by the law to allow any person in charge of a state government building to post NO GUN signs. Look on the following page and you will see an example that I photographed myself at the State Tax Commission.

ATTENTION

Carrying Of A Pistol Or Revolver Is Prohibited.
Carrying Of Any Other Deadly Weapons Is Also Prohibited.

Persons Entering This Building With Such A Weapon May Be Subject To An Action For Trespass.

More than anything, I am appalled that the Governor can't go to the agency heads in state government and require them to comply with the law.

So what else was wrong with House Bill 314? Well the Circuit Judges of the counties have already shown us how they will violate the law and issue orders that are in direct conflict with 97-37-7. So guess who has to hear the cases if the AG finds a County Board in violation of the law with their ordinances and/or signs? You got it, the Circuit Judge. So what if he decides he doesn't want to hear the case or issues his own order like so many already have?

Again, House Bill 314 only focused on City boards and County boards, not state agencies or Judges. George County was faced with an AG Complaint on July 7, 2014 and they got all the Chancery Judges to issue a court order against carrying guns into George, Jackson and Green County courthouses so as to circumvent the new law under HB-314.

I also think until we get an Attorney General who will go after these Judges on the part of citizens we will have problems with them even greater than we have now. I have done my part by filing an action in the Supreme Court against Judges in the Columbus (Lowndes County area) and I await the results. As with most bills they affect more than one statute but the main one is this one which has changed once again since my last publication. Changes from both years are included:

§ 45-9-53. Exceptions; procedure for challenging ordinances; county or municipal programs to purchase weapons from citizens

(1) This section and Section 45-9-51 do not affect the authority that a county or municipality may have under another law:

(a) To require citizens or public employees to be armed for personal or national defense, law enforcement, or another lawful purpose;

(b) To regulate the discharge of firearms within the limits of the county or municipality. A county or municipality may not apply a regulation relating to the discharge of firearms or other weapons in the extraterritorial jurisdiction of the county or municipality or in an area annexed by the county or municipality after September 1, 1981, if the firearm or other weapon is:

(i) A shotgun, air rifle or air pistol, BB gun or bow and arrow discharged:

1. On a tract of land of ten (10) acres or more and more than one hundred fifty (150) feet from a residence or occupied building located on another property; and

2. In a manner not reasonably expected to cause a projectile to cross the boundary of the tract; or
(ii) A center fire or rim fire rifle or pistol or a muzzle-loading rifle or pistol of any caliber discharged:

1. On a tract of land of fifty (50) acres or more and more than three hundred (300) feet from a residence or occupied building located on another property; and

2. In a manner not reasonably expected to cause a projectile to cross the boundary of the tract;

(c) To regulate the use of property or location of businesses for uses therein pursuant to fire code, zoning ordinances, or land-use regulations, so long as such codes, ordinances and regulations are not used to circumvent the intent of Section 45-9-51 or paragraph (e) of this subsection;

(d) To regulate the use of firearms in cases of insurrection, riots and natural disasters in which the city finds such regulation necessary to protect the health and safety of the public. However, the provisions of this section shall not apply to the lawful possession of firearms, ammunition or components of firearms or ammunition;

(e) To regulate the storage or transportation of explosives in order to protect the health and safety of the public, with the exception of black powder which is exempt up to twenty-five (25) pounds per private residence and fifty (50) pounds per retail dealer;

(f) To regulate the carrying of a firearm at: (i) a public park or at a public meeting of a county, municipality or other governmental body; (ii) a political rally, parade or official political meeting; or (iii) a non-firearm-related school, college or professional athletic event; or

(g) To regulate the receipt of firearms by pawnshops.

(2) The exception provided by subsection (1)(f) of this section does not apply if the firearm was in or carried to and from an area designated for use in a lawful hunting, fishing or other sporting event and the firearm is of the type commonly used in the activity.

(3) This section and Section 45-9-51 do not authorize a county or municipality or their officers or employees to act in contravention of Section 33-7-303.

(4) No county or a municipality may use the written notice provisions of Section 45-9-101(13) to prohibit concealed firearms on property under their control except:

(a) At a location listed in Section 45-9-101(13) indicating that a license issued under Section 45-9-101 does not authorize the holder to carry a firearm into that location, as long as the sign also indicates that carrying a firearm is unauthorized only for license holders without a training endorsement or that it is a location included in Section 97-37-7(2) where carrying a firearm is unauthorized for all license holders; and

(b) At any location under the control of the county or municipality aside from a location listed in subsection (1)(f) of this section or Section 45-9-101(13) indicating that the possession of a firearm is prohibited on the premises, as long as the sign also indicates that it does not apply to a person properly licensed under Section 45-9-101 or Section 97-37-7(2) to carry a concealed firearm or to a person lawfully carrying a firearm that is not concealed.

(5) (a) A citizen of this state, or a person licensed to carry a concealed pistol or revolver under Section 45-9-101, or a person licensed to carry a concealed pistol or revolver with the endorsement under Section 97-37-7, who is adversely affected by an ordinance or posted written notice adopted by a county or municipality in violation of this section may file suit for declarative and injunctive relief against a county or municipality in the circuit court which shall have jurisdiction over the county or municipality where the violation of this section occurs.

(b) Before instituting suit under this subsection, the party adversely impacted by the ordinance or posted written notice shall notify the Attorney General in writing of the violation and include evidence of the violation. The Attorney General shall, within thirty (30) days, investigate whether the county or municipality adopted an ordinance or posted written notice in violation of this section and provide the chief administrative officer of the county or municipality notice of his findings, including, if applicable, a description of the violation and specific language of the ordinance or posted written notice found to be in violation. The county or municipality shall have thirty (30) days from receipt of that notice to cure the violation. If the county or municipality fails to cure the violation within that thirty-day time period, a suit under paragraph (a) of this subsection may proceed. The findings of the Attorney General shall constitute a "Public Record" as defined by the Mississippi Public

Records Act of 1983, Section 25-61-1 et seq.

(c) If the circuit court finds that a county or municipality adopted an ordinance or posted written notice in violation of this section and failed to cure that violation in accordance with paragraph (b) of this subsection, the circuit court shall issue a permanent injunction against a county or municipality prohibiting it from enforcing the ordinance or posted written notice. Any elected county or municipal official under whose jurisdiction the violation occurred may be civilly liable in a sum not to exceed One Thousand Dollars ($ 1,000.00), plus all reasonable attorney's fees and costs incurred by the party bringing the suit. Public funds may not be used to defend or reimburse officials who are found by the court to have violated this section.

(d) It shall be an affirmative defense to any claim brought against an elected county or municipal official under this subsection (5) that the elected official:

(i) Did not vote in the affirmative for the adopted ordinance or posted written notice deemed by the court to be in violation of this section;

(ii) Did attempt to take recorded action to cure the violation as noticed by the Attorney General in paragraph (b) of this subsection; or

(iii) Did attempt to take recorded action to rescind the ordinance or remove the posted written notice deemed by the court to be in violation of this section.

(6) No county or municipality or their officers or employees may participate in any program in which individuals are given a thing of value provided by another individual or other entity in exchange for surrendering a firearm to

the county, municipality or other governmental body unless:

(a) The county or municipality has adopted an ordinance authorizing the participation of the county or municipality, or participation by an officer or employee of the county or municipality in such a program; and

(b) Any ordinance enacted pursuant to this section must require that any firearm received shall be offered for sale at auction as provided by Sections 19-3-85 and 21-39-21 to federally licensed firearms dealers, with the proceeds from such sale at auction reverting to the general operating fund of the county, municipality or other governmental body. Any firearm remaining in possession of the county, municipality or other governmental body after attempts to sell at auction may be disposed of in a manner that the body deems appropriate.

AMENDMENT NOTES. --The 2006 amendment rewrote (1)(b); and added the last sentence in (1)(d).

The 2014 amendment, in (1)(b)(ii)2, inserted "the" following "to cross the boundary of"; in (1)(c), substituted "paragraph" for "subparagraph" and "subsection" for "section" at the end; in (1)(d), substituted "ammunition or components of firearms or ammunition" for "in the home, place of business or in transit to and from the home or place of business"; and added (3), (4), (5), and (6).

The 2015 amendment, in the introductory paragraph of (4), inserted "concealed," and deleted "in the locations listed in subsection (1)(f) of this section. Nothing in this subsection shall limit the ability of a county or municipality to post signs" from the end. No changes in 2016 or 2017.

Chapter Eleven
Attorney General Opinions 2011

Office of the Attorney General
State of Mississippi

Opinion No. 2011-00094

March 21, 2011

Re: MCA 97-37-17

Dean Bearden
Chief of Campus Police
Northeast Mississippi Community College
101 Cunningham Blvd.
Booneville, MS 38829

Dear Chief Bearden:

Attorney General Jim Hood has received your request and has assigned it to me for research and reply. **Your question concerns an interpretation of Section 97-37-17(6) of the Mississippi Code, which you quote:**

(6) It shall not be a violation of this section for any person to possess or carry, whether openly or concealed, any gun, rifle, pistol or other firearm of any kind on educational property if:

(a) The person is not a student attending school on any educational property;

(b) The firearm is within a motor vehicle; and

(c) The person does not brandish, exhibit or display the firearm in any careless, angry or threatening manner.

ISSUE

Must all three subsections (a), (b), and (c) be met to not be a violation of 97-37-17?

RESPONSE

Yes. Section 97-37-17 authorizes a person to possess, openly or concealed, a firearm on educational property if (1) the person is not a student, (2) the firearm is within a motor vehicle, and (3) the person does not brandish, exhibit or display the firearm in any careless, angry or threatening manner.

Thus, a person not a student might still be in violation of the statute if he possessed the firearm outside the vehicle on educational property and/ or brandished the firearm in a careless manner whether inside or outside the vehicle.

By: James Y. Dale
Special Assistant Attorney General

Office of the Attorney General
State of Mississippi

Opinion No. 2011-00063

March 23, 2011

Re: Concealed Weapons in Vehicle

Gene Barton, Esquire
City of Okolona
Post Office Box 147
Okolona MS 38860

Dear Mr. Barton:

Attorney General Jim Hood has received your request for an opinion and has assigned it to me for research and reply. Your letter asks:

QUESTION

Specifically, the question has arisen as to whether or not under the statute as amended may a person carry, without a permit, a concealed weapon inside their vehicle which would include on the dashboard, on the seat, or in the glove compartment, or on their person if they are inside the vehicle and also may the person maintain in their own home a concealed weapon.

Our particular question has arisen concerning carrying a concealed weapon inside an automobile for example on the seat, under the seat, in the glove compartment or in the compartment between the seats.

RESPONSE

None of the factual situations described above would be a violation of the concealed weapons statute, assuming the defendant is 18 or older.

ANALYSIS

Section 97-37-1 of the Mississippi Code prohibits the carrying of a concealed weapon, but adds it shall not be a violation of this section for any person over the age of eighteen (18) years to carry a firearm or deadly weapon concealed in whole or in part within the confines of his own home or his place of business, or any real property associated with his home or business or within any motor vehicle.

Miss. Code Ann. Section 97-37-1 (2).

Under this statute, having a pistol concealed under a blanket inside a van while driving around is not a crime. Knight v. State, 983 So.2d 348 (Miss. App. 2008) (ineffective assistance of counsel to allow defendant to plead guilty to concealed weapon charge under these facts).

Likewise, it is our opinion that none of the instances cited in your letter would constitute a violation of 97-37-1 by a person over the age of 18.

By: Mike Lanford
Deputy Attorney General

Office of the Attorney General
State of Mississippi

Opinion No. 2011-00205

May 27, 2011

Re: Firearms on Educational Property

Don Thompson
Executive Director
Department of Human Resources
P. O. Box 352
Jackson, MS 39205

Dear Director Thompson:

Attorney General Jim Hood has received your request and has assigned it to me for research and reply. **Your letter provides in full:**

During preparations for emergency situations, MDHS and MEMA work in conjunction with State Superintendent, Dr. Tom Burnham, to secure housing for evacuees on educational property. Educational property is used during times of emergency because it is in compliance with the Americans with Disabilities Act. Recently, in emergency preparedness meetings for the current flood situation, the question of whether or not evacuees could bring their personal weapons, registered or not, onto educational property was presented to the Sheltering Task Force. The Department of Public Safety advised that allowing evacuees to bring weapons onto educational property could possible subject them to criminal charges. As you are aware Mississippi Code Annotated Section 97-37-17(2) specifically states that "it shall be a felony for any person to possess or carry, whether openly or concealed any gun, rifle, pistol or other firearm of any kind, or any dynamite cartridge, bomb, grenade, mine or powerful explosive on educational property...." At this time, I am requesting an official opinion from the Attorney General's office regarding the following:

1.   Whether in emergency situations when the need for evacuation arises there are measures and/or procedures that can be put in place to allow the evacuees to lawfully bring their personal firearms onto educational property, i.e, either by surrender of weapons upon check-in and placement/holding in a secure facility; or

2. Upon execution of an emergency waiver by Superintendents or other authorized public official in the affected areas which allows the evacuees to lawfully bring their personal firearms onto educational property?

If the listed options are inappropriate and/or unavailable at this time, I'd request further information and/or guidance on how to handle the evacuees' possession of firearms on educational property during emergency situations.

RESPONSE

Section 97-37-17(6) of the Mississippi Code provides an answer to your questions:

6) It shall not be a violation of this section for any person to possess or carry, whether openly or concealed any gun, rifle, pistol or other firearm of any kind on educational property if:

(a) The person is not a student attending school on any educational property;

(b) The firearm is within a motor vehicle; and

(c) The person does not brandish, exhibit or display the firearm in any careless, angry or threatening manner.

Thus, evacuees in motor vehicles may possess a firearm within a vehicle on educational property provided the firearm remains in the vehicle and the person does not brandish, exhibit or display the firearm in any careless, angry or threatening manner. See MS AG Op., Bearden (March 21, 2011).

In the event an evacuee does not have a motor vehicle, the entity in charge of the housing could furnish a motor vehicle for firearm storage.

In response to your second question, there is no authority which would allow the Superintendent or other public official to waive the terms of Section 97-37-17.

By: James Y. Dale
Special Assistant Attorney General

Office of the Attorney General
State of Mississippi

Opinion No. 2011-00163

June 17, 2011

Re: Forfeiture Weapons and Gambling Monies

Gene Barton, Esquire
P. O. Box 147
Okolona, MS 38860

Dear Mr. Barton:

Attorney General Jim Hood has received your request and has assigned it to me for research and reply. You ask four questions concerning forfeitures:

ISSUES AND RESPONSES

1. In the event an individual is charged with a crime, such as simple assault or a similarly related crime, does the individual forfeit his right to the gun or weapon which has been taken as evidence as a part of the crime?

RESPONSE: Section 97-37-3 of the Mississippi Code answers your question:

(1) Any weapon used in violation of Section 97-37-1, or used in the commission of any other crime, shall be seized by the arresting officer, may be introduced in evidence, and in the event of a conviction, shall be ordered to be forfeited, and shall be disposed of as ordered by the court having jurisdiction

(2) of such offense. In the event of dismissal or acquittal of charges, such weapon shall be returned to the accused from whom it was seized.

(2)(a) If the weapon to be forfeited is merchantable, the court may order the weapon forfeited to the seizing law enforcement agency.

(b) A weapon so forfeited to a law enforcement agency may be sold at auction as provided by Sections 19-3-85 and 21-39-21 to a federally-licensed firearms dealer, with the proceeds from such sale at auction to be used to buy bulletproof vests for the seizing law enforcement agency.

2. The gambling statutes provide that monies that are proceeds from gambling activities are to be forfeited. However, under the gambling statutes there are no precise procedures set up dealing with the forfeiture of these funds. Is this handled by the city judge or are there other applicable provisions I am missing?

RESPONSE: Section 97-33-1 provides in part:

If any person shall encourage, promote or play at any game, play or amusement, other than a fight or fighting match between dogs, for money or other valuable thing, or shall wager or bet, promote or encourage the wagering or betting of any money or other valuable things, upon any game, play, amusement, cockfight, Indian ball play or duel, other than a fight or fighting match between dogs, or upon the result of any election, event or contingency whatever, upon conviction thereof, he shall be fined in a sum not more than Five Hundred Dollars ($500.00); and, unless such fine and costs be immediately paid, shall be imprisoned for any period not more than ninety (90) days. However, this section shall not apply to betting, gaming or wagering:

A violation of this statute is a misdemeanor. Therefore, municipal court would have jurisdiction of this offense if committed in the municipality. Section 97-33-17 provides for seizure of gambling monies by law enforcement:

(1) All monies exhibited for the purpose of betting or alluring persons to bet at any game, and all monies staked or betted, shall be liable to seizure by any sheriff, constable, or police officer, together with all the appliances used or kept for use in gambling, or by any other person; and all the monies so seized shall be accounted for by the person making the seizure, and all appliances seized shall be destroyed; provided, however, this section shall not apply to betting, gaming or wagering on: ....

Although there are no statutes dealing with the forfeiture of these funds, it is the opinion of this office that the municipal court judge could provide an order forfeiting the funds to the law enforcement agency(s) responsible for the seizure. The funds should be used for any law enforcement purpose, but must be used to augment and not supplant the existing budget.

3. It was my understanding that under the concealed weapons statute the weapon is to be forfeited. Is there some specific practice or procedure to be followed in this case?
+
RESPONSE: See the answer to question number 1.

4. In the event the local police and other law enforcement agencies arrest an individual under a drug charge and desire to forfeit money as part of the arrest or perhaps the vehicle or cash that is found with the drugs, what are exactly the proper procedures to follow to forfeit this money or property?

RESPONSE: The drug forfeiture statutes provide specific instructions on the procedures to be used:

1. Section 41-29-176 concerns administrative forfeiture procedures for property, the value of which does not exceed ten thousand dollars.

2. Sections 41-29-177 and 41-29-179 concern judicial forfeiture of property not included in Section 41-29-176.

3. Section 41-29-181 provides the procedure for disposition of seized property including the mathematical division among participating law enforcement agencies of property, including cash, which is forfeited. It is divided among the participating law enforcement agencies to be used for law enforcement purposes and is not forfeited to the city.

By: James Y. Dale
Special Assistant Attorney General

Office of the Attorney General
State of Mississippi

Opinion No. 2011-00295

August 31, 2011

RE: House Bill 506

The Honorable Jim Johnson
Lee County Sheriff
510 Commerce Street
Tupelo MS 38805

Dear Sheriff Johnson:

Attorney General Jim Hood has received your request for an opinion and has assigned it to me for research and reply. Your letter asks the following regarding House Bill 506 of the 2011 regular session of the Legislature:

QUESTION:

Prior to House Bill 506, Mississippi Code 45-9-101 did not allow a concealed weapon to be carried in a courthouse, polling place, any meeting place of the governing body of any governmental entity, schools and other locations. It also provided that the carrying of a concealed weapon may be disallowed in the discretion of the person or entity exercising control over the physical location of such place by placing of a written notice clearly readable at a distance of not less than (10) feet that the "carrying of a pistol or revolver is prohibited."

Does any part of House Bill 506 take away the right of a person or entity exercising physical control over a location to disallow the carry of a concealed weapon? For example, can a county board of supervisors disallow the carry of concealed weapons in a county courthouse or other county property?

RESPONSE:

House Bill 506 takes away the power of the county to post the statutory written notice and thereby trigger criminal penalties under 97-37-1 et seq. against persons with the training endorsement on their firearms permit. A firearms permit holder with training endorsement will not violate Section 97-37-1 by carrying a concealed handgun into the courthouse or other county property, even if the county posts the notice stating "carrying of a pistol or revolver is prohibited."

APPLICABLE LAW:

Section 97-37-1 of the Mississippi Code makes it a crime to carry a concealed weapon, including a pistol or revolver, "except as otherwise provided in Section 45-9-101." Section 45-9-101 authorizes the Department of Public Safety to issues licenses[1] to carry concealed weapons. Section 97-37-7 of the Code, as amended by HB 506, states in pertinent part:

A person licensed under Section 45-9-101 to carry a concealed pistol, who has voluntarily completed an instructional course in the safe handling and use of firearms offered by an instructor certified by a nationally recognized organization that customarily offers firearms training, or by any other organization approved by the Department of Public Safety, shall also be authorized to carry weapons in courthouses except in courtrooms during a judicial proceeding, and any location listed in subsection (13) of Section 45-9-101, except any place of nuisance as defined in Section 95-3-1, any police, sheriff or highway patrol station or any detention facility, prison or jail. The department shall promulgate rules and regulations allowing concealed pistol permit holders to obtain an endorsement on their permit indicating that they have completed the aforementioned course and have the authority to carry in these locations. This section shall in no way interfere with the right of a trial judge to restrict the carrying of firearms in the courtroom.

(Emphasis added).

Therefore, a holder of a permit with a training endorsement from the Department of Public Safety may carry a concealed pistol or revolver in the courthouse and same will not constitute a violation of the concealed weapons statute.

When read together, the statutes create 2 classes of permits which exempt holders of the permit from the criminal penalties of 97-37-1. A permit which does not have the endorsement created by HB 506 is not valid in any of the places listed in Section 45-9-101 (13). A permit which does have the endorsement is valid in those places listed in subsection (13)(with a few listed exceptions). Those places are:

any courthouse; any courtroom, except that nothing in this section shall preclude a judge from carrying a concealed weapon or determining who will carry a concealed weapon in his courtroom; any polling place; any meeting place of the governing body of any governmental entity; any meeting of the Legislature or a committee thereof; any school, college or professional athletic event not related to firearms; any portion of an establishment, licensed to dispense alcoholic beverages for consumption on the premises, that is primarily devoted to dispensing alcoholic beverages; any portion of an establishment in which beer or light wine is consumed on the premises, that is primarily devoted to such purpose; any elementary or secondary school facility; any junior college, community college, college or university facility unless for the purpose of participating in any authorized firearms-related activity; inside the passenger terminal of any airport, except that no person shall be prohibited from carrying any legal firearm into the terminal if the firearm is encased for shipment, for purposes of checking such firearm as baggage to be lawfully transported on any aircraft; any church or other place of worship; or any place where the carrying of firearms is prohibited by federal law. In addition to the places enumerated in this subsection, the carrying of a stun gun, concealed pistol or revolver may be disallowed in any place in the discretion of the person or entity exercising control over the physical location of such place by the placing of a written notice clearly readable at a distance of not less than ten (10) feet that the "carrying of a pistol or revolver is prohibited." No license issued pursuant to this section shall authorize the participants in a parade or demonstration for which a permit is required to carry a stun gun, concealed pistol or revolver.

(Emphasis added).

A location with a sign reading "carrying of a pistol or revolver is prohibited" is one of the locations listed in subsection (13); therefore, it is also not a violation of the concealed weapons statute for an endorsement permit holder to carry concealed weapons on county property, including the courthouse, which has such a sign posted on it.

Of course, persons with or without weapons and with or without firearms permits may be excluded from non-public areas of the courthouse, such as judges' or clerks' personal offices, areas behind the counter, etc.

By: Michael Lanford
Deputy Attorney General

Footnotes

1or "permits" - the words appear to be used interchangeably in the statutes. Since the Department of Public Safety uses 'permit', we will do the same.

Office of the Attorney General
State of Mississippi

Opinion No. 2011-00470

November 14, 2011

Re: Expungement Misdemeanors

Robert R. Morris III, Esquire
City Prosecutor
P. O. Drawer 1586
Batesville, MS 38606

Dear Mr. Morris:

Attorney General Jim Hood has received your request and has assigned it to me for research and reply. Your letter concerns the expungement of two misdemeanor offenses (shoplifting and possession of a concealed weapon) for an individual who was convicted of both charges on the same date at the same time. You state that prior to that date the individual had no convictions. You state that the individual has filed a petition to expunge the misdemeanor convictions, alleging that he is a first offender and therefore qualifies for expungement pursuant to Section 99-19-71 (1) of the Mississippi Code.

ISSUE

Would the petitioner be eligible to have both convictions expunged, or would he lack standing as a "first offender" to expunge one or both of these convictions? Said another way, can a person who previously had no convictions expunge two misdemeanor offenses that occurred on the same date, arising from the same incident pursuant to Section 99-19-71 (1)?

RESPONSE

Section 99-19-71 (1) provides:

(1) Any person who has been convicted of a misdemeanor, excluding a conviction for a traffic violation, and who is a first offender, may petition the justice, county, circuit or municipal court in which the conviction was had for an order to expunge any such conviction from all public records.

This statute allows for the expungement of only one misdemeanor for a first offender. Therefore the petitioner may only have one of the convictions expunged. In that the convictions occurred at the same date and time, it is the opinion of this office that the petitioner must choose one of the convictions to be expunged. Once that has occurred he is no longer a first offender and cannot have the other charge expunged under Section 99-19-71 (1).

By: James Y. Dale
Special Assistant Attorney General

Office of the Attorney General
State of Mississippi

Opinion No. 2011-00507

December 9, 2011

Re: Weapons Forfeiture

W. Eugene Henry, Esquire
Municipal Court Judge
170 Porter Street
Biloxi, MS 39530

Dear Judge Henry:

Attorney General Jim Hood has received your request and has assigned it to me for research and reply. Your letter concerns the seizure and forfeiture of weapons pursuant to Section 97-37-1 of the Mississippi Code.

ISSUE

If a person is convicted of carrying a concealed weapon can forfeiture of the weapon as required by Section 97-37-3 be suspended by a municipal judge under authority of section 21-23-7(5)?

RESPONSE

Yes. This office has opined in MS AG Op., Jenkins (June 28, 1985): ".... that while Section 97-37-3, supra, mandates a forfeiture, Section 21-23-7 [5], supra, authorizes a municipal court judge to suspend sentences in whole or in part. Therefore, a municipal court judge may order the weapon in question forfeited and then suspend the order of forfeiture and return said weapon."

By: James Y. Dale
Special Assistant Attorney General

Chapter Twelve
Attorney General Opinions 2012

Office of the Attorney General
State of Mississippi

Opinion No. 2

011-00365

January 5, 2012

Re: Firearms and Permits on Campus

Hank M. Bounds
Commissioner of Higher Education
3825 Ridgewood Road
Jackson MS 39211

Dear Commissioner:

Attorney General Jim Hood has received your request for an Official opinion and has assigned it to me for research and reply. We set out your questions followed by our response.

Question No. 1: Can university police departments, institutional security officers, and other Mississippi law enforcement officials continue to enforce Section 97-37-17 notwithstanding the amendment of Section 97-37-7?

Answer: Yes, but not against a holder of a firearms permit with the training endorsement. See discussion below.

Question No. 2: Since Section 97-37-17 is not ambiguous, should not the statute be applied according to its plain meaning or terms, thus allowing university police department, institutional security officers, and other law enforcement officials to enforce that statute as to all persons notwithstanding the issuance of a permit license with endorsement?

Answer: No. When statutes deal with the same subject matter, as here, there must be applied the well-established rule that statutes in parimateria, although in apparent conflict, should, so far as reasonably possible, be construed in harmony with each other so as to give force and effect to each. Greaves v. Hinds County, 166 Miss. 89, 145 So.900 (1933).

Section 97-37-17 broadly prohibits possession of a firearm on any educational property, which includes property owned, used or operated by any university. Several exceptions exist, including one for "any person as authorized in Section 97-37-7 while in the performance of his official duties." We believe that this exception is limited to those persons listed in 97-37-7 having official duties inherent in their position, and does not apply to "enhanced permit" holders. Nevertheless, the language of 97-37-7 itself creates the exception for enhanced permit holders:

A person licensed under Section 45-9-101 to carry a concealed pistol, who has voluntarily completed an instructional course in the safe handling and use of firearms offered by an instructor certified by a nationally recognized organization that customarily offers firearms training, or by any other organization approved by the Department of Public Safety, shall also be authorized to carry weapons in courthouses except in courtrooms during a judicial proceeding, and any location listed in subsection (13) of Section 45-9-101.

(Emphasis added). Listed in subsection (13) of Section 45-9-101 is "any junior college, community college, college or university facility" as well as "any school, college or professional athletic event not related to firearms," as well as meetings of the Legislature, elementary and secondary schools, and airport terminals.

The prohibition against possession of firearms applies to all educational property owned, used or operated by a university. The exception is somewhat less broad, being limited to any university facility and athletic event. In any case, Section 97-37-17 continues to operate against all persons, with endorsement permit holders being excepted therefrom. As stated in White v. Lowry, 162 Miss. 751, 758, 139 So. 874, 876 (1932), "Where a statute contains both a particular and a general enactment, and the general enactment in its most comprehensive sense would include what is embraced in the particular one, the latter must be given effect as to all cases which fall within the particular provision, and the general enactment must be taken to embrace only such cases within its general language as are not within the provisions of the particular enactment."

Reading the statutes together, it is our opinion that Section 97-37-7 of the Mississippi Code constitutes an exception to Section 97-37-17.

Question No. 3: Section 45-9-101(13) provides in part "... In addition to the places enumerated in this subsection, the carrying of a stun gun, concealed pistol or revolver may be disallowed in any place in the discretion of the person or entity exercising control over the physical location of such place by the placing of a written notice clearly readable at a distance of not less than ten (10) feet that the 'carrying of a pistol or revolver is prohibited.'" Under applicable law, does a university have the option of preventing weapons on its campus, notwithstanding the amendment to Section 97-37-7, by posting notices as authorized by Section 45-9-101(13)?

Answer: No. See MS AG Op., Johnson (Aug. 31, 2011)(Sheriff may not outlaw endorsement permit holders by erecting sign forbidding firearms in courthouse since the exception applies to places where signs are erected).

Question No. 4: If Section 97-37-7 allows persons with a valid license with endorsement to carry a pistol, revolver or weapon onto a university campus, can university police departments or institutional security officers require permitted individuals to visit the police or security department upon entering campus for the purpose of producing the license with endorsement and thereby verifying lawful authority to possess and carry pursuant to the license?

Answer: No. However, the "licensee must carry the license, together with valid identification, at all times in which the licensee is carrying a stun gun, concealed pistol or revolver and must display both the license and proper identification upon demand by a law enforcement officer. Miss. Code Ann. Section 45-9-101 (1)(b) (emphasis added). It is our opinion that this statute only requires the licensee to produce the license where the licensee is found, upon individual demand. The licensee cannot be required to visit a police department. We note that the University may restrict the general public, including persons with or without firearms and with or without permits, from entering non-public areas and buildings of the University. See MS AG Op., Johnson (Aug. 31, 2011).

The above opinion addresses the application of Mississippi's criminal statutes to persons visiting or otherwise present on university campuses. It does not prohibit IHL or the various universities from adopting admissions, employment or resident hall policies which administratively address the possession of firearms by enrolled students, university employees, dormitory residents etc. See Miss. Constitution of 1890, Section 213-A (Board of Trustees for the Institutions of Higher Learning has Constitutional authority to manage and control the various universities; and Section 37-101-15 (IHL to supervise university buildings and grounds and to prescribe rules and regulations for policing same).

By: Mike Lanford
Deputy Attorney General

Office of the Attorney General
State of Mississippi

Opinion No. 2012-00102

April 6, 2012

Re: Disposition Property Obtained in Criminal Cases

Robert M. Logan, Esquire
P. O. Box 218
Newton, MS 39345

Dear Mr. Logan:

Attorney General Jim Hood has received your request and has assigned it to me for research and reply. Your letter provides:

ISSUE

Over the years the Newton Police Department has obtained a large number of firearms, collected as evidence or contraband in various closed criminal cases. Generally speaking, no court orders have been entered with respect to their disposition. We need to know if we have authority to place these on the City's property rolls or declare them surplus property to be disposed of as other surplus property of the City. As to either alternative, please direct us to the proper procedures to be followed.

RESPONSE

The manner in which to dispose of the property you describe must be determined on a case by case basis considering the type of property and the circumstances surrounding the method by which the property was acquired and kept by the police. Some methods of disposal are:

If applicable, the city must follow the provisions of Section 97-37-3 of the Mississippi Code:

(1) Any weapon used in violation of Section 97-37-1, or used in the commission of any other crime, shall be seized by the arresting officer, may be introduced in evidence, and in the event of a conviction, shall be ordered to be forfeited, and shall be disposed of as ordered by the court having jurisdiction of such offense. In the event of dismissal or acquittal of charges, such weapon shall be returned to the accused from whom it was seized.

(2)(a) If the weapon to be forfeited is merchantable, the court may order the weapon forfeited to the seizing law enforcement agency.

(b) A weapon so forfeited to a law enforcement agency may be sold at auction as provided by Sections 19-3-85 and 21-39-21 to a federally-licensed firearms dealer, with the proceeds from such sale at auction to be used to buy bulletproof vests for the seizing law enforcement agency.

Property seized as a result of drug offenses should be forfeited pursuant to Section 41-29-176 if the value does not exceed ten thousand dollars. Sections 41-29-177 and 41-29-179 relate to forfeiture of property not included in Section 41-29-176. See MS AG Op., Barton (June 17, 2011).

Property deemed abandoned in the possession of the police should be disposed of pursuant to the provisions of Section 21-39-21.

Office of the Attorney General
State of Mississippi

Opinion No. 2012-00250

June 13, 2012

Re: Disposal Firearms

Susan O. Carr, Esquire
P. O. Box 1100
Tupelo, MS 38802-1100

Dear Ms. Carr:

Attorney General Jim Hood has received your request and has assigned it to me for research and reply. Your question relates to disposal of firearms that have been entered into evidence.

ISSUE

My question is whether law enforcement agencies may sell or use the evidence, specifically firearms or must they physically destroy them?

RESPONSE

Section 97-37-3 of the Mississippi Code answers your question:
(1) Any weapon used in violation of Section 97-37-1, or used in the commission of any other crime, shall be seized by the arresting officer,

may be introduced in evidence, and in the event of a conviction, shall be ordered to be forfeited, and shall be disposed of as ordered by the court having jurisdiction of such offense. In the event of dismissal or acquittal of charges, such weapon shall be returned to the accused from whom it was seized.

(2)(a) If the weapon to be forfeited is merchantable, the court may order the weapon forfeited to the seizing law enforcement agency.

(b) A weapon so forfeited to a law enforcement agency may be sold at auction as provided by Sections 19-3-85 and 21-39-21 to a federally-licensed firearms dealer, with the proceeds from such sale at auction to be used to buy bulletproof vests for the seizing law enforcement agency.

Furthermore, this office opined in MS AG Op., Price (January 31, 1990):

Those firearms that are seized as concealed pursuant to Section 97-37-1 are to be disposed of in accordance with Section 97-37-3, which places the responsibility of disposing of said firearms at the discretion of the judge. This office in the past has issued opinions that a judge may lawfully order those firearms not returned to the acquitted defendant disposed of at public auction, destroyed, or placed upon the property roles of the county for the benefit of a law enforcement unit.

By: James Y. Dale
Special Assistant Attorney Genera

Office of the Attorney General
State of Mississippi

Opinion No. 2012-00248

June 14, 2012

Re: Concealed Weapons

Chief Robert B. Russell
Ellisville Police Department
104 West Holly Street
Ellisville, MS 39437

Dear Chief Russell:

Attorney General Jim Hood has received your request and has assigned it to me for research and reply. Your letter concerns the carrying of weapons in Mississippi.

ISSUE

Is there a law in Mississippi that requires a permit holder to completely cover his weapon in public by means of a shirt, jacket or other piece of clothing?

RESPONSE

Yes. The authority to legally carry a pistol or revolver is derived from Section 45-9-101 of the Mississippi Code which provides in the first sentence: "(1)(a) The Department of Public Safety is authorized to issue licenses to carry stun guns, concealed pistols or revolvers to persons qualified in this section."

This provision does not authorize a person to carry a pistol "concealed in part", but requires that it be totally concealed. This conclusion is succinctly set forth in Section 45-9-101 (18): "... Further, nothing in this section shall be construed to allow the open and unconcealed carrying of any stun gun or deadly weapon as described in Section 97-37-1, Mississippi Code of 1972."

Section 97-37-1 prohibits the carrying of listed weapons "concealed in whole or in part":

(1) Except as otherwise provided in Section 45-9-101, any person who carries, concealed in whole or in part, any bowie knife, dirk knife, butcher knife, switchblade knife, metallic knuckles, blackjack, slingshot, pistol, revolver, or any rifle with a barrel of less than sixteen (16) inches in length, or any shotgun with a barrel of less than eighteen (18) inches in length, machine gun or any fully automatic firearm or deadly weapon, or any muffler or silencer for any firearm, whether or not it is accompanied by a firearm, or uses or attempts to use against another person any imitation firearm, shall upon conviction be punished as follows:

Thus, it is illegal to carry the weapons described in Section 97-37-1(1) without securing a license as provided in Section 45-9-101, which license authorizes the carrying of a concealed pistol or revolver. The securing of the "'enhanced" permit provided in Section 97-37-7 does not abrogate the requirement that the weapons be carried totally concealed.[1]

By: James Y. Dale
Special Assistant Attorney General

Footnotes

<u>1</u>

Section 12 of the Mississippi Constitution of 1890 states, "The right of every citizen to keep and bear arms in defense of his home, person, or property, or in aid of the civil power when thereto legally summoned, shall not be called in question, but the legislature may regulate or forbid carrying concealed weapons." In addition, it is a violation of Section 97-37-1 of the Mississippi Code, except as provided in Section 45-9-101, to carry a weapon described in the statute "concealed in whole or in part". See also Martin v. State, 47 So. 426 (Miss. 1908); Powell v. State,184 So. 2d866 (Miss. 1966); Reed v. State, 199 So.2d 803 (Miss. 1967) and the dissent of Justice Roy Noble Lee in L. M., Jr. V. State, 600 So.2d 967 (Miss. 1992). (Even if weapon is visible, there is still violation since statute prohibits carrying of weapon only part of which is concealed.)

The manner in which to dispose of the property you describe must be determined on a case by case basis considering the type of property and the circumstances surrounding the method by which the property was acquired and kept by the sheriff's office.

In the first scenario, the firearms referenced in your opinion request are those firearms that are seized as a result of criminal activity. These firearms are to be disposed of in accordance with Miss. Code Ann., Section 97-37-3, which states:

(1) Any weapon used in violation of Section 97-37-1, or used in the commission of any other crime, shall be seized by the arresting officer, may be introduced in evidence, and in the event of a conviction, shall be ordered to be forfeited, and shall be disposed of as ordered by the court having jurisdiction

of such offense. In the event of dismissal or acquittal of charges, such weapon shall be returned to the accused from whom it was seized.

(2)(a) If the weapon to be forfeited is merchantable, the court may order the weapon forfeited to the seizing law enforcement agency.

(b) A weapon so forfeited to a law enforcement agency may be sold at auction as provided by Sections 19-3-85 and 21-39-21 to a federally-licensed firearms dealer, with the proceeds from such sale at auction to be used to buy bulletproof vests for the seizing law enforcement agency.

Furthermore, this office opined in MS AG Op., Price (January 31, 1990):
Those firearms that are seized as concealed pursuant to Section 97-37-1 are to be disposed of in accordance with Section 97-37-3, which places the responsibility of disposing of said firearms at the discretion of the judge. This office in the past has issued opinions that a judge may lawfully order those firearms not returned to the acquitted defendant disposed of at public auction, destroyed, or placed upon the property roles of the county for the benefit of a law enforcement unit.

If the firearms are placed on the property rolls by a judge, the firearms could then be declared surplus and sold under Miss. Code Ann., Section 19-7-5 and Section 17-25-25 (2012).

The second group of firearms you mention in your opinion request are surplus county property. These firearms are to be disposed of in accordance with Miss. Code Ann., Section 19-7-5 (2012), which states:

The board of supervisors shall have the power to sell and dispose of any personal property belonging to the county or any subdivision thereof according to the uniform personal property disposal requirements for local governments in Section 17-25-25. Nothing contained in this section shall be construed to prohibit, restrict or to prescribe conditions with regard to the authority granted under Section 17-25-3.

Miss. Code Ann., Section 17-25-25 states:

(1) General. The governing authority of a county or municipality may sell or dispose of any personal property belonging to the governing authority when the property has ceased to be used for public purposes or when, in the authority's judgment, a sale thereof would promote the best interest of the governing authority.

(2) Public sale. At least ten (10) days before bid opening, the governing authority shall advertise its acceptance of bids by posting notices at three (3) public places located in the county or municipality that the governing authority serves. One of the three (3) notices shall be posted at the governing authority's main office. The governing authority may designate the manner by which the bids will be received, including, but not limited to, bids sealed in an envelope, bids made electronically or bids made by any other method that promotes open competition. The proceeds of the sale shall be placed in a properly approved depository to the credit of the proper fund.

(3) Private sale. Where the personal property does not exceed One Thousand Dollars ($ 1,000.00) in value, the governing authority, by a unanimous approval of its members, may sell or dispose of the property at a private sale. The proceeds of the sale shall be placed in a properly approved depository to the credit of the proper fund.

(4) If the governing authority finds that the fair market value of the personal property is zero and this finding is entered on the minutes of the authority, then the governing authority may dispose of the personal property in the

manner it deems appropriate and in its best interest, but no official or employee of the governing authority shall derive any personal economic benefit from such disposal.

(5) If the personal property may be of use or benefit to any federal agency or authority, another governing authority or state agency of the State of Mississippi, or a state agency or governing authority of another state, it may be disposed of in accordance with Section 31-7-13(m)(vi).

(6) Nothing contained in this section shall be construed to prohibit, restrict or to prescribe conditions with regard to the authority granted under Section 17-25-3.

Lastly, your opinion request references firearms that have been deemed abandoned property. These firearms are also disposed of in accordance with Miss. Code Ann., Section 19-3-85.

Consequently, it is evident that county board of supervisors are authorized to dispose by public auction firearms that have been either forfeited to the county, are surplus county property, or have been abandoned.

However, the question of whether the county has the authority to contract with a private auction company to dispose of the property in accordance with the above referenced statutes must be addressed. Miss. Code Ann., Section 19-3-69(h) authorizes county boards of supervisors to contract with auctioneers to sell county personal property pursuant to the provisions of Section 19-7-5 and in conformance with regulations established by the Office of the State Auditor. MS AG Op., Webb (May 19, 2006). Thus, Section 19-3-69(h) specifically limits county board of supervisors to contracting with an auctioneer to those public auctions held pursuant to Section 19-7-5, which provides for the disposal of surplus county personal property pursuant to

Section 17-25-25. Furthermore, state law requires that firearms that have been either forfeited to a law enforcement agency or abandoned are to be sold pursuant Miss. Code Ann., Section 19-3-85, which "designate[s] the sheriff to make the sale." We can find no other authority that would authorize county boards of supervisors to contract with an auctioneer for a sale conducted pursuant to Section 19-3-83.

Conclusion

A county board of supervisors may contract with an auction company for the sale of firearms that have been determined by the board of supervisors to be surplus personal property pursuant to Miss. Code Ann., Section 19-7-5 and Section 17-25-25. Public sale of abandoned personal property, including firearms, conducted pursuant to Miss. Code Ann., Section 19-3-85, are to be conducted by the sheriff of the county.

If this office may be of further assistance to you, please let us know.

By: Avery Mounger Lee
Special Assistant Attorney General

Office of the Attorney General
State of Mississippi

Opinion No. 2012-00475

October 12, 2012

Re: Disposition of Property Forfeited to Municipality Pursuant to the Uniform Controlled Substance Law (Section 41-29-101 et. seq. of the Mississippi Code)

Bryan E. Dye, Esquire
900 Pigeon Roost
Olive Branch, MS 38645

Dear Mr. Dye:

Attorney General Jim Hood has received your request and has assigned it to me for research and reply. Your questions concern the applicability of newly enacted Section 17-25-25 of the Mississippi Code pertaining to disposition of personal property under the drug forfeiture laws contained in Sections 41-29-176, 177, 179 and 181 of the Mississippi Code.

ISSUES AND ANSWERS

1(a). Does the new section 17-25-25 enacted by 2012 Senate Bill 2534 have any applicability to the disposition of personal property forfeited to a municipality pursuant to the Uniform Controlled Substances Law?

(b). May motor vehicles forfeited to the city be sold pursuant to the public sale provisions of 17-25-25(2), including receipt of bids made electronically in a method that promotes open competition(for example, online auctions such as Govdeals)?

ANSWER: The provisions of forfeiture of the Uniform Controlled Substances Law, Sections 41-29-176, 177, 179 and 181 control the disposition of property as set forth in those statutes. Section 41-29-181(7)(c) specifically provides that if a motor vehicle forfeited to a municipal law enforcement agency becomes obsolete or is no longer needed for official or governmental purposes it may be disposed of in the manner provided by law for disposing of municipal property (which would include the provisions of Section 17-25-25). However, although motor vehicles may be disposed of pursuant to Sections 41-29-181 or17-25-25, the disposal of all other personal property shall be disposed of in the manner set forth in section 41-29-181, particularly subsection 6:

(6) All other property that has been forfeited shall, except as otherwise provided, be sold at a public auction for cash by the chief law enforcement officer of the initiating law enforcement agency, or his designee, to the highest and best bidder after advertising the sale for at least once each week for three (3) consecutive weeks, the last notice to appear not more than ten (10) days nor less than five (5) days prior to such sale, in a newspaper having a general circulation in the jurisdiction in which said law enforcement agency is located. Such notices shall contain a description of the property to be sold and a statement of the time and place of sale. It shall not be necessary to the validity of such sale either to have the property present at the place of sale or to have the name of the owner thereof stated in such notice. The proceeds of the sale shall be disposed of as follows:

(a) To any bona fide lien holder, secured party, or other party holding an interest in the property in the nature of a security interest, to the extent of his interest; and

(b) The balance, if any, remaining after deduction of all storage, court costs and expenses of liquidation shall be divided, forwarded and deposited in the same manner set out in subsection (2) of this section.

2. From time to time the City of Olive Branch comes into possession of firearms which have been forfeited pursuant to the administrative forfeiture procedures of Section 41-29-176. In such cases there is often no court order pertaining to the disposition of the firearms in the associated criminal case, and of course there is no court order in the forfeiture proceeding since the City came into possession of the firearm by administrative procedures.

a. Does the November 30, 2004 Opinion to W. Price Elliott remain the opinion of your office as it pertains to the disposition of firearms forfeited to a municipality under administrative procedures?

ANSWER: Seized weapons forfeited by administrative procedure under Section 41-29-176 shall be disposed of pursuant to Section 41-29-181(6). Weapons used in violation of section 97-37-1 or used in commission of any other crime shall be seized by the arresting officer pursuant to Section 97-37-3 and upon conviction ordered forfeited and disposed of as ordered by the court. This procedure is separate from disposal of weapons forfeited pursuant to the drug forfeiture procedures, under Sections 41-29-176.

MS AG Op., Elliot (November 30, 2004) does not reference disposition under administrative procedures. The facts in the opinion relate to seized firearms in regard to drug-related cases which "are now property of the City." It does not indicate how the firearms became property of the city.

b. For firearms forfeited by the City pursuant to the Uniformed Controlled Substances Law, do Sections 97-37-3 or 21-39-21 have any applicability to the disposal of such firearms given that there are more specific procedures outlined in Section 41-29-181(6) and the new uniform requirements of Section 17-25-25?

ANSWER: See the answer to no 1.

c. May the proceeds from the sale of firearms forfeited to the City pursuant to the Uniform Controlled Substance Law be used for law enforcement purposes other than the purchase of bulletproof vests?

ANSWER: Yes. The provision contained in Section 97-37-3 concerning purchase of bulletproof vests does not apply to disposal under Section 41-29-181.

By: James Y. Dale
Special Assistant Attorney General

Chapter Thirteen
Attorney General Opinions 2013

Office of the Attorney General
State of Mississippi

Opinion No. 2013-00026

March 1, 2013

Re: Firearm on School Property

Chief Joedy Pennington
P. O. Box 307
Decatur, MS 39327

Dear Chief Pennington:

Attorney General Jim Hood has received your request and has assigned it to me for research and reply. Your question concerns a school employee with an enhanced permit carrying a firearm on school property.

ISSUE

Is it legal for a school employee that has an enhanced carry permit to carry a firearm on school property if the school board allows it?

RESPONSE

Yes. When read in parimateria Sections 45-9-101(13) and Section 97-37-7(2) authorize an individual with the required instructional training which results in an "enhanced permit" to carry a concealed pistol on school property.

APPLICABLE LAW

Section 45-9-101(13) prohibits a person with a regular conceal carry permit issued under that section from carrying a concealed pistol or revolver on any elementary or secondary school facility. However, Section 97-37-7(2) authorizes a person with advanced training as set forth in the statute, known as an enhanced permit, to carry a weapon on the locations listed in subsection (13) of Section 45-9-101 which includes any elementary or secondary school facility.

Although the carrying of a weapon on school facilities is authorized for an individual with an enhanced permit, the school board or, if applicable, the conservator under the direction of the State Board of Education could under the terms of its contract with the school employee disallow the school employee from carrying a weapon on the school facility or in certain areas or buildings. MS AG Op., Bounds (January 5, 2012). A school employee violating the terms of the contract would not be criminally liable but would be subject to penalties as provided by contract.

It should be noted that this opinion is based upon Mississippi law and this office issues no opinion on the effect of Federal law, if any.

By: James Y. Dale
Special Assistant Attorney General

Office of the Attorney General
State of Mississippi

Opinion No. 2013-00114

June 13, 2013

Re: House Bill 2

Sheriff Brad Lance
1 Justice Drive
Senatobia, MS 38668

Dear Sheriff Lance:

Attorney General Jim Hood has received your request and has assigned it to me for research and reply. You ask several questions about House Bill 2 of the 2013 Regular Session.

At the outset it should be noted that since your questions specifically address the open carry provisions of this Bill, the following answers do not include a discussion of the carrying of a concealed weapon with a standard permit or enhanced permit. Different rules apply to carrying a concealed weapon with a permit or enhanced permit. Also, a convicted felon is still not allowed to possess a weapon unless he is authorized by Section 97-37-5 which includes a pardon for such felony, has received a relief from disability pursuant to Section 925 (c) of Title 18 of the U. S. Code, or has received a certificate of rehabilitation.

House Bill 2 provides:

97-37-1. (1) Except as otherwise provided in Section 45-9-101, any person who carries, concealed * * * on or about one's person, any bowie knife, dirk knife, butcher knife, switchblade knife, metallic knuckles, blackjack, slingshot, pistol, revolver, or any rifle with a barrel of less than sixteen (16) inches in length, or any shotgun with a barrel of less than eighteen (18) inches in length, machine gun or any fully automatic firearm or deadly weapon, or any muffler or silencer for any firearm, whether or not it is accompanied by a firearm, or uses or attempts to use against another person any imitation firearm, shall, upon conviction, be punished as follows:

(a) By a fine of not less than One Hundred Dollars ($100.00) nor more than Five Hundred Dollars ($500.00), or by imprisonment in the county jail for not more than six (6) months, or both, in the discretion of the court, for the first conviction under this section.

(b) By a fine of not less than One Hundred Dollars ($100.00) nor more than Five Hundred Dollars ($500.00), and imprisonment in the county jail for not less than thirty (30) days nor more than six (6) months, for the second conviction under this section.

(c) By confinement in the custody of the Department of Corrections for not less than one (1) year nor more than five (5) years, for the third or subsequent conviction under this section

(d) By confinement in the custody of the Department of Corrections for not less than one (1) year nor more than ten (10) years for any person previously convicted of any felony who is convicted under this section.

(2) It shall not be a violation of this section for any person over the age of eighteen (18) years to carry a firearm or deadly weapon concealed * * * within the confines of his own home or his place of business, or any real property associated with his home or business or within any motor vehicle.

(3) It shall not be a violation of this section for any person to carry a firearm or deadly weapon concealed * * * if the possessor of the weapon is then engaged in a legitimate weapon-related sports activity or is going to or returning from such activity. For purposes of this subsection, "legitimate weapon-related sports activity" means hunting, fishing, target shooting or any other legal * * * activity which normally involves the use of a firearm or other weapon.

(4) For the purposes of this section, "concealed" means hidden or obscured from common observation and shall not include any weapon listed in subsection (1) of this section, including, but not limited to, a loaded or unloaded pistol carried upon the person in a sheath, belt holster or shoulder holster that is wholly or partially visible, or carried upon the person in a scabbard or case for carrying the weapon that is wholly or partially visible

This bill becomes law on July 1, 2013, and the answers below will be applicable at that time. The statute must be read in light of MISS. CONST. art. 3, Section 12, which states, "The right of every citizen to keep and bear arms in defense of his home, person, or property, or in aid of the civil power when thereto legally summoned, shall not be called in question, but the legislature may regulate or forbid carrying concealed weapons." Further, U.S. CONST. amend. II states, "A well regulated militia being necessary to the security of a free state, the right of the people to keep and bear arms shall not be infringed." Your specific questions are set out below, followed by our answers:

1. Under House Bill 2 as signed by the Governor, can an individual carry a firearm without a permit as long as part of the firearm is visible?

ANSWER; An individual may carry a firearm without violating Section 97-37-1 (the concealed weapon statute) as long as it is not "concealed"; i.e., "hidden or obscured from common observation." Terms used in a statute should be given their common and ordinary meaning. Miss. Code Ann. Section 1-3-65. Merriam-Webster's Dictionary defines "hidden" as "being out of sight or not readily apparent: concealed," and defines the verb "obscure" as "to conceal or hide by or as if by covering." Whether a weapon is "hidden or obscured from common observation" will depend on the facts of each case. Generally however, if enough of the firearm is visible so that it is readily apparent to "common observation," then the firearm is not concealed.

After providing a definition of "concealed" the statute gives examples of what is NOT considered to be a concealed weapon, namely:
any weapon listed in subsection (1) of this section, including, but not limited to, a loaded or unloaded pistol carried upon the person in a sheath, belt holster or shoulder holster that is wholly or partially visible, or carried upon the person in a scabbard or case for carrying the weapon that is wholly or partially visible.

Therefore, weapons carried as described above - in a wholly or partially visible sheath, holster, scabbard or case, even though no part of the firearm is visible - are not "concealed" weapons, the carrying of which is prohibited by 97-37-1.

2. If the answer to question # 1 is yes, does that include carrying openly on public educational property?

ANSWER: No. Although carrying a weapon in a visible belt holster on educational property would not violate the concealed weapon statute,

(97-37-1), it would violate Section 97-37-17.[1] The term "educational property" includes public and private schools, colleges and universities.

3. Can law enforcement approach an individual carrying a visible firearm and ask for identifying information that would allow a criminal history check to see if that person is a convicted felon?

ANSWER: We read your question to be whether a law enforcement officer may *ask for (not require)* identifying information. A law enforcement officer may certainly ask for the information. However, the individual is not *required* to provide it. As stated by the U.S. Supreme Court in *Florida v. Royer*, 460 U.S. 491 (1983):

Law enforcement officers do not violate the Fourth Amendment by merely approaching an individual on the street or in another public place, by asking him if he is willing to answer some questions, by putting questions to him if the person is willing to listen, or by offering in evidence in a criminal prosecution his voluntary answers to such questions, [citations omitted]. * * * The person approached, however, need not answer any question put to him; indeed, he may decline to listen to the questions at all and may go on his way.

Id. at 497.

To be clear, the mere fact that a person is openly carrying a weapon, without anything more, does not give the officer grounds to detain that person, or to require him to submit to questioning. For further discussion of an officer's authority to briefly detain persons based upon reasonable suspicion of criminal activity, as well as traffic stops and community care-taking functions, please see Appendix A, attached hereto.

4. Under HB 2 will an individual be allowed to carry a long gun (i.e. shotgun or rifle) openly as well?

ANSWER: Yes.

5. Can an individual carry a firearm in the waistband of his/her pants or in the pocket of his/her pants or coat as long as part of the grip, or any other part, of the firearm is visible or must it be carried in a holster?

ANSWER: As stated generally in our answer to No. 1, if enough of the firearm is visible so that it is readily apparent to common observation, then the firearm is not concealed and there is no violation of 97-37-1.

We note also that Section 97-37-19, as amended by HB 2, states in part:

If any person, having or carrying any dirk, dirk-knife, sword, sword-cane, or any deadly weapon, or other weapon the carrying of which concealed is prohibited by Section 97-37-1, shall, in the presence of another person, brandish or wield the same in a threatening manner, not in necessary self-defense, or shall in any manner unlawfully use the same in any fight or quarrel, the person so offending, upon conviction thereof, shall be fined in a sum not exceeding Five Hundred Dollars ($500.00) or be imprisoned in the county jail not exceeding three (3) months, or both.

"Brandish" is not defined by state statute, but is defined in Webster's Third New International Dictionary as "to shake or wave (as a weapon) menacingly; to exhibit in an ostentatious, shameless, or aggressive manner." ""Wield" is defined by Merriam Webster as, "to handle (as a tool) especially effectively." There is authority from other jurisdictions that a weapon need not be pointed at a victim in order to be threatening. See 79 Am Jur 2d, *Weapons and Firearms*, Section 32 (2013).

6. Can an individual carry a firearm openly on private property such as a retail store, grocery store or restaurant?

At the core of this question, as well as question 7., is whether the change to the concealed weapons statute alters the power of private property owners and of custodians of public property generally to prohibit conduct on that property that is not criminal, in particular, the carrying of unconcealed weapons. Our answer is that it does not.

A private property owner or manager of a retail store, grocery store or restaurant may exercise his property rights and deny entry to persons carrying weapons on his property (verbally, by posting a sign or by other means). A private property owner may even prohibit enhanced concealed permit holders from their property. As stated by the Mississippi Supreme Court in *Biglane v. Under the Hill Corporation*, 949 So.2d 9, at 16 (Miss. 2007);

It is a basic tenet of property law that a landowner or tenant may use the premises they control in whatever fashion they desire, so long as the law is obeyed. This leads to the logical conclusion that a landowner or valid tenant may forbid any other persons from using their property. This ideal is protected in our law to the point that there are both civil and criminal prohibitions against trespassing.

See also, *GeorgiaCarry.Org v. Georgia*, 687 F.3d 1244 (11th Cir. 2012)(2nd amendment right to bear arms is limited by equally fundamental rights of private property owners to control their property). Depending on the facts, violation of a private property owner's prohibition of weapons might constitute a violation of 97-17-97

1(trespass after warning), 97-17-93 (entry without permission) or other statute.

7. Can an individual carry a firearm openly inside a courthouse, or other public buildings?

Custodians or owners of public property generally have the authority and duty, express or necessarily implied, to manage that property in the public interest. This often includes the authority to deny entry to the property, to place conditions upon entry onto the publicly-owned property, and to otherwise regulate and govern that property short of enforcing the state criminal laws. For example, a municipality may prohibit smoking in the city hall and a public library may prohibit loud speech. These activities are perfectly legal, but the municipality and the state library have the statutory authority to prohibit them and to exclude persons who do not comply. See, *Bigham v. Huffman*, 199 WL 33537149 (N.D. Miss. 1999)(Criminal trespass laws applied to public property). The authority of state or local officials to govern and manage government property may be separate and apart from any power to enact police-power ordinances or regulations having criminal or misdemeanor penalties.

Unlike private property owners, however, the authority of custodians of public property to disallow a lawful activity on land controlled by them requires a case-by-case analysis of the authority of the public body or official under state law. If the public body or official has such authority, then the question is whether the restriction or prohibition is Constitutional. This is a fact-specific and regulation or state action-specific inquiry.

Specifically with regard to courthouses, the sheriff is in charge of and responsible for the security of the courthouse. MS AG Op., Meadows (Feb. 14, 2003). Miss. Code Ann, Section 19-25-69 states:

The sheriff shall have charge of the courthouse and jail of his county, of the premises belonging thereto, and of the prisoners in said jail. He shall preserve

0 the said premises and prisoners from mob violence, from any injuries or attacks by mobs or otherwise, and from trespasses and intruders. He shall keep the courthouse, jail, and premises belonging thereto, in a clean and comfortable condition, and it shall be his duty to prosecute all persons who are guilty of injuring or defacing same. If, after a hearing by the governor, held in accordance with due process of law, it shall be ascertained that the sheriff has willfully failed, neglected or refused to preserve the courthouse, or the jail, or any prisoners lawfully in his custody from injuries by mob violence, then the governor shall have the power and it shall be his duty to remove such sheriff from office.

This statute authorizes the sheriff to exclude from the courthouse premises county employees whom he believes are stealing county property or are intoxicated. MS AG Op., Barrett (Sept. 18, 1992). The sheriff is also the jailer and is responsible for the safekeeping of ail prisoners being brought before the courts.

Thus, it is our opinion that the sheriff has the state-law authority, if he determines it reasonable and necessary to the security of the courthouse, to disallow the open carry of firearms in the courthouse. As stated above, the second part of the question is whether such action by the sheriff is constitutional. Please note that an official opinion of the Attorney General does not provide immunity from liability for violations of federal law, including possible violations of individual rights under the U.S. Constitution. See Miss. Code Section 7-5-25. Therefore, the following is provided for informational purposes only.

The United States Supreme Court has addressed this question in a limited fashion, saying that "longstanding" laws prohibiting firearms in government buildings are presumptively constitutional. In *District of Columbia v. Heller*, 128 S.Ct. 2783 (2008), a 5-4 majority of the Supreme Court held that the

Second Amendment protects an individual's right to possess and carry a loaded handgun in case of confrontation and as an inherent right of self-defense. The Court extended the *Heller* holding in *McDonald v. City of Chicago*, 130 S.Ct. 3020 (2010), ruling that the Second Amendment right to bear arms applies to the states, thus limiting the ability of states and local government to regulate firearm possession.

These lengthy opinions provided few explicit holdings and left open many issues relating to the constitutionality of gun-control laws by not defining the scope of the right to bear arms, by not providing a standard of review for firearms regulation, and by including, without elaboration, a non-exhaustive list of examples of laws that are "presumptively lawful" and which can be exceptions to the right:

[N]othing in our opinion should be taken to cast doubt on longstanding prohibitions on the possession of firearms by felons and the mentally ill, or laws forbidding the carrying of firearms in *sensitive places such as* schools and *government buildings*, or laws imposing conditions and qualifications on the commercial sale of arms.

(italics added). *Heller* at 2816-2817. See also, *McDonald v. City of Chicago, III.*, 130 S. Ct. 3020, at 3047(2010}(Court does not question "longstanding regulatory measures" which prohibit carrying firearms in sensitive places such as schools and government buildings). This statement is consistent with other statements in *Heller*, such as the right to keep and bear arms (like other rights conferred by the Bill of Rights) is not unlimited. Moreover, *James v. State*, 731 So.2d 1135 (Miss.1999) recognized that the right to bear arms under our state constitution may be limited by reasonable regulation, such as prohibiting possession of firearms by convicted felons.

Of course, the designation of the three categories as "presumptively lawful" means there exists the possibility that a regulation can be unconstitutional under particular circumstances. The *Heller* Court acknowledged that its opinion left much doubt to be clarified, but that it would further expound upon the historical justifications for the exceptions that it had mentioned if and when those exceptions came before the Court. In the meantime, states and local governmental entities are left with the task of deciding whether existing or contemplated restrictions violate state and federal constitutional rights.

Neither *Heller* nor *McDonald* provide a clear framework for deciding whether a restriction is an impermissible infringement on the right to bear arms. However, the *Heller* opinion eight times drew parallels between the First and Second Amendments. Consequently, several courts have analyzed restrictions in light of First Amendment principles - most notably, the doctrines of strict scrutiny and intermediate scrutiny. *See e.g., Ezell v. City of Chicago,* 651 F.3d 684 (7th Cir. 2011)(whether government regulation infringes the Second Amendment requires the court to evaluate the regulatory means the government has chosen and the public-benefits end it seeks to achieve, and the rigor of this judicial review will depend on how close the regulation comes to the core of the Second Amendment right and the severity of the regulation's burden on the right). In *Ezell*, the court found that city ordinances effectively banned private possession of firearms by simultaneously requiring range training in order to lawfully possess, while also forbidding firing ranges within the city limits. In addition, the city offered no evidence of a governmental purpose being served by the ordinances. Therefore, the court ruled the ordinances to be invalid under the Second Amendment.

Several other court cases addressing the "sensitive places" language of *Heller* have upheld partial restrictions,. See *United States v. Masciandaro,* 638 F.3d 458 (4th Cir. 2011)(federaf regulation banning loaded - but not unloaded - firearms in vehicles in National Parks upheld); *GeorgiaCarry.Org v. Georgia,*

687 F.3d 1244 (11ᵗʰ Cir. 2012)(law banning guns from churches upheld, but church leadership had private property right to grant permission); *DiGiacinto v. Rector & Visitors of George Mason*, 704 S.E.2d 365 (Va. 2011)(upheld state university regulation banning guns from specified college buildings and events but not from open grounds).

Others who have written on the subject of sensitive places observe that some "facilities would qualify as sensitive places because security personnel electronically screen persons entering these facilities to determine whether persons are carrying firearms, or weapons of any kind. Equally important, security personnel restrict access to these facilities to only those persons who have been screened and determined to be unarmed." James M. Manley, *Defining the Second Amendment Right to Carry: Objective Limits on a Fundamental Right*, 14 T.M. Cooley J. Prac. & Clinical L. 81, 100 (2012).

In answer to question 7., it is our opinion that a county courthouse would easily be characterized as a "sensitive place." It is a "government building" per *Heller* and *McDonald*, and is the scene of emotionally charged disputes such as child custody battles, criminal prosecutions, property forfeitures, tax sales, etc. Opposing parties are often in close contact with one another. Judges, prosecutors and other elected officials who routinely make unpopular decisions affecting persons have their offices there and are vulnerable. Further, the ban, being limited to the courthouse, is reasonably tailored to serve the governmental interest in preserving security for courthouse proceedings and personnel. The provision by the county of security measures such as the presence of deputies and metal detector checkpoints would further support the Constitutionality of the sheriff's action.

In any case, the sheriff should be able to articulate the government interest being served by such a ban, and why the ban is a reasonable means to achieve that interest. The same applies to any ban imposed by other state or local custodians of government property pursuant to lawful authority. Any ordinance adopted by a county or municipality pursuant to Miss. Code Ann. Section 45-9-53 should be supported by similar findings, preferably reflected in the minutes. Any regulation adopted by a state agency which restricts firearm possession on state property should be supported by similar findings, preferably placed in the administrative record.

By: Mike Lanford
Deputy Attorney General

APPENDIX A

TERRY STOPS AND TRAFFIC STOPS

Under *Terry v. Ohio*, 392 U.S. 1 (1968), a law enforcement officer may briefly detain an individual if he has a reasonable, articulable suspicion that the person to be detained is involved or is about to be involved in criminal activity. Where such a detention occurs, the officer may frisk the outer clothing of the person detained to be sure the person is not armed, if the officer has a reasonable belief that the person may be armed and presently dangerous. *See also Ybarra v. Illinois*, 444 U.S. 85 (1979); *Adams v, Williams*, 407 U.S. 143 (1972); *Sibron v. New York*, 392 U.S. 40 (1968). If the officer feels a weapon, he may take it from the person to ensure the safety of the officer. The reason an officer is permitted to frisk for weapons, where he has a reasonable belief that the person detained may be armed and presently dangerous, is to ensure officer safety. *Terry, supra.*

Terry frisks normally involve instances in which a police officer believes that a person detained has a weapon concealed on his person. Where a person is carrying a weapon in a non-concealed fashion, the question, assuming a valid *Terry* stop, is simply whether the officer may temporarily seize that weapon during the period of the detention.

There have been a number of decisions nationwide that hold that an officer may temporarily seize a weapon that is in plain view in order to ensure the safety of the officer as well as the safety of others who may be nearby, where there is a legitimate or reasonable concern for safety. *E.g. United States v. Antwine* 882 F.2nd 1144, 1147 (8ᵗʰ Cir. 1989)(Officer may seize weapons when justified by the officer's legitimate concern for the safety of others); *United States v. Malacheson*, 597 F.2d 1232 (8ᵗʰ Cir. 1979); *United States v. Rodriquez*, 601 F.3rd 402 (5ᵗʰ Cir. 2010)(Officers justified in temporarily seizing weapons in plain view where officers were reasonably concerned about safety); *United States v. Bishop*, 338 F.3rd 623 (6th Cir.) (and cases cited therein). What factual circumstances would be sufficient to give rise to a legitimate concern for safety of an officer or others is a question that can only be addressed on a case - by - case basis.

As stated above, If an officer observes a person carrying a weapon included in Miss. Code Ann, Section 97-37-1(1) in a way that is not "hidden or obscured from common observation", this, without more, will not give rise to a reasonable suspicion of criminal activity. Nor will it of itself present a reasonable or legitimate concern about safety. The fact of carrying such a weapon in such a manner will not in and of itself provide a lawful basis for a *Terry* stop, or provide a lawful basis to remove the weapon from the person carrying it. However, there could be circumstances in which the carrying of such a weapon could be a factor which, when taken together with other factors, could give rise to a reasonable suspicion of criminal activity.

In the instance of a valid traffic stop, an officer may conduct a limited *Terry* search for weapons in the areas of the passenger compartment of an automobile where a weapon may be placed or hidden, if the officer possesses a reasonable belief, based upon specific, articulable facts, that the occupant or occupants are dangerous, and may take immediate control of a weapon in the car. *Michigan v. Long*, 463 U.S. 1032(1983). It is our view that where a weapon is in plain view in an automobile, and, where an officer has a reasonable concern about his safety or the safety of others, he may seize the weapon for that reason. He may also order the driver out of the vehicle, *Pennsylvania v. Minis*, 434 U.S. 106 (1977), and he may order the passengers out of the vehicle, *Maryland v, Wilson*, 519 U.S. 408 (1997).

In all instances in which the detention ends without arrest, the weapon seized is to be returned by the officer.

COMMUNITY CARETAKING

Law enforcement officers have "complex and multiple tasks to perform in addition to identifying and apprehending persons committing serious criminal offenses"; by design or default, the police are also expected to "reduce the opportunities for the commission of some crimes through preventive patrol and other measures," "aid individuals who are in danger of physical harm," "assist those who cannot care for themselves," "resolve conflict," "create and maintain a feeling of security in the community," and "provide other services on an emergency basis." 3 Wayne R. LaFave, A Treatise on the Fourth Amendment, § 6.6, p. (5th ed.)

In *Cady v. Dombrowski*, 93 S.Ct. 2623, 2528 (1973), the Supreme Court used the term "community caretaking function" to refer to police responsibilities that were "totally divorced from the detection, investigation, or acquisition of evidence relating to the violation of a criminal statute."

When law enforcement officers are not "identifying and apprehending persons committing" criminal offenses, but instead are performing non-investigative duties characterized as part of the "community caretaking function," their actions must be reasonable. For instance, an officer may stop an individual with a firearm who is believed to be mentally deranged and a danger to himself or others if "a reasonable person, given the totality of the circumstances, would believe [the individual] is in need of help or that the safety of the public is endangered." [internal quotations omitted] *Trejo v. State*, 76 So.3d 684 (Miss. 2011). Should a stop under the community caretaking function disclose evidence that is later used for criminal prosecution, courts will carefully analyze the circumstances to ensure that this doctrine is not "abused or used as a pretext for conducting an investigatory [stop and] search for criminal evidence." *Trejo* at 689.

Footnotes

1

"It shall be a felony for any person to possess or carry, whether openly or concealed, any gun, rifle, pistol or other firearm of any kind, or any dynamite cartridge, bomb, grenade, mine or powerful explosive on educational property. However, this subsection does not apply to a BB gun, air rifle or air pistol. Any person violating this subsection shall be guilty of a felony and, upon conviction thereof, shall be fined not more than Five Thousand Dollars ($5,000.00), or committed to the custody of the State Department of Corrections for not more than three (3) years, or both." Miss. Code Ann. Section 97-37-17(2).

Office of the Attorney General
State of Mississippi

Opinion No. 2013-00023

October 1, 2013

Re: Concealed Weapon on a Public School Campus

Scott Cantrell
Superintendent of Education
Monroe County School District
P.O. Box 209
Amory, MS 38821

Dear Superintendent Cantrell:

Attorney General Jim Hood has received your opinion request and has assigned it to me for research and reply.

Issues Presented

Your questions are:

1. Does Mississippi law allow an individual with an "enhanced conceal/carry permit" to carry a concealed weapon on a Mississippi public school campus?

Yes, but the school may restrict individuals to parts of the campus generally open to the public. See MS AG Op., Bounds (Jan. 5, 2012) and MS AG Op., Johnson (Aug. 31, 2011). We note initially that the concealed carry of weapons, as opposed to the open carry of weapons, enjoys no constitutional protections. See *District of Columbia v. Heller*, 554 U.S. 570, 626 (2008)("the majority of the 19th—century courts to consider the question held that prohibitions on carrying concealed weapons were lawful under the Second Amendment or state analogues."); and *Robertson v. Baldwin,165 U.S. 275, 281 (1897).* The Mississippi Constitution of 1890 specifically provides that "... the legislature may regulate or forbid carrying concealed weapons." See *Wilson v. State*, 81 Miss. 404, 33 So. 171 (Miss. 1903). Therefore, questions regarding concealed carry of weapons must be answered solely by referring to statutory law.

Mississippi has had a statutory prohibition against the concealed carry of weapons since at least 1878. See *Tipler v. State*, 57 Miss. 685 (1880). This statute as well as section 12 of the 1890 Constitution were likely adopted to address the problems reported to the governor of Mississippi by Attorney General Morris:

There remains, however, several very effective and very certain agencies and aids to crime and bloodshed. I refer now, on the one hand, to the practice among a large proportion of our male inhabitants of carrying concealed lethal weapons, and, on the other hand, to the universal and ever-present Drinking-Houses. These are the causes of at least nine-tenths of the rowdyism, violence, and crime in the state, and upon them the laws have, as yet, imposed no restraint. [Etc.]

Annual Report of the Attorney General, Jan. 1, 1872. Historically it was considered a cowardly act to carry a weapon concealed rather than openly,[1] and the use of a concealed weapon in a fight constituted attempted murder at common law. *Price v. State*, 7 George 531, 5 So. 99 (Miss. 1858).

Currently, Section 97-37-1 of the Mississippi Code (Supp. 2013) makes it a crime to carry certain concealed weapons, including handguns, but provides an exception for persons who obtain a license (sometimes called a "permit") from the Department of Public Safety pursuant to Section 45-9-101. Subsection (13) of the latter statute lists a number of places in which persons holding a standard license are prohibited from carrying concealed handguns. Therefore, it is a violation of Section 45-9-101 (13) and of 97-37-1 for persons with a standard concealed weapon license to carry a pistol or revolver at those places.

Section 97-37-7 (2) was amended in 2011 to create a second category of concealed carry license, commonly called an "enhanced license." This authorizes the enhanced licensee to carry a concealed pistol or revolver even in the places named in Section 45-9-101 (13). In other words, the person holding an *enhanced license* may carry concealed handguns in the listed locations without violating the concealed weapons law (Section 97-37-1), whereas the carrying of a concealed handgun in those locations with a *standard license* does violate that law.

Two of the listed locations are "any elementary or secondary school facility" as well as "any school, college or professional athletic event not related to firearms." Therefore, the holder of an *enhanced license* does not violate the concealed weapon statute, 97-371, by carrying a firearm into a public school facility or non-firearm related athletic event. Further, as we stated in our opinion to Bounds, dated January 5, 2012, it is our opinion that the enhanced permit law is an exception to Section 97-37-17, which otherwise makes it a felony to possess a firearm on educational property.[2]

2. If Mississippi law does not prohibit an individual with an enhanced conceal/carry permit from carrying a concealed weapon on a Mississippi public school campus, may the local School Board establish a policy that

prohibits the carrying of concealed weapons on campus by school district employees or outside individuals with enhanced conceal/carry certification?

The school board may establish employment policies and enter employment contracts which prohibit the carrying of concealed weapons by employees, even with enhanced carry certification. MS AG Op., Pennington (March 1, 2013).

The answer to the second part of your question, whether the district can prohibit the carrying of concealed weapons by outside individuals with enhanced permits, is problematic. It is problematic due to the legislative language of Section 97-37-7 (2), adopted in 2012 by way of a floor amendment, referring back to but not amending the prohibitory language of Section 45-9-101 (13) for the kinds of conduct that would be permitted by the enhanced permit. This legislative construct, if read literally, leads to several results that we do not think the legislature intended.

For example:

Section 97-37-7 (2) states that an enhanced permit holder "shall also be authorized to carry weapons in... any location listed in subsection (13) of Section 45-9-101" which includes "any place where the carrying of firearms is prohibited by federal law." No citation of authority is needed to know that our state statute cannot authorize the concealed carry of weapons where prohibited by federal law.

Further, the same combination of statutes could be read as authorizing enhanced permit holders to carry weapons on private property where the owner or proprietor has posted a sign forbidding the same. We do not believe such a reading is reasonable since it would result in the violation of a person's private property rights. Further, the result would be that enhanced permit holders could legally carry at a business where a sign using the exact statutory language ("carrying of a pistol or revolver is prohibited") was posted, but could not carry where signage using some other language was posted or where the permit holder was verbally or otherwise forbidden to enter the property with a weapon. In other words, the next-to-last sentence of subsection 13 containing the sign language would be negated by a literal reading of the enhanced permit statute. We do not believe this was the intent of the legislature.

In addition, the same combination of statutes would authorize enhanced permit holders to carry concealed weapons at "any school, college or professional athletic event not related to firearms." (Emphasis added). Read literally, the school or college could not prohibit the enhanced permit holder from attending the school or college athletic event not related to firearms, but could prohibit the enhanced permit holder from attending a school athletic event which is related to firearms.

As noted, to read the statute as written in this manner requires that the statute be read to be in direct conflict with federal law. Given the Supremacy Clause of the United States Constitution and the requirement that state law yield to federal law, this reading logically leads one to conclude that the Section 97-37-7 is unconstitutional under the federal constitution. However, the rules of statutory interpretation require that "[i]f possible, courts should construe statutes so as to render them constitutional rather than unconstitutional ...." *City of Jackson v. Rebuild America, Inc.*, 77 So.3d 1105, 1119 (Miss. App. 2011). Courts will not impute to the legislature an absurd result. *Teche Lines, Inc., v. Danforth*,195 Miss. 226, 12 So.2d 784 (Miss. 1943).

Following this principle, and reading Sections 97-37-1, 45-9-101 and 97-37-7 *in parimateria*, we conclude that the legislature intended, at most, that enhanced permit holders not be subject to prosecution for violating the state concealed weapons statute (97-37-1) when firearms are possessed in places prohibited by federal law - not that licensees are granted an absolute right of entry to those places by virtue of holding the enhanced permit.

This analysis also applies to private property owners or custodians. An enhanced permit cannot constitutionally take away the rights of property owners to exclude persons from their property if that is their wish. As stated by the Mississippi Supreme Court in *Biglane v. Under the Hill Corporation*, 949 So.2d 9, at 16 (Miss. 2007):

It is a basic tenet of property law that a landowner or tenant may use the premises they control in whatever fashion they desire, so long as the law is obeyed. This leads to the logical conclusion that a landowner or valid tenant may forbid any other persons from using their property. This ideal is protected in our law to the point that there are both civil and criminal prohibitions against trespassing.

See also, *GeorgiaCarry.Org v. Georgia*, 687 F.3d 1244 (11th Cir. 2012)(2nd amendment right to bear arms is limited by equally fundamental rights of private property owners to control their property). See generally our discussion of same in MS AG Op., Lance (June 13, 2013). Therefore, private property owners, including but not limited to owners or custodians of those types of property listed in section 45-9-101 (13)(e.g., bars, churches, restaurants serving alcohol, private schools, professional athletic event property) may exclude from their premises persons carrying weapons pursuant to an enhanced permit. They may do this by posting a sign[3] as described in 45-9-101 (13), by giving verbal notice or through notice by other means. The enhanced permit holder would not violate the concealed weapon law (97-37-1) by disregarding such an exclusion; but, depending on the facts, disregard of a private property owner's prohibition of weapons could constitute a violation of Section 97-17-97 (trespass after warning), Section 97-17-93 (entry without permission) or other statute.[4]

Of course, your question is whether the public School District may prohibit enhanced permit holders from carrying weapons onto school property. The same argument as above could be made that the Legislature did not intend to take away the duty and authority of school districts to hold, control and manage school property in the public interest, but merely intended that enhanced permit holders would not violate the concealed carry law by carrying on school property. However, the property rights of state and local governmental entities are purely statutory, not constitutional. Therefore, the constitutional considerations discussed above with regard to federal or private property are not present when applying a literal reading of the statute to public school property.

As shown from all of the above discussion, the amendment to Section 97-37-7 (2), adopted in 2012 by way of a floor amendment, referring back to but not amending the prohibitory language of Section 45-9-101 (13) for the kinds of conduct that would be permitted by the enhanced permit, has resulted in a confused state of law containing conflicting provisions. The intent of the legislature regarding the authority of property owners, including government property owners, to control and manage access to property is unclear and clarification of these statutes is needed. Nevertheless, the legislature has expressly stated in section 97-37-7 (2) that an enhanced permit holder "shall also be authorized to carry weapons in... any location listed in subsection (13) of section 45-9-101," including "any elementary or secondary school facility" and "any school ... athletic event...." In light of this language, our conclusion is that the school district may not bar enhanced permit holders with concealed pistols and revolvers from entry into a school facility or school athletic event to which the general public is otherwise normally permitted.

We discussed with you on the phone a potential situation where an armed parent and enhanced license holder wishes to meet with a teacher or administrator about what the parent feels is unfair discipline or grades given to the parent's child; the teacher or administrator does not wish to meet with the parent while armed. Although an enhanced licensee may carry into the public areas of a school facility, the enhanced license does not authorize him to enter onto parts of property where the public is not generally allowed. As we have stated in previous opinions, even persons carrying a weapon with an enhanced permit may be barred from parts of a government-owned property listed in section 45-9-101 (13) to which the public is normally not allowed. See MS AG Op., Bounds (Jan. 5, 2012) and MS AG Op., Johnson (Aug. 31, 2011). In that regard, we note that unlike a public street or sidewalk, an elementary or secondary school is not considered to be open to the general public, although it may be made so for school plays, concerts, athletic events and the like. See *Digiacinto v. Rector and Visitors of George Mason University*, 704 S.E. 2d 365, 370 (Va. 2011)(A university, unlike a public street or park, is not traditionally open to the public). In fact, since the 1997 school shooting in Pearl, MS, public schools in Mississippi and across the nation have adopted security measures severely limiting public access to school buildings. In Mississippi, controlled visitor access procedures are required for accreditation. Dept. of Education, *Mississippi School Safety Manual*, rev'd, 2008; Miss. Code Ann Section 37-3-83(2). Therefore, the school may, in its discretion, refuse access to an armed, enhanced license holder for a meeting with a teacher or administrator in a non-public area of the school.

2. **If Mississippi law allows school district employees with an "enhanced conceal/carry permit" to carry a concealed weapon on a Mississippi public school campus, may the local school board, for campus security purposes, allow MAEP expenditures for district employees to attend enhanced conceal/carry certification courses and to be carried on the**

campus by these employees after the enhanced conceal/carry training has been successfully completed?

Yes. Miss. Code Ann. Section 37-7-301.1, the "home rule" statute, provides that a school board may adopt any order, resolution or ordinance with respect to district affairs, property and finances which is not inconsistent with some other state law. Our research indicates there is no constitutional or statutory prohibition on using district funds as you described. Previous opinions by this office have emphasized the discretion local school boards have in making expenditures for security and safety—related purposes. MS AG Op., Taylor (July 7, 2003). See also MS AG Op., Higginbottom (September 11, 1991). Further, school districts have the authority to make expenditures with MAEP funds for items which are part of the MAEP formula as well as items which are not components of the formula. MS AG Op., Chaney (June 18, 2004).

You may also wish to review Senate Bill 2659 of the 2013 regular session of the Legislature, which provides that the school board of a district that is financially unable to participate in the MCOPS program may develop a school security plan (which must be approved by the State Board of Education and the Mississippi Department of Public Safety) and may apply for grants under the MCOPS program for training of security personnel employed by the school district.

CONCLUSION

A school district may, in its discretion, prohibit its employees who hold enhanced carry licenses from possessing weapons at the school. In the alternative, a school district may, in its discretion, allow its employees with enhanced carry licenses to carry weapons and may expend funds for those employees to be trained for such purpose.

Other persons with enhanced carry licenses may enter onto school facilities without violating the concealed weapons statutes; and may enter onto the public areas of those schools without being subject to a possible charge of trespass. School districts may bar persons, including persons with enhanced carry permits, from areas of the school to which the general public is not allowed.

By: Michael Lanford
Deputy Attorney General

Footnotes

1

"The policy underlying the prohibition against concealed weapons is based on the protection of those persons who may come into contact with a weapon bearer, compelling persons who carry weapons to so wear them about their persons that others who come in contact with them might see that they are armed and dangerous persons to be avoided in consequence. If a weapon is not concealed, one may take notice of the weapon and its owner and govern oneself accordingly, but no such opportunity for cautious behavior or self—preservation exists for one encountering the bearer of a concealed weapon." 94 C.J.S. Weapons, section 48 (2013).

2

Section 97-37-17 contains other exceptions, including the possession of firearms in a motor vehicle by non-students.

3

Section 45-9-101 (13) prescribes the form of a sign by which persons or entities exercising control over property may disallow the carrying of a concealed pistol or revolver (namely, "carrying of a pistol or revolver is prohibited."). Posting of such a sign, readable from 10 feet, constitutes statutorily sufficient notice to persons, the violation of which would constitute a trespass. Posting of a differently worded sign could also be sufficient but actual notice might have to be proved.

4

It is our opinion that posting the sign described in 45-9-101 (13) conclusively asserts the property owner's right to exclude persons with pistols or revolvers (with either a regular permit or enhanced permit) but does not trigger criminal penalties for concealed weapon under 97-37-1. Our prior opinions to Johnson dated August 21, 2011 and to Bounds dated January 5, 2012 assumed that property owners could trigger criminal penalties under 97-37-1 for regular permit holders by posting the statutory sign. Those opinions are hereby modified in accordance with this opinion.

Office of the Attorney General
State of Mississippi

Opinion No. 2013-00215

October 23, 2013

Re: Application of Open Carry Laws to Mississippi Fair Commission and Department of Agriculture Properties

Cindy Hyde-Smith
Commissioner of Agriculture & Commerce
121 North Jefferson Street
Jackson, MS 39201

Dear Commissioner:

Attorney General Hood is in receipt of your request for an official opinion and has assigned it to me for reply.

Issues Presented

Your letter requests our office's opinion on the following issues:

In light of recent amendments to Miss. Code Ann. Section 97-37-1 (House Bill 2, 2013 Regular Session), can the MFC and the Department prohibit the carrying of weapons, concealed or not concealed, on the Mississippi State Fairgrounds Complex and at properties of the Department, including but not limited to the Mississippi Farmers' Market and the Mississippi Agriculture & Forestry Museum, by posting signage prohibiting the carrying of a weapon?

We understand that the Mississippi Fair Commission ("MFC") and Department of Agriculture Properties ("Department") do not intend to prohibit concealed carry by those individuals with enhanced concealed weapons permits, and accordingly, this opinion does not address that issue.[1]

Legal Analysis and Discussion

A. Concealed Carry

With regard to concealed weapons,[2] your question is readily answerable by reference to Miss. Code Ann. Section 45-9-101(13) which states in relevant part:

In addition to the places enumerated in this subsection, the carrying of a stun gun, concealed pistol or revolver may be disallowed in any place in the discretion of the person or entity exercising control over the physical location of such place by the placing of a written notice clearly readable at a distance of not less than ten (10) feet that the "carrying of a pistol or revolver is prohibited."

It is the opinion of this office that MFC and the Department can disallow the carry of concealed weapons by concealed permit holders by following the notice provisions of Section 45-9-101(13). Thus, with regard to regular concealed carry permit holders, a public body can prohibit the concealed carrying of weapons in all locations by posting the signage referenced in Section 45-9-101, other signage that provides actual notice or otherwise providing actual notice to individuals.

We note that disregard of such a sign or other notice would not be a concealed-weapons violation.[3] Rather, depending on the facts, disregard of the sign could constitute a violation of Section 97-17-97 (trespass after warning), Section 97-17-93 (entry without permission) or other statutes.[4]

B. Open Carry

With regard to open carry on state property, that issue was recently addressed in our opinion, MS AG Op. Lance, June 13, 2013. In Lance, we noted that whether or not the open carrying of weapons on public property can be prohibited is a two-prong inquiry based first on state law authority and second on whether such a prohibition would violate the Second Amendment to the United States Constitution. With regard to state law authority, the Lance Opinion stated:

Custodians or owners of public property generally have the authority and duty, express or necessarily implied, to manage that property in the public interest. This often includes the authority to deny entry to the property, to place conditions upon entry onto the publicly-owned property, and to otherwise regulate and govern that property short of enforcing the state criminal laws. For example, a municipality may prohibit smoking in the city hall and a public library may prohibit loud speech. These activities are perfectly legal, but the municipality and the state library have the statutory authority to prohibit them and to exclude persons who do not comply. See, *Bigham v. Huffman*, 199 WL 33537149 (N.D. Miss. 1999)(Criminal trespass laws applied to public property). The authority of state or local officials to govern and manage government property may be separate and apart from any power to enact police-power ordinances or regulations having criminal or misdemeanor penalties.

Unlike private property owners, however, the authority of custodians of public property to disallow a lawful activity on land controlled by them requires a case-by-case analysis of the authority of the public body or official under state law.

MS AG Op. Lance at p. 6. We have previously opined that "the Legislature has given full authority to regulate the State Fairgrounds to the Mississippi Fair Commission under Section 69-5-3, Mississippi Code of 1972." MS AG Op. White (June 2, 2006). Likewise, responsibility for operations of the Mississippi Agricultural and Forestry Museum is vested in the Department. Miss. Code Ann. Section 69-1-203. Based on this authority and our Lance Opinion, it is our opinion that the Department and MFC are respectively authorized by statute to regulate the open carry of weapons on a person onto properties such as the Mississippi Farmer's Market, the Mississippi Agriculture and Forestry Museum the Mississippi State Fairgrounds Complex[5] if the responsible entity determines that such a prohibition is necessary to secure the properties and to ensure the safety of the public.

With regard to prohibitions against carrying a weapon passing federal constitutional muster, this office in the Lance Opinion discussed the applicable federal law.[6] In Lance, we noted that the federal courts have recognized certain areas as sensitive areas in which prohibitions against firearms will be upheld. Included as sensitive places in the federal case law are locations such as schools and government buildings. Whether the places you describe are "sensitive places" as described by the United States Supreme Court is a determination which must be made by the state agency having control of the property.

As we stated in the Lance opinion, a state agency should be able to articulate the government interest being served by such a ban, and why the ban is a reasonable means to achieve that interest. Any regulation adopted by a state agency which restricts open firearm possession on state property should be supported by such findings, preferably placed in the administrative record. In your case, the following factors may be appropriate to consider in making your determination: the nature of the functions at the locations identified in your letter; the potential for hundreds and in some cases thousands of patrons, including children, to be on site; the presence of armed as well as mounted law enforcement officers; the general need to protect the safety of those on public property, the presence and nature of controlled access points to the area, etc. See *United States v. Masciandaro*, 638 F.3d 458 (4th Cir. 2011)(finding that a parking lot on a National Parkway was a sensitive area in sustaining a federal regulation banning loaded - but not unloaded - firearms in vehicles).

You also ask our opinion about other procedures that might be deemed to be random searches of individuals entering the gates at the State Fairgrounds Complex. This issue is only answerable by reference to federal law and cases construing the Fourth Amendment to the United States Constitution. Accordingly a full discussion of federal constitutional requirements is beyond the scope of this opinion and could only be effectively completed upon fully discussing the searches and search protocol proposed by the MFC, the factors concerning necessity and so forth. Our office is available to assist the MFC and Department in any efforts it may undertake to implement a search or controlled access protocol for the State Fairgrounds Complex and to analyze the issues both under state and federal law.

Conclusion

Based on the foregoing discussion, it is the opinion of this office that the Department and MFC can restrict the concealed carrying of weapons by regular permit holders by posting the statutorily authorized signage, other signage that provides actual notice or otherwise providing actual notice to persons entering onto the subject properties.

By: Ricky G. Luke
Assistant Attorney General

Footnotes

1

This office's opinion with regard to restrictions and the validity of posting signage restricting the concealed carrying of weapons by enhanced permits holders is set forth in MS AG Op. Cantrell (Oct. 1, 2013) at p. 6. In Cantrell we noted that schools could not post signs to prevent enhanced permit holders from carrying concealed weapons in areas generally open to the public because schools are locations in which enhanced permit holders are specifically authorized by statute to carry. We note that the Fair Grounds and grounds operated by the Department are not locations on which enhanced permit holders are specifically authorized to carry in Section 45-9-101(13)

2

A license to carry a concealed weapon under Mississippi law applies only to the carry of "stun guns, concealed pistols or revolvers." See Miss. Code Ann. Section 45-9-101. Section 97-37-1 provides criminal penalties for carrying of a weapon concealed "except as otherwise provided in Section 45-9-101." Thus, the authority of public body to generally prohibit the carrying of concealed weapons, other than stun guns and concealed pistols or revolvers remains rooted in Section 97-37-1. Thus, when discussing the carrying of concealed weapons in this opinion, the use of the word weapon(s) relates to stun guns, pistols or revolvers.

3

However, Section 45-9-101 does not authorize a regular concealed permit holder to carry in the following locations:

"any police, sheriff or highway patrol station; any detention facility, prison or jail; any courthouse; any courtroom, except that nothing in this section shall preclude a judge from carrying a concealed weapon or determining who will carry a concealed weapon in his courtroom; any polling place; any meeting place of the governing body of any governmental entity; any meeting of the Legislature or a committee thereof; any school, college or professional athletic event not related to firearms; any portion of an establishment, licensed to dispense alcoholic beverages for consumption on the premises, that is primarily devoted to dispensing alcoholic beverages; any portion of an establishment in which beer or light wine is consumed on the premises, that is primarily devoted to such purpose; any elementary or secondary school facility; any junior college, community college, college or university facility unless for the purpose of participating in any authorized firearms-related activity; inside the passenger terminal of any airport, except that no person shall be prohibited from carrying any legal firearm into the terminal if the firearm is encased for shipment, for purposes of checking such firearm as baggage to be lawfully transported on any aircraft; any church or other place of worship; or any place where the carrying of firearms is prohibited by federal law."

Thus, a regular concealed carry permit holder would violate Section 97-37-1 by carrying a concealed weapon into these listed locations.

4

Our prior opinions to Johnson dated August 21, 2011 and to Bounds dated January 5, 2012 assumed that property owners could trigger criminal penalties under Section 97-37-1 for regular permit holders by posting the statutory sign referenced in Section 45-9-101. We, however, now modify our opinion to state that that a concealed carry permit holder would not violate Section 97-37-1 by carrying a concealed weapon merely because a sign prohibiting weapons is posted. Our prior opinions are hereby modified in accordance with this opinion.

<u>5</u>

Your opinion request asked for our opinion on areas "including but not limited" to these three specifically identified areas. We do not know what properties would be listed on a full listing of properties owned or controlled by the Department and MFC and cannot opine as to any other locations other than those specifically identified.

<u>6</u>

For a full discussion of the federal law issues, see the Lance Opinion at pp. 7-9, a copy of which is attached hereto.

Office of the Attorney General
State of Mississippi

Opinion No. 2013-00219

November 15, 2013

Re: Clarification of statutory requirements regarding the return of firearms to patients upon discharge from treatment at Pine Grove Behavioral Health Psychiatric and/or addiction units

Mr. V. Wayne Landers
Director
Department of Public Safety
Forrest General Hospital
P.O. Box 16389
Hattiesburg, MS 39404-6389

Dear Mr. Landers:

Attorney General Hood is in receipt of your request for an official opinion and it has been assigned to me for research and reply.

Background and Questions Presented

Your letter states:

The Forrest General Hospital Police has under its jurisdiction Pine Grove Behavioral Health, which has various programs; two of which are the psychiatric unit and the addiction unit. When a patient is admitted to either of these programs a search of their person and property is conducted. If a weapon is found, it is secured by the police department for safekeeping.

With the knowledge that an individual participated in either of these programs; when the individual discharges and requests their weapon returned, do we have any legal standing on refusing to return the weapon? If so, how long would the department be obligated to hold the weapon before either returning it to the owner or disposing of it?

Response

Pursuant to Miss. Code Ann. Section 7-5-25, the Attorney General is authorized to issue official opinions regarding questions of law. The questions you present relate primarily to federal law and are subject to a number of different factual scenarios and interpretations; therefore, we are unable to respond to your question with an official opinion. For informational purposes, we offer the following information.

Applicable Law and Conclusion

* * *

18 U.S.C.A. Section 922 addresses federal crimes regarding the possession and distribution of firearms by certain persons and states in part:

(d) It shall be unlawful for any person to sell or otherwise dispose of any firearm or ammunition to any person knowing or having reasonable cause to believe that such person-

(3) is an unlawful user of or addicted to any controlled substance (as defined in section 102 of the Controlled Substances Act (21 USC 802));

* * *

(4) has been adjudicated as a mental defective or has been committed to any mental institution

* * *

(g) It shall be unlawful for any person-

*p * *

(3) who is an unlawful user of or addicted to any controlled substance (as defined in Section 102 of the Controlled Substances Act (21 U.S.C. 802));

* * *

(4) who has been adjudicated as a mental defective or who has been committed to a mental institution;

* * *

to ship or transport in interstate or foreign commerce, or possess in or affecting commerce, any firearm or ammunition; or to receive any firearm or ammunition which has been shipped or transported in interstate or foreign commerce.

In addition to the scenarios listed above, the federal statute addresses a number of other instances in which it is unlawful for a person to possess or ""dispose of" firearms or ammunition to another person. You may wish to consult with the U.S. Attorney's Office or the Bureau of Alcohol, Tobacco,

Firearms and Explosives regarding the interpretation and enforcement of these federal provisions.

Mississippi law specifically prohibits persons from selling, giving or lending to "any minor under eighteen (18) years of age or person intoxicated, knowing him to be a minor under eighteen (18) years of age or in a state of intoxication, any deadly weapon, or other weapon the carrying of which concealed is prohibited, or pistol cartridge; and, on conviction thereof, he shall be punished by a fine not more than One Thousand Dollars ($1,000.00), or imprisoned in the county jail not exceeding one (1) year, or both." See Miss. Code Ann. Section 97-37-13.

I am enclosing complete copies of both statutes for your reference. Please let us know if this office can be of further assistance.

Sincerely,

By: Chuck Rubisoff
Assistant Attorney General

Office of the Attorney General
State of Mississippi

Opinion No. 2013-00217

December 2, 2013

Re: City Ordinance Prohibiting the Carrying of Firearms

Wendell H. Trapp, Jr., Esq.
Mitchell, McNutt &Sams, P.A.
Post Office Box 1200
Corinth, MS 38835-1200

Dear Mr. Trapp:

Attorney General Jim Hood has received your request for an official opinion and assigned it to me for research and response. An Attorney General's opinion can neither validate nor invalidate past action of a municipality. Therefore, this opinion is given on a prospective basis only.

Factual Background

Your letter states that the City of Corinth (the "City") prohibits the possession of firearms, with no distinction between concealed or openly carried weapons,[1] in the following areas:

1. A public park or at a public meeting of a municipality or other governmental body:
2. A non-firearm related political rally, parade or public meeting;

3. A non-firearm related school, college or professional event including, but not limited to, an athletic event, concert, or other group assembly;

4. In or upon the premises of any financial institution;

5. In or upon the premises of any establishment which permits on-premises consumption of beer, wine or alcoholic beverages; or in or upon any city, county or other governmental owned building or property.

In a subsequent telephone conversation, you confirmed that Corinth's ordinance imposes misdemeanor penalties.

Issues Presented

Your letter notes the prohibitions found in Section 45-9-101(13)[2] and asks the following questions: Does Subsection (13) apply to "openly carried firearms" or apply only to "concealed" weapons? You also question whether the City can use signage as authorized under Section 45-9-101(13). You next ask whether, assuming that Subsection (13) does not prohibit open carry in those places enumerated in the City's ordinance, is the City nonetheless entitled to enforce its ordinance relating to open and concealed carry with regard to such places. To restate your questions we understand them to be (1) whether, and if so how, Section 45-9-101(13) applies to open carry of weapons, (2) can the City use the signage authorized by Section 45-9-101(13) to prevent carrying of firearms on certain property and (3) whether the City's ordinance as written is enforceable.

Response and Legal Analysis

In response to your first question, Section 45-9-101 does not apply to open carrying of weapons. This statute is devoted in its entirety and facially applies only to licensing issues and authority to carry "stun guns,[3] concealed pistols or revolvers." Therefore, it is the opinion of this office that the licensing and other requirements set forth in Subsection (13) do not apply to or restrict in any manner the open carry of any firearm.[4]

In response to your second question and with regard to the use of signage by a municipality, the opinion of this office depends on whether the person is carrying concealed with a permit, carrying concealed with an enhanced permit or carrying openly. As to regular concealed permit holders, it is the opinion of this office that a municipality can prohibit regular permit holders from entry into *property owned or controlled by the municipality* by posting the signage set out in Section 45-9-101(13).

With regard to enhanced permit holders a municipality *has limited* authority to prohibit enhanced permits holders from entry *into property owned or controlled by the municipality* by posting the signage set out in Section 45-9-101(13). This authority is limited because enhanced permit holders are specifically authorized by Section 97-37-7(2) to carry "weapons" as follows:

A person licensed under Section 45-9-101 to carry a concealed pistol [and who has also obtained an enhanced permit endorsement on his license] shall also be authorized to carry weapons in courthouses except in courtrooms during a judicial proceeding, and any location listed in subsection (13) of Section 45-9-101, except any place of nuisance as defined in Section 95-3-1, any police, sheriff or highway patrol station or any detention facility, prison or jail.

Reading Section 97-37-7(2) in conjunction with Section 45-9-101(13), it is the opinion of this office that an enhanced permit holder can carry a stun gun or a concealed pistol or revolver (even where governmental entities have posted signage) in the following locations found in Section 45-9-101(13):

1. Any polling place. — (Other than the Section 45-9-101(13) prohibiting regular permit holders from carrying in polling places, Mississippi Code Sections 23-15-895 (relating to armed candidates) and 97-13-29 (military officer keeping armed troops within one mile of an election) are the only other state law restrictions regarding firearms in polling places.)

2. Any meeting place of the governing body of any governmental entity.

— (It is the opinion of this office that the phrase meeting place means the room in which a meeting transpires as opposed to the entire building. Thus, although an enhanced permit holder would be entitled to carry a concealed pistol or revolver into a meeting place, that individual would not have unfettered gun carrying access to places within the building that are not generally open to the general public. *See* MS AG Op. Cantrell (Oct. 1, 2013)).

1. Any meeting of the Legislature or a committee thereof. — (Notwithstanding this language, it is the understanding of this office that the House and the Senate have each passed rules or regulations restricting the right of individuals to carry weapons at meetings of the Legislature or its committees.)

4. Any school, college or profession athletic event not related to firearms.

— (This provision authorizes an enhanced permit holder to carry a stun gun, concealed pistol or revolver into non-firearm related events even if signage is posted pursuant to Section 45-9-101(13). However, if signage were posted relating to a ***firearm related*** school, college or professional event, enhanced permit holders would not be authorized to carry their weapons.)

5. Any portion of an establishment, licensed to dispense alcoholic beverages for consumption on the premises, that is primarily devoted to dispensing alcoholic beverages.

— (This provision would only have applicability to governmental entities to the extent that such entities owned an establishment that was primarily devoted to consuming alcoholic beverages.)

6. Any portion of an establishment in which beer or light wine is consumed on the premises, that is primarily devoted to such purpose.

— (This provision would only have applicability to governmental entities to the extent that such entities owned an establishment that was primarily devoted to consuming beer or light wine.)

7. Any elementary or secondary school facility. — (*See* MS AG Op. Cantrell (Oct. 1, 2013)).

8. Any junior college, community college, college or university facility.

9.   Inside the passenger terminal of any airport.

— (Any person may bring a weapon into a passenger terminal if brought in for the purposes of properly lawfully checking or shipping such weapon. An enhanced permit holder could of course still be arrested under federal law for possessing a weapon in areas prohibited by federal law.)

10.   Any church or other place of worship. (Practically speaking this provision would not apply to public entities who do not own or control places of worship. This provision has little practical value because private land owners

can generally always allow or disallow anyone from carrying a weapon on their private property regardless of whether the state has granted a license.

— *See* MS AG Op. Cantrell (Oct. 1, 2013)).

11. Any place where the carrying of firearms is prohibited by federal law. (This provision can only be read to mean that an enhanced permit holder carrying a weapon on prohibited federal property would not be subject to prosecution for state law violations. The federal government certainly could and probably would prosecute anyone bringing a weapon into an unauthorized area regardless of the person's possession of a state permit.).

12. In a parade or demonstration for which a permit is required.

13. In courthouses except in courtrooms during a judicial proceeding.

— (The right to carry in courthouses except in courtrooms during judicial proceedings is granted to enhanced permit holders expressly by Section 97-37-7 without reference to Section 45-9-101(13). Section 45-9-101(13) states that regular permit holders may not carry in "courthouses" or "courtrooms" with the caveat that nothing contained therein precludes a judge from determining who "will" carry a weapon "in his courtroom." Presumably under this authority, a judge has authority to determine who will, who can and who cannot carry a weapon in his courtroom. However, the governing authority of the jurisdiction, whether municipal or county could restrict a regular permit holder from initial entry into the courthouse, as opposed to the courtroom, by posting a sign. However, such signage could not prevent an enhanced permit holder from entry into the courthouse. Under no interpretation of the law would either a regular or enhanced permit holder be authorized to carry a firearm into a courtroom during a judicial proceeding unless authorized by the judge. Likewise, as noted above, an individual would not have unfettered gun carrying access to places within the building that are not generally open to the general public. *See* MS AG Op. Cantrell (Oct. 1, 2013)).

If an enhanced permit holder ignores such signs, we previously opined in MS AG Op. Cantrell (Oct. 1, 2013) that the permit holder could be liable for a violation of Section 97-17-97 (trespass after warning), Section 97-17-93 (entry without permission) or other statute. Also in Cantrell, we opined that while a property owner can use the signage set forth in statute, "[p]osting of a differently worded sign could also be sufficient but actual notice might have to be proved."

Both Section 97-37-7(2) and Section 45-9-101(13) make it clear that neither an enhanced nor regular permit holder can carry into the following locations:

1. Any place of nuisance defined in Section 95-3-1 which would include "any place ... in or upon which lewdness, assignation or prostitution is conducted, permitted, continued or exists or any other place ... or upon which a controlled substance as defined in section 41-29-105 ... is unlawfully used, possessed, sold or delivered and the personal property and contents used in conducting or maintaining any such place for any such purpose. See Miss. Code Ann. Section 95-3-1 (as amended).

2. Any police, sheriff or highway patrol station.

3. Any detention facility, prison or jail.

With regard to posting of signs pursuant to Section 45-9-101(13), a municipality is acting pursuant to state law and not exercising its independent regulatory authority. As discussed herein below, the Legislature has placed substantial limitations on a municipality's authority to regulate the possession of firearms. This principle is important because as we noted above Section

45-9-101(13) applies only to the carrying of concealed weapons and not openly carried weapons. Thus, we find no authority for a municipality to restrict the open carrying of firearms by use of signs or any means other than the express and limited authority given by Section 45-9-53 discussed below. Your third question is whether the City's pre-existing ordinance is enforceable. With regard to municipal ordinances, this office has opined as follows:

The Attorney General's Office generally does not interpret municipal ordinances by way of official opinion. We have previously recognized that the interpretation and application of municipal ordinances are more appropriately determined by the governing authority of the municipality. MS AG Op., Jones (July 27, 2012); MS AG Op., Adams (March 25, 2011); MS AG Op., Doty (Oct. 6, 2000).

MS AG Op. Trapp (April 5, 2013). Moreover a municipality only has "authority under home rule to enact an ordinance ... provided the ordinance does not conflict with state statutes." MS AG Op. Povall (Dec. 18, 2009). In *Green v. Cleary Water, Sewer & Fire Dist.*, 910 So.2d 1022, 1031 (Miss. 2005) the Supreme Court reversed an order granting summary judgment because a genuine issue of material fact exist[ed] as to whether the ... Ordinance conflict[ed] with Department of Health regulations." With regard to the City's ordinance, it is apparent that the ordinance in some instances does and perhaps in many instances could conflict with state law thus causing the ordinance to be preempted. Any attempt by this office to discuss each aspect of the ordinance and the multiple factual scenarios to which it could be applied would be hopelessly complex and confusing. For this reason, and because opinions of this office must avoid factual determinations and opining on past acts and because we cannot possibly anticipate each factual scenario in which enforcement of the ordinance might be attempted, this opinion will instead attempt to set out affirmatively what we believe is the permissible scope for municipal ordinances relating to carrying of weapons.

Section 45-9-51, subject to limited exceptions, prohibits municipalities from regulating the carrying of firearms as follows:

Subject to the provisions of Section 45-9-53, no county or municipality may adopt any ordinance that restricts ... the possession ... of firearms ...

Section 45-9-53 authorizes limited regulations by stating:

(1) This section and Section 45-9-51 *do not affect the authority that a county or municipality may have under another law*:

* * * * *

(f) To regulate the carrying of a firearm at: (i) a public park or at a public meeting of a county, municipality or other governmental body; (ii) a political rally, parade or official political meeting; or (iii) a non-firearm-related school, college or professional athletic event;[5]

Our reading of these statutes is that a municipality may regulate, by ordinance, the carrying of any firearm, whether concealed or not, at only the locations or events identified in Section 45-9-53 if, as the statute notes, the municipality is authorized by "another law" to enact such an ordinance. Our research has found no law that expressly authorizes municipalities to regulate the carrying of a firearm. However, it is the opinion of this office that the Home Rule Statute, Miss. Code Ann. Section 21-17-5, provides such authority and would constitute "another law" as referenced in Section 45-9-51.

Based on this authority, it is the opinion of this office that a municipality could pass an ordinance prohibiting concealed carry under a regular carry permit or open carrying of weapons only at the following locations: (1) a public park or at a public meeting of the municipality or other municipal governmental body;[6] (2) a political rally, parade or official political meeting; or (3) a non-firearm-related school, college or professional athletic event. This opinion and a municipality's authority, however, are limited with regard to enhanced permit holders because such enhanced permit holders are expressly authorized via Section 97-7-7(2) and Section 45-9-101(13) to carry concealed pistols in a "meeting place" of a governmental entity or to a "non-firearm related school, college or professional athletic event." Thus, a municipality could not prohibit enhanced permit holders from carrying in these locations by ordinance.

Additionally, any municipal ordinance that regulates the open carry of weapons in the places enumerated in Section 45-9-53(f) must meet constitutional muster. While many courts have considered restrictions on concealed carry of firearms to be either presumptively valid or not involving constitutional protections granted under the Second Amendment to the United States Constitution,[7] a ban on the open carry of firearms at least potentially impinges on rights granted under both Article 3, Section 12 of the Mississippi Constitution and the Second Amendment. In MS AG Op. Lance (June 13, 2013), this office opined on the factors that must be considered in determining whether open carry of weapons can be restricted on public property. In Lance, we noted that each individual property and restriction or regulation must be considered on a case-by-case basis in light of both Mississippi state law and federal constitutional law. With regard to this aspect of the applicable law, we refer you to the Lance opinion as our best analysis on that topic.

If our office can be of further assistance, please feel free to contact us.

By: Ricky G. Luke
Assistant Attorney General

Footnotes

<u>1</u>

The discussion of open carrying of firearms would relate to pistols, revolvers, handguns, rifles or shotguns. Under Mississippi's concealed weapons permitting statutes, permits are available only for stun guns or "concealed pistols or revolvers."

<u>2</u>

Section 45-9-101(13) states in relevant part: "In addition to the places enumerated in this subsection, *the carrying of a stun gun, concealed pistol or revolver may be disallowed in any place in the discretion of the person or entity exercising control over the physical location of such place by the placing of a written notice clearly readable at a distance of not less than ten (10) feet that the 'carrying of a pistol or revolver is prohibited.'* No license issued pursuant to this section shall authorize the participants in a parade or demonstration for which a permit is required to carry a stun gun, concealed pistol or revolver."

<u>3</u>

The statute's reference to "stun guns, concealed pistols or revolvers" without placing "concealed" before stun guns leaves some question as to whether the licensing applies to open or concealed carry stun guns. However the recent amendment by H.B. 2 to Section 45-9-101(14) now clarifies that the licensing applies only to "concealed" stun guns. This recent amendment stated: "The licensing requirements of this section do not apply to the carrying ... of a stun gun, pistol or revolver, knife, or other deadly weapon that is not concealed as defined in Section 97 -37-1." Thus we conclude that the licenses granted by Sections 45-9-101 and 97-37-7(2) are to carry a concealed stun gun and no license is needed to openly carry a stun gun.

<u>4</u>

Section 45-9-101(13) expressly states that "in addition to the places enumerated in this subsection, the carrying of a stun gun, concealed pistol or revolver may be disallowed ... by the posting of a written notice ... "There is no language in Section 45-9-101 that attempts to make the law applicable to open carry, and indeed, subsection (14) was amended by H.B. 2 to state "[t] he licensing requirements of this *section* do not apply to the carrying by any person of a stun gun, pistol or revolver, knife, or other deadly weapon that is not concealed ..." Notably, this amendment discussed the applicability of the ""section" as opposed to any one subsection.

<u>5</u>

We take the legislative language at its face value. By this statute, the Legislature clearly indicated that it did not intend to "affect the authority" of a municipality granted by another law to regulate guns in the enumerated categories found in (i) through (iii). W e therefore logically conclude that to the extent additional regulatory authority over possession of firearms in places other than (i) through (iii) could be gleaned from a statute such as the Home Rule Statute, that authority is stripped or rescinded by virtue of Sections 45-9-51 and 45-9-53.

<u>6</u>

The current version of the City's ordinance purports to prohibit the right of citizens to carry weapons on governmental property controlled by other governmental entities. This office has previously opined that one governmental entity cannot usurp control over facilities owned by a separate governmental entity. *See eg.*, MS AG Op. White (June 2, 2006)(Opining that "the Jackson City Council has no authority to ban gun shows on the Mississippi State Fairgrounds.") Thus, this office does not believe that a municipality could by ordinance restrict carry rights on property owned or controlled by other local or state governmental entities.

7

See Peterson v. Martinez, 707 F.3d 1197 (10th Cir.2013) (holding Second Amendment does not provide the right to carry a concealed firearm); *Kachalsky v. County of Westchester*, 701 F.3d 81 (holding New York legislation limiting concealed firearms in public does not violate the Second Amendment); *Hightower v. City of Boston*, 693 F.3d 61, 73 (1st Cir.2012) (holding revocation of license to carry concealed firearm did not violate Second Amendment); *United States v. Rene E.*, 583 F.3d 8, 12 (1st Cir.2009) ("laws prohibiting the carrying of concealed weapons" are an "example [] of 'longstanding' restrictions that [are] 'presumptively lawful' under the Second Amendment") (quoting Heller, 554 U.S. at 626); *Richards v. County of Yolo*, 821 F.Supp.2d 1169, 1174 (E.D. Cal.2011) ("[T]he Second Amendment does not create a fundamental right to carry a concealed weapon in public"); *Martinkovich v. Oregon Legislative Body*, 2011 W L 7693036, at p. 2 (D. Or. Aug. 24, 2011) ("The Second Amendment does not prohibit regulations on carrying a concealed weapon."); *Dorr v. Weber*, 741 F.Supp.2d 993, 1005 (N.D. La. 2010) ("a right to carry a concealed weapon under the Second Amendment has not been recognized to date").

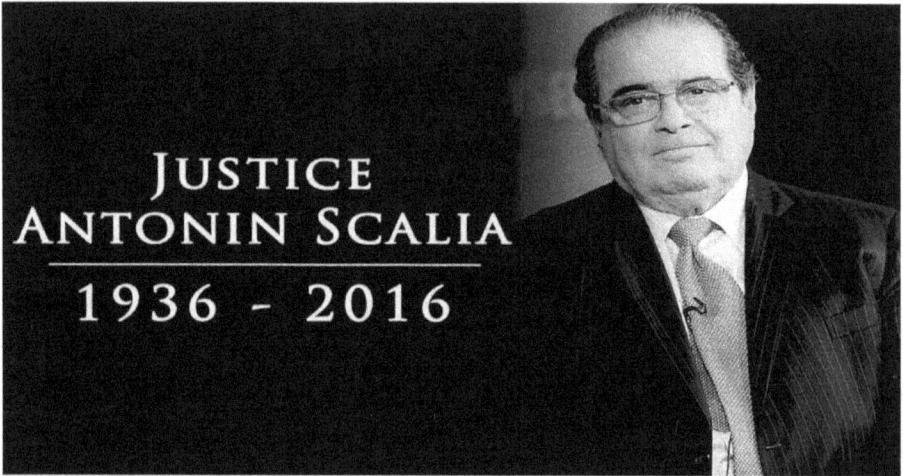

JUSTICE
ANTONIN SCALIA
1936 - 2016

The best gun rights advocate we have ever had on the US Supreme Court.

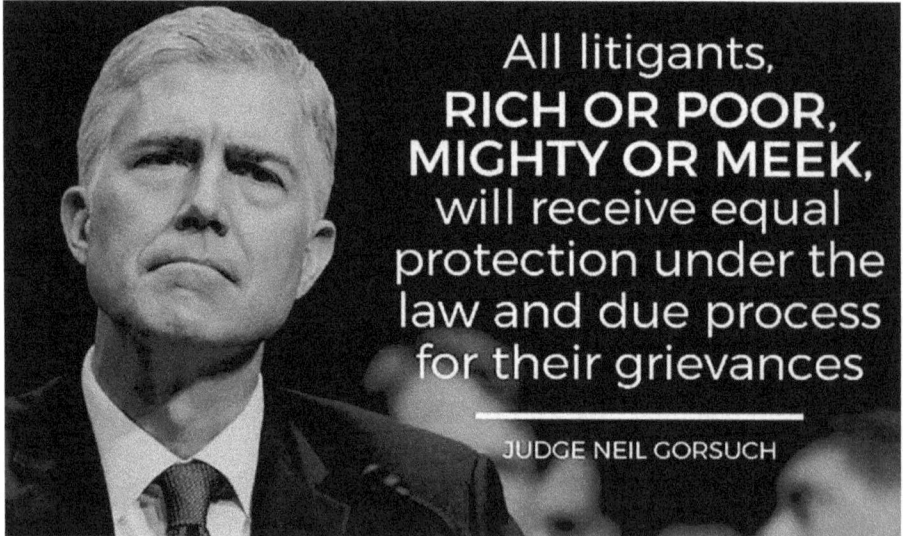

All litigants, **RICH OR POOR, MIGHTY OR MEEK,** will receive equal protection under the law and due process for their grievances

JUDGE NEIL GORSUCH

Judge Scalia's replacement appointed by President Donald John Trump.

Chapter Fourteen
Attorney General Opinions 2014

Office of the Attorney General
State of Mississippi

Opinion No. 2013-00233

February 10, 2014

Re: Banning of Openly Carried Weapons on Property Under the Jurisdiction of the Department of Finance and Administration ("DFA")

Kevin Upchurch
Department of Finance and Administration
P.O. Box 267
Jackson, MS 39205

Dear Mr. Upchurch:

Attorney General Jim Hood has received your request for an official opinion and assigned it to me for research and response.

Issue Presented

Your letter requests this office opinion on the following questions:

1. Can the DFA adopt a written policy that would impose a ban on the open carrying of weapons by anyone other than authorized law enforcement

officials, on state owned property that falls under its jurisdiction; provided that an articulated governmental interest for doing so has been established?

2. If your answer is yes, can the DFA impose a ban, in consultation with the landlord, on the open carrying of weapons on property that is being leased under the provisions of [Miss. Code Ann.] Section 29-5-2(c) provided an articulated governmental interest for doing so has been established?

3. Assuming your answers to 1 and 2 are in the affirmative, can the DFA post signage similar to that authorized in [Miss. Code Ann.] Section 45-9-101(13) notifying the public of the ban on open carrying of weapons on state owned property and on property that is being leased pursuant to [Miss. Code Ann.] Section 29-5-2(c)?

Response and Legal Analysis

Your letter cites to Miss. Code Ann. Section 29-5-2 for the purpose of identifying those buildings over which DFA has "general supervision and care." This section identifies specific buildings by name. Additionally Section 29-5-2(a)(iv) gives DFA the right of general supervision and care over "any property purchased, constructed or otherwise acquired by the State of Mississippi for conducting state business" which is "not specifically under the supervision and care by any other state entity." Your letter also cites to this office's opinion in MS AG Op. Lance (June 13, 2013) for the proposition that open carrying of weapons may be restricted by state and local governments under appropriate circumstances and conditions. On this discrete point, the Lance Opinion can be distilled to its essence to state that a state or local entity can regulate open carrying of weapons on property controlled by the entity if (1) authorized by state law and (2) the regulation meets federal constitutional muster.

With regard to your first question, it is the opinion of this office that DFA has requisite state law authority over those properties specifically listed in Section 29-5-2(a). Additionally, DFA has similar authority over those properties identified generally in Section 29-5-2(a)(iv) to the extent that such properties are not under the "supervision and care" of another "state entity." Whether a property not specifically identified is under the care of another state entity would potentially be a mixed question of law and fact on which this office cannot opine in a general manner without additional facts including the specific identity of the property.

As this office noted in Lance, whether a particular restriction is reasonable and permissible under federal constitutional constraints is a matter that must be determined on a case-by-case analysis in the first instance by the agency implementing the regulation. Because this issue turns on federal law, this office cannot provide an official opinion as to the validity of any particular regulation or restriction on the open carrying of weapons in a particular location. Our opinion in Lance provides our analysis of the federal constitutional considerations which should be helpful in assisting DFA in making these determinations.

Your second question asks whether DFA can impose a ban, "in consultation with the landlord" on property being leased by the State under the provisions of Miss. Code Ann. Section 29-5-2(c). This section sets forth the authority of DFA in part as follows:

To approve or disapprove with the concurrence of the Public Procurement Review Board, any lease or *rental agreements by any state agency or department*, including any state agency financed entirely by federal and special funds, *for space outside the buildings under the jurisdiction of the Department of Finance and Administration* ...

Miss. Code Ann. Section 29-5-2(c)(emphasis added). The wording of the statute seems to clearly contemplate that the leases under this section are for buildings "outside" the jurisdiction of DFA.

It is the opinion of this office that absent some type of memorandum of understanding between DFA and the renting agency, such leased properties would be properties under the supervision and care of another state entity as contemplated in Section 29-5-2(a)(iv).[1] Of course it would still be possible for DFA to consult with the landlord and renting agencies regarding restrictions relating to open carrying of weapons.

Your third question asks whether DFA can post signage similar to that authorized in Miss. Code Ann. Section 45-9-101(13). It should be noted that the signage specified in Section 45-9-101(13) relates specifically to prohibiting the **concealed** carry of weapons onto premises by a person holding a concealed carry permit. For this reason, simply posting the signage prescribed in Section 45-9-101(13) would not, in our opinion, presumptively establish notice to a person carrying a weapon openly, and the agency in any legal proceeding or challenge might be required to prove actual notice. Additionally, it is our opinion that providing notice other than by, or in conjunction with, signage would be appropriate. In the context of notice to concealed carry permit holders, the office has previously opined that notice can be provided by "by posting a sign ..., by giving verbal notice or through notice by other means." MS AG Op. Cantrell (Oct. 1, 2013). We believe the same logic would apply to notice regarding open carrying of weapons. Of course, the ability of DFA to post signs is dependent on whether DFA has jurisdiction over the property in question.

Conclusion

In summary, it is the opinion of this office that DFA can prohibit the open carrying of weapons on state property that is controlled by and under the jurisdiction of DFA. Any such restrictions would, of course, have to meet federal constitutional muster. DFA may post signage on properties controlled by it. Such signs could be similar to the signage referenced in Section 45-9-101(13) or different so long as the signs are sufficient to provide notice to people entering the property. Additionally, DFA could provide notice through verbal or other means. It is our opinion that DFA's power to approve an agency's lease of property, which would place the property under the agency's control, does not authorize DFA to determine whether weapons may be openly carried on such property.

If this office can be of further assistance, do not hesitate to contact us.

By: Ricky G. Luke
Assistant Attorney General

Footnotes

1
You also cite Miss. Code Annotated Section 29-5-77 and 29-5-81. Both of these code provisions likewise contain the exclusionary language for properties under the control of another state agency. Section 29-5-81 specifically gives DFA the authority to enforce state law on certain state property but excludes from that jurisdiction properties "under the supervision and care by any other state entity."

Office of the Attorney General
State of Mississippi

Opinion No. 2013-00241

February 10, 2014

**Re: Classification of Mississippi Department of Human Services ("dhs")
Offices as Sensitive Places for Purposes of Restricting Open Carry of
Weapons**

Richard A. Berry
Department of Human Services
P.O. Box 352
Jackson, MS 39205

Dear Mr. Berry:

Attorney General Jim Hood has received your request for an official opinion
and assigned it to me for research and response.

Issue Presented

Your letter requests this office opinion on the following issues:
Are MDHS offices considered "a sensitive place" where "openly carrying" all
the weapons listed in House Bill 2 may be prohibited?

Your letter then asks, assuming the answer to the above question is yes, (1)
what constitutes "legally sufficient" notice to the public of the proposed ban
on open carry of weapons; (2) will signs readable at a distance of not less than
ten feet suffice to prohibit weapons; (3) do the signs have to read "carrying of

pistol or revolver is prohibited" or is "firearms prohibited" sufficient; (4) if the signs are required to say "pistol or revolver" how does the agency prohibit other weapons; and (5) is a security guard verbally warning a person openly carrying sufficient?

Response and Legal Analysis

Your letter relates to the ability of a state agency to prohibit openly carried weapons. In an opinion issued concurrently with this one to the Department of Finance and Administration, this office opined as follows:

Your letter also cites to this office's opinion in MS AG Op. Lance (June 13, 2013) for the proposition that open carrying of weapons may be restricted by state and local governments under appropriate circumstances and conditions. On this discrete point, the Lance Opinion can be distilled to its essence to state that a state or local entity can regulate open carrying of weapons on property controlled by the entity if (1) authorized by state law and (2) the regulation meets federal constitutional muster.

MS AG Op. Upchurch (Feb. 10, 2014). Your letter did not ask us about state law authority regarding banning of openly carried weapons, and we assume for purposes of this opinion that DHS has such authority as the owner or controlling entity over the buildings in question.

Your first question focuses on whether DHS offices are sensitive places. The concept of sensitive places for purposes of firearm regulation is a federal constitutional issue. *See* MS AG Op. Lance (June 13, 2013)(discussing federal constitutional considerations). Not only does this issue turn on federal constitutional law, it requires various factual determinations to determine whether a building would fit within the definition of a sensitive place. Our office does not opine on federal law issues or questions of fact, and we restrict our opinions to questions of state law. In MS AG Op Hyde-Smith (Oct. 23, 2013) we stated that "[w]hether the places ... describe[d] are 'sensitive places"D' under constitutional analysis of firearm regulation "is a determination which must be made by the state agency having control of the property." Our opinions in Lance and Hyde- Smith[1] should provide informational guidance on these federal issues.

Because the determination of whether a building is a sensitive place is a factual matter and based on federal law, we must accordingly refrain from opining by way of official opinion. Your remaining questions were contingent on our providing an affirmative answer to your first question. However, we will nonetheless address the notice issues that are at the center of your remaining questions. The majority of your questions on notice center on the requirement in Miss. Code Ann. Section 45-9-101(13). That particular statute deals with concealed weapons and the notice provisions for prohibiting concealed weapon permit holders from entry onto a property. A concealed weapon permit by definition is issued only for a concealed pistol, revolver or stun gun. Thus the signage set out in Section 45-9-101(13) makes reference to the "carrying of a pistol or revolver." There is no concealed weapons permit for a rifle, shotgun or other weapon.

Outside one statute's reference to open carry on educational property, there are no statutes that generally prohibit the open carrying of weapons or that describe the type of notice required. Our prior opinions have based the right to restrict the open carry of weapons on the rights of a property owner. Thus, any criminal penalties or enforcement mechanism relating to prohibitions on open carry derive from the State's law on trespass. The "elements of trespass include willfully and maliciously entering another's property without permission or remaining on his or her property after being told to leave."

Hill v. State, 929 So.2d 338, 341 (Miss. App. 2005). Thus, any agency that chooses to prohibit open carry on its premises must determine how it can best provide notice to a person that they are not allowed on the property while carrying a weapon. It is our opinion that such notice should be actual notice.

In the Upchurch Opinion we noted an agency could provide notice by posting signs, giving verbal notice or using these methods in conjunction with one another. There is, however, no statute which provides a notice provision that would provide a presumption of notice as is the case in Section 45-9-101(13). Each building may present different situations. In the case of limited access buildings, it may be that simply posting a sign is sufficient. However, people who cannot see or read may need some other type of notice. This office cannot opine as to what method would best provide notice in each situation and the question of notice would likely be a question of fact in each case. However, there is no requirement that DHS follow the signage requirements of Section 45-9-101(13) since DHS is prohibiting open carry and prohibiting all weapons and not simply pistols and revolvers.

Conclusion

Unfortunately, we are unable to provide an opinion on whether specific DHS offices are sensitive places. With regard to notice of prohibitions on open carry, it is our opinion that agencies should provide actual notice of the open carry prohibitions. How best to do so with regard to each location is a matter that is best left to the discretion of the agency.

By: Ricky G. Luke
Assistant Attorney General

Office of the Attorney General
State of Mississippi

Opinion No. 2014-00090

March 21, 2014

Re: Open/concealed Carry in Municipal Park

Andrew W. Stuart, II, Esq.
Attorney, City of Guntown
Post Office Box 1266
Tupelo, Mississippi 38802

Dear Mr. Stuart:

Attorney General Jim Hood has received your request for an opinion and has assigned it to me for research and response.

Issues Presented

You inquire as to whether a citizen may reserve a municipal park for the purpose of holding a political rally where the open carry of firearms is visible and encouraged. Specifically, you provide the following:

Please accept this letter as notification that I am the municipal attorney for the board of aldermen of the city of Guntown, Mississippi. I also serve as the prosecuting attorney for that municipality.

First, subject to the applicable ordinance in the city of Guntown, Mississippi, which I have enclosed, together with Mississippi Code Ann. Section 97-37-1;

Mississippi Code Ann. Section 45-9-101, *et al.*, may a private citizen reserve the municipal park, together with the state and community center, paying all applicable fees and costs, hold a political and gun (firearms) rally, and welcome open carry of visible firearms, and encourage attendees to wear firearms?

Next, if the answer to your question is yes, would the municipality be liable for the intentional and/or unintentional torts of attendees that may or may not occur, related to intentional and/or unintentional discharge of a firearm?

Last, could a private individual and/or entity, adhering to applicable municipal ordinance mandates, rent the municipal park and/or community center to hold what is commonly referred to as a "gun show", where firearms and other inherently dangerous weapons are displayed and/or offered for sale?

Response

In regard to your first and third inquiries, we know of no state statute that would prohibit a gun rally or gun show on municipal property. With respect to potential liability, our office does not generally opine on questions of liability because they involve mixed issues of law and fact.

With respect to the application of the provisions of the municipal ordinance, we generally do not by official opinion interpret municipal ordinances, which are best interpreted by the governing authority who adopts such

By: Leigh TricheJanous
Special Assistant Attorney General

Office of the Attorney General
State of Mississippi

Opinion No. 2014-00293

August 1, 2014

Re: Recognition of Concealed Weapon Carry Weapons Licenses Issued by Other States

Odis Easterling
Director
Firearms Unit
Mississippi Department of Public Safety
Post Office Box 958
Jackson, MS 39205-0958

Dear Mr. Easterling:

Attorney General Jim Hood has received your request for an official opinion and assigned it to me for research and response.

Facts and Issues Presented

Your letter states that the Mississippi Department of Public Safety ("DPS") recently received an inquiry from the State of Idaho concerning recognition of that state's regular and enhanced carry licenses. You note that Idaho law, unlike Mississippi law, allows applicants that are at least 18 years of age to receive a regular carry permit. In this regard, this office notes that recent amendments to Section 45-9-101(13) do allow applicants who are 18 years of age to obtain a Mississippi concealed carry license if the person is a member or veteran of the United States Armed Forces and the applicant holds a valid Mississippi driver's license with the "Veteran" designation. Under Idaho law, a holder of an enhanced license must be at least 21 years of age.[1]

Your letter notes that pursuant to Section 45-93-101(19) the Legislature has authorized "any person holding a valid unrevoked and unexpired license to carry stun guns, concealed pistols, or revolvers issued in another state shall have such license recognized by this state to carry stun guns, concealed pistols or revolvers." Your letter notes that Section 97-37-7(2) does not contain similar language.

Your precise opinion request states as follows:

Please render an opinion stating whether Mississippi's recognition of out- of-state concealed weapons licenses is limited to regular licenses or if it applies to enhanced licenses as well. Also, please render an opinion whether Mississippi may recognize an Idaho concealed carry license issued to a person who is under 21 years of age.

Response and Legal Analysis

With regard to your second request concerning whether Mississippi would recognize a sister state's concealed carry license issued to a person over 18[2] but younger than 21, it is the opinion of this office that the answer is yes. Section 45-9-101(18) specifically states that anyone holding a "valid unrevoked and unexpired license to carry stun guns, concealed pistols, or revolvers issued in another state shall have such license recognized by this state to carry stun guns, concealed pistols or revolvers ..." The statute does not authorize officials to go beyond the face of an out-of-state license to determine what requirements that other state may have placed on obtaining the concealed weapons license. If the license is valid, unrevoked and applies to the concealed carry of stun guns, pistols and revolvers, then the license ""shall be recognized" in this state. This would apply even if the holder were only 18 years of age.[34]

The first part of your question seeks our opinion on whether recognition of out-of-state concealed weapons licenses applies only to regular concealed licenses or enhanced licenses as well. Your letter suggests that because Section 45-9-101 contains out-of- state recognition language and Section 97-37-7(2) does not, out-of-state recognition should only be given to regular concealed licenses. The premise of your letter appears to be that there are two distinct Mississippi concealed carry licenses. We do not read the statute in that manner. In our opinion, all licenses are issued pursuant to Section 45-9-101. Section 97-37-7(2) simply provides that "[a] person licensed under Section 45-9-101" who voluntarily completes an instructional course may carry in additional places such as courtrooms except during a judicial proceeding, and locations listed in Section 45-9-101(13). Thus, it is our opinion that all licenses, enhanced and regular, are issued pursuant to Section 45-9-101, and the fact that Section 97-37-7 does not contain language concerning out-of-state recognition does not govern whether this state will recognize out-of-state licenses.

However, we do not believe that the fact that Mississippi would recognize an ""enhanced" out-of-state permit requires that the designation of the out-of-state license as "enhanced" controls where that person may carry a weapon while in this State. Section 45-9-101(13) states where a concealed license holder cannot carry a concealed pistol, revolver or stun gun. Section 97-37-7(2) grants additional carry rights to certain individuals. Those individuals, however, are only those persons who are "licensed under Section 45-9-101" and who complete a voluntary course of instruction. Individuals with out-of-state concealed licenses, of any type, are not licensed "under Section

45-9-101." For this reason, it is the opinion of this office that out-of-state concealed license holders are not authorized to carry weapons in those places listed in Section 45-9-101(13).[2]

Conclusion

To summarize, it is the opinion of this office that Mississippi law requires the recognition of a valid, unrevoked out-of-state concealed carry license properly issued to an individual 18 years or older under the law of another state. Additionally, it is the opinion of this office that out-of-state concealed license holders are not authorized to carry weapons in those places listed in Section 45-9-101(13), which is limited to enhanced license holders licensed under Section 45-9-101 with the enhanced carry rights granted under Section 97-37-7(2).

If this office can be of further assistance, do not hesitate to contact us.

By: Ricky G. Luke
Assistant Attorney General

Footnotes

[1]
Your letter states that Mississippi law also only allows enhanced licenses to be issued to applicants over 21 years old. Our review of the statutes indicated no restrictions on a person who is 18 years of age and otherwise eligible for a concealed carry license from being able to obtain an enhanced carry endorsement under Section 97-37-7(2) to his concealed carry license.

2

See generally, Section 97-37-13 regarding providing weapons to minors under the age of 18..

3

Our opinion could be different if another state allowed permits to be issued to minors. By statute, Mississippi makes the providing of such a weapon to a minor a crime. Where accepting another state's permit would directly violate penal statutes of this state such as prohibitions against minors having weapons, our opinion would most likely be different. This issue is not raised by your request and, accordingly, not answered herein.

4

Mississippi law only allows for the licensed carry of concealed stun guns, pistols and revolvers. Idaho law, according to the Idaho Attorney General's webpage allows concealed license holders to also carry, concealed the following: "[A]ny dirk, dirk knife, bowie knife, dagger, pistol, revolver or any other deadly or dangerous weapon." An Idaho concealed license holder in this State would not be authorized to carry concealed "any bowie knife, dirk knife, butcher knife, switchblade knife, metallic knuckles, blackjack, slingshot, pistol, revolver, or any rifle with a barrel of less than sixteen (16) inches in length, or any shotgun with a barrel of less than eighteen (18) inches in length, machine gun or any fully automatic firearm or deadly weapon, or any muffler or silencer for any firearm ..." *See* Miss. Code Ann. Section 97-37-1 (as amended).

5

Stated otherwise, the carry rights of out-of-state concealed licensed holders are governed by Mississippi law, not the law of the issuing jurisdiction. As previously noted, Idaho, as an example, authorizes holders of its enhanced licenses to carry concealed weapons other than pistols, revolvers or stun guns. An Idaho licensee would not be authorized to carry those other weapons in

Mississippi nor would that person be authorized to carry in those places authorized only for Mississippi licensees who have completed an instructional course.

Office of the Attorney General
State of Mississippi

Opinion No. 2013-00250

September 18, 2014

Re: Opinion Request Concerning Application of Gun Laws

David Ringer, Esq.
Ringer Law Firm
Post Office Box 737
Florence, MS 39073

Dear Mr. Ringer:

Attorney General Jim Hood has received your request for an official opinion and assigned it to me for research and response.

Issues Presented and Responses

On behalf of the Town of Florence, your letter asks the following questions which this opinion will respond to seriatim.

1. We are mindful of Miss. Code Ann. Section 45-9-101(13) which lists the places where a concealed weapons license holder is not allowed to carry his/her concealed weapon. We are also mindful of Miss. Code Ann. Section 45-9-53(1)(f), which clarifies that a municipality may regulate the carrying of a firearm at: "(I) a public park or at a public meeting of a county, municipality or other governmental body; (ii) a political rally, parade or official political meeting; or(iii) a non-firearm-related school, college or

professional athletic event[.]" Our concern is that there is no authority that would allow the City to prevent people from openly carrying weapons inside such places as City Hall, the police station, municipal courtroom, etc. Is there any authority that would allow the Governing Authority to prevent people from openly carrying weapons on City property?

In MS AG Op. Trapp (Dec. 2, 2013), this office opined that the only places that a municipality may regulate the possession of firearms are those places and events listed in Section 45-9-53(1)(f). This remains our opinion, and we are unaware of any other authority under which a municipality can regulate the possession of firearms. Although not specifically asked in your opinion request, we did discuss in the Trapp Opinion the authority of a municipality to use the signage provisions of Section 45-9-101(13) to prevent concealed carry of weapons in certain instances. The Trapp opinion has been supplanted in part by the recent enactment of H.B. 314, effective July 1, 2014, which contains very specific and express limits and/or requirements on municipalities' authority to post signage to prevent concealed carry.

2. We are also mindful that Miss. Code Ann. Section 45-19-101(13) further provides that:

the carrying of a stun gun, concealed pistol or revolver may be disallowed in any place in the discretion of the person or entity exercising control over the physical location of such place by the placing of a written notice clearly readable at a distance of not less than (10) feet that the "carrying of a pistol or revolver is prohibited."

Is there similar authority that would allow a private property owner (or even a county or municipality) to post similar signs in regards to openly carrying a weapon, and if so what are the criminal penalties (if any) if a person who is openly carrying disregards such a sign.

We are aware of no statutory authority that specifically provides for a private person to post signs to prevent the open carrying of weapons on his or her property. However, with regard to private property owners, they have, as a matter of property rights, the ability to control the use of their land, including the ability to prevent individuals from possessing either concealed or openly carried weapons on the property. The answer to your question can be found in our discussion in Lance as follows:

At the core of this question, as well as question 7., is whether the change to the concealed weapons statute alters the power of private property owners and of custodians of public property generally to prohibit conduct on that property that is not criminal, in particular, the carrying of unconcealed weapons. Our answer is that it does not.

A private property owner or manager of a retail store, grocery store or restaurant may exercise his property rights and deny entry to persons carrying weapons on his property (verbally, by posting a sign or by other means). A private property owner may even prohibit enhanced concealed permit holders from their property. As stated by the Mississippi Supreme Court in Biglane v. Under the Hill Corporation, 949 So.2d 9, at 16 (Miss. 2007):

It is a basic tenet of property law that a landowner or tenant may use the premises they control in whatever fashion they desire, so long as the law is obeyed. This leads to the logical conclusion that a landowner or valid tenant may forbid any other persons from using their property. This ideal is protected in our law to the point that there are both civil and criminal prohibitions against trespassing.

See also, GeorgiaCarry.Org v. Georgia, 687 F.3d 1244 (11th Cir. 2012)(2nd amendment right to bear arms is limited by equally fundamental rights of private property owners to control their property). Depending on the facts, violation of a private property owner's prohibition of weapons might constitute a violation of 97-17-97 (trespass after warning), 97-17-93 (entry without permission) or other statute'

MS AG Op. Lance (June 13, 2013)(emphasis added).

In our Trapp opinion, we opined that where municipalities post signs to prohibit the carrying of weapons they do so under state law and not municipal authority. We also opined that Section 45-9-101(13) signage applied only to concealed weapons. Thus we concluded in Trapp as follows:

With regard to posting of signs pursuant to Section 45-9-101(13), a municipality is acting pursuant to state law and not exercising its independent regulatory authority. As discussed herein below, the Legislature has placed substantial limitations on a municipality's authority to regulate the possession of firearms. This principle is important because as we noted above Section 45-9-101(13) applies only to the carrying of concealed weapons and not openly carried weapons.

Thus, we find no authority for a municipality to restrict the open carrying of firearms by use of signs or any means other than the express and limited authority given by Section 45-9-53

MS AG Op., Trapp (Dec. 2, 2013)(emphasis added)..

3. May the agents of a business require that someone, who has entered the premises of the business while otherwise lawfully openly carrying a weapon,

to leave the premises of the building and not return unless he/she leaves the weapon outside the premises?

Because this question applies to private entities and not municipal officers we cannot answer by way of an official opinion. We believe that the answer is generally that a private person has resort to the State's trespass law to either prevent a person from entering property or requiring the person to leave. The ultimate answer would depend on the facts of any given circumstances, and private entities faced with such issues should seek private legal advice.

4. During a traffic stop or while making other contact, may a police officer take possession of the weapon of someone who is otherwise lawfully openly carrying a weapon so as to ensure the safety of the officer, driver, passengers, and bystanders?

5. During a traffic stop or while making other contact, may a police officer take possession of the weapon of someone who is lawfully carrying a concealed weapon so as to ensure the safety of the officer, driver, passengers, and bystanders?

Questions 4 and 5 raise questions which would be dependent on the individual factual scenario of each case. Moreover, the answer would be determined by reference to and application of federal constitutional law including the prohibitions against unlawful search and seizures. Our office does not opine on factual matters and does not opine on questions of federal law. For these reasons, we must decline to respond to these questions. For informational purposes, I am enclosing the Appendix to our Lance Opinion which provides research and discussion of federal case law touching on these issues. If you have further questions regarding these matters and would like to discuss the issues further, I suggest you contact one of our attorneys working in the criminal law area.

If this office can be of further assistance, feel free to contact us.

By: Ricky G. Luke
Assistant Attorney General

APPENDIX A

TERRY STOPS AND TRAFFIC STOPS

Under *Terry v. Ohio*, 392 U.S. 1 (1968), a law enforcement officer may briefly detain an individual if he has a reasonable, articulable suspicion that the person to be detained Is involved or is about to be involved in criminal activity. Where such a detention occurs, the officer may frisk the outer clothing of the person detained to be sure the person is not armed, if the officer has a reasonable belief that the person may be armed and presently dangerous. See *also Ybarra v. Illinois*, 444 U.S. 85 (1979); *Adams v. Williams*, 407 U.S. 143 (1972); *Sibron iv. New York*, 392 U.S. 40 (1968). If the officer feels a weapon, he may take he from the person to ensure the safety of the officer. The reason an officer is permitted to frisk for weapons, where he has a reasonable belief that the person detained may be armed and presently dangerous, is to ensure officer safety. *Terry, supra.*

Terry frisks normally involve instances in which a police officer believes that a person detained has a weapon concealed on his person. Where a person is carrying a weapon in a non-concealed fashion, the question, assuming a valid *Terry* stop, is simply whether the officer may temporarily seize that weapon during the period of the detention.

There have been a number of decisions nationwide that hold that an officer may temporarily seize a weapon that is in plain view in order to ensure the safety of the officer as well as the safety of others who may be nearby, where there is a legitimate or reasonable concern for safety. *E.g., United States v. Antwine* 882 F.2nd 1144, 1147 (8th Cir. 1989)(Officer may seize weapons when justified by the officer's legitimate concern for the safety of others); *United States v. Malacheson*, 597 F.2d 1232 (8th Cir. 1979); *United States v. Rodriquez*, 601 F.3rd 402 (5th Cir. 2010)(Officers justified in temporarily seizing weapons in plain view where officers were reasonably concerned about safety); *United States v. Bishop*, 338 F.3rd 623 (6th Cir.) *(and cases cited therein)*. What factual circumstances would be sufficient to give rise to a legitimate concern for safety of an officer or others is a question that can only be addressed on a case - by - case basis.

As stated above, if an officer observes a person carrying a weapon included in Miss. Code Ann. Section 97-37-1(1) in a way that is not "hidden or obscured from common observation", this, without more, will not give rise to a reasonable suspicion of criminal activity. Nor will it of itself present a reasonable or legitimate concern about safety. The fact of carrying such a weapon in such a manner will not in and of itself provide a lawful basis for a *Terry* stop, or provide a lawful basis to remove the weapon from the person carrying it. However, there could be circumstances in which the carrying of such a weapon could be a factor which, when taken together with other factors, could give rise to a reasonable suspicion of criminal activity.

In the instance of a valid traffic stop, an officer may conduct a limited *Terry* search for weapons in the areas of the passenger compartment of an automobile where a weapon may be placed or hidden, if the officer possesses a reasonable belief, based upon specific, articulable facts, that the occupant or occupants are dangerous, and may take immediate control of a weapon in the car. *Michigan v. Long*, 463 U.S. 1032 (1983). It is our view that where a weapon is in plain view in an automobile, and, where an officer has a reasonable concern about his safety or the safety of others, he may seize the weapon for that reason. He may also order the driver out of the vehicle, *Pennsylvania v. Mims*, 434 U.S. 106 (1977), and he may order the passengers out of the vehicle, *Maryland v. Wilson*, 519 U.S. 408 (1997).

In all instances in which the detention ends without arrest, the weapon seized is to be returned by the officer.

COMMUNITY CARETAKING

Law enforcement officers have "complex and multiple tasks to perform in addition to identifying and apprehending persons committing serious criminal offenses"; by design or default, the police are also expected to "reduce the opportunities for the commission of some crimes through preventive patrol and other measures," "aid individuals who are in danger of physical harm," "assist those who cannot care for themselves," "resolve conflict," "create and maintain a feeling of security in the community," and "provide other services on an emergency basis." 3 Wayne R. LaFave, A Treatise on the Fourth Amendment, § 6.6, p. (5th ed.)

In *Cady v. Dombrowski*, 93 S.Ct 2623, 2528 (1973), the Supreme Court used the term "community caretaking function" to refer to police responsibilities that were "totally divorced from the detection, investigation, or acquisition of evidence relating to the violation of a criminal statute,"

When law enforcement officers are not "identifying and apprehending persons committing" criminal offenses, but instead are performing non-investigative duties characterized as part of the "community caretaking function," their actions must be reasonable. For instance, an officer may stop an individual with a firearm who is believed to be mentally deranged and a danger to himself or others if "a reasonable person, given the totality of the circumstances, would believe [the individual] is in need of help or that the safety of the public is endangered." [internal quotations omitted] *Trejo v. State*, 76 So.3d 684 (Miss. 2011). Should a stop under the community caretaking function disclose evidence that is later used for criminal prosecution, courts will carefully analyze the circumstances to ensure that this doctrine is not "abused or used as a pretext for conducting an investigatory [stop and] search for criminal evidence." *Trejo* at 689.

Office of the Attorney General
State of Mississippi

Opinion No. 2013-00262

September 18, 2014

Re: Regulation of Firearms on the Longleaf Trace

Lynn Cartlidge
President
Board of Directors
Pearl & Leaf Rivers Rails-to-Trails
Recreational District
P.O. Box 15187
Hattiesburg, MS 39404

Dear Ms Cartlidge:

Attorney General Jim Hood has received your request for an official opinion
and assigned it to me for research and response.

Issues Presented

Your letter states that you are President of the Board of Directors of the Pearl
& Leaf Rivers Rails-to-Trails Recreational District (the "District"). The District
was formed pursuant to Miss. Code Ann. Section 55-25-1, *et seq.* Under the
authorizing statutes, districts may be formed by one or more counties and one
or more municipalities. Once formed, a district has the authority to publish
rules and regulations pursuant to Section 55-25-6, and once adopted and
published in accordance with that statute, the rules and regulations have the

force and effect of general law and violations may be punished as a misdemeanor. Municipalities within a district are mandated to enforce a district's regulations within the municipality and may task their municipal police forces to assist in enforcement within the municipality and for a distance not to exceed five (5) miles outside of the municipality. Counties are authorized to levy a tax for support of a district. You note that the District has already passed a rule or regulation which states "firearms of any kind are prohibited on the trail except for authorized personnel, law enforcement officers or by permit." You letter asks the following questions:

1. Can the district prohibit open carry of firearms on and along the trail?

2. If yes, will signage "FIREARMS OR WEAPONS ALLOWED WITH PERMIT[1] ONLY" located at the trail's nine (9) trailheads and/or gateways adequately serve the prohibition, and in further view of the fact entrances can be made throughout the trails length and particularly at highway roads, and street crossings, and at private crossings?

Legal Analysis and Discussion

Your letter asks only about restrictions on open carrying of firearms and for this reason, this opinion will not and does not address any authority the District may have to regulate concealed carry of weapons by either regular or enhanced carry permit holders granted such rights by Section 45-9-101 or Section 97-37-7(2). This office has previously opined that whether a public entity in this state may regulate the open carrying of weapons on public property "is a two-prong inquiry based first on state law authority and second on whether such a prohibition would violate the Second Amendment to the United States Constitution." MS AG Op Hyde-Smith (Oct. 23, 2013). In MS AG Op., Lance (June 13, 2013) we opined that custodians or owners of public property generally have the authority and duty, express or necessarily implied, to manage that property in the public interest. This often includes the authority to deny entry to the property, to place conditions upon entry onto the publicly-owned property, and to otherwise regulate and govern that property short of enforcing the state criminal laws. For example, a municipality may prohibit smoking in the city hall and a public library may prohibit loud speech. These activities are perfectly legal, but the municipality and the state library have the statutory authority to prohibit them and to exclude persons who do not comply. See, *Bigham v. Huffman*, 199 WL 33537149 (N.D. Miss. 1999)(Criminal trespass laws applied to public property). The authority of state or local officials to govern and manage government property may be separate and apart from any power to enact police-power ordinances or regulations having criminal or misdemeanor penalties.

Unlike private property owners, however, the authority of custodians of public property to disallow a lawful activity on land controlled by them requires a case-by-case analysis of the authority of the public body or official under state law.

The District's enabling statute does not make it a state agency, so we believe that it is a local government unit much like a county or municipality. The Legislature has both granted and limited the authority either a county or municipality has to regulate the possession of firearms on county or municipality property. With regard to both entities, the Legislature has granted authority to regulate the possession of firearms specifically in regard to a "public park." Miss. Code Ann. Section 45-9-53(1)(f).[2] The District's enabling statutes grant it authority "to establish rules and regulations for the use of the recreational facilities of the district." Miss. Code Ann. Section 55-25-5. It is the opinion of this office that such authority extends to regulations that require that use of the District's facilities be without possession of a firearm. We believe that the District's property is in the nature of a public park. Because municipalities and counties are authorized to regulate possession of weapons in public parks, we are of the opinion that this supports our conclusion that the District, as a local government entity, should be able under state law to regulate, at a minimum, the open carry of weapons on its property which is either, in fact, a public park or analogous to one.

However, as we noted earlier, regulation of open carrying of weapons must be proper under federal constitutional provisions and the Second Amendment to the United States Constitution. As discussed in our Lance opinion, the regulation of open carry of firearms will be upheld where such areas are properly characterized as "sensitive areas." Whether an area is a "sensitive area" is a determination that must made in the first instance by the agency or entity having control over the property. Such determinations must be made based on the facts with reference to federal law. Our office does not make these types of factual determinations, and we do not opine on matters of federal law. Both the Lance and Hyde-Smith opinions discuss factors that may be considered by a public body in reaching a conclusion regarding whether an area is a "sensitive area." Accordingly, we refer you to those opinions for guidance in this matter. Furthermore, we previously opined that a public body making a determination that an area is a "sensitive area" should articulate the government interest served by the ban as well as its rationale supporting the reasonableness of the ban. Like our prior opinions, we suggest that any findings and determinations that the District make in this regard be included in the administrative record and/or minutes of any meeting approving or making such determinations.

Thus, it is the opinion of this office that the District may regulate open carrying of weapons on the District's property under state law. However, such regulations must be consistent with federal constitutional principles which would require that the area in which a firearms ban is imposed be properly designated as a "sensitive area." This office cannot make that determination on the District's behalf, and because such determinations must be made under federal law, we cannot provide an official opinion as to whether such a determination would be appropriate. We note that your letter states that a regulation is already in existence. This office only opines on prospective matters, and for this reason, this opinion may not be used to either validate or invalidate the previously promulgated rule or regulation.

Your second question asks whether particular language and locations of signs is adequate to "serve the prohibition" in the regulation against open carrying of weapons. We understand your question to be whether the verbiage and locations of the signage is adequate to provide notice to patrons. This question is inherently a factual question on which this office cannot opine. We, instead, limit our opinions to matters of law. Moreover, the regulation and signage are already in place. For your information we do note that Section 55-25-6 provides for the notice to be given when the District passes a rule or regulation, and as we noted once passed such rules and regulations carry the force and effect of law. Generally speaking once a public body passes a regulation or law and complies with the notice provisions, no further notice or actual notice need be given as a prerequisite to enforcement thereof. Of course, the District would have to have complied with the notice provisions when such regulations were enacted, and such regulations should be maintained as a record of the District available for public inspection. These matters all involve past actions upon which we are unaware of the factual circumstances. Accordingly, we decline to opine whether the District followed proper notice procedures when it adopted its regulations.

Conclusion

If this office may be of further assistance, do not hesitate to contact us.

By: Ricky G. Luke
Assistant Attorney General

Footnotes

1

We understand that "PERMIT" refers to the conceal carry license (regular or enhanced) issued by the Mississippi Department of Public Safety.

2

The Legislature in the 2014 Regular Session enacted and the Governor recently signed H.B. 314 which amends Section 45-9-53. The amended statute leaves in place a county or municipality's authority "[t]o regulate the carrying of a firearm at ... a public park" among other places. The District has no specific statute addressing either its rights to regulate weapons or restricting any such right.

Office of the Attorney General
State of Mississippi

Opinion No. 2014-00328

September 18, 2014

Re: City of Diamondhead Proposed Firearm/deadly Weapon Ordinance

Sean Tindell, Esq.
Tindell Law Firm, PLLC
2200 25th Avenue
Gulfport, MS 39501-4520

Dear Mr. Tindell:

Attorney General Jim Hood has received your request for an official opinion and assigned it to me for research and response.

Facts and Issues Presented

Your letter states that the City of Diamondhead (the "City") received an ""opinion"[1] from Deputy Attorney General Whitley in which she determined that the City's prior firearm/deadly weapon ordinance violated Section 45-9-53. The Deputy Attorney General's letter was issued pursuant to the statutory duty to investigate citizens' complaints regarding non-compliant firearm signs and ordinances placed on this office by the recent amendments to Section 45-9-53. *See* H.B. 314 (2014 Reg. Sess.). The purpose of such letters or notices is to provide the conclusions and findings of this office regarding whether a violation exists[2] and to allow local governments an opportunity to cure any violations prior to a citizen bringing suit. In response to Deputy Attorney General Whitley's letter, the City rescinded its prior ordinance. Your letter attaches a proposed new ordinance and asks the following questions:

(1) Does the proposed Ordinance satisfy or meet the requirements of Mississippi Law; and

(2) If, not, what changes should be made to satisfy and cure any deficiencies.

Response and Legal Analysis

As a general matter, response to your initial question would require that we interpret the ordinance to determine how the ordinance would be applied and perhaps to determine the intent or meaning of the ordinance. Our office has repeatedly opined that "[w]ith respect to the application of the provisions of ... municipal ordinance[s], we generally do not by official opinion interpret municipal ordinances, which are best interpreted by the governing authority." MS AG Op. Stuart (March 21, 2014). Because "we cannot possibly anticipate each factual scenario in which enforcement of the ordinance might be attempted," we are limited to a more general discussion of the general scope of permissible regulation. See MS AG Op. Trapp (Dec. 2, 2013)(Declining to interpret and pass on enforceability of a gun ordinance).[2]

In general the City's Ordinance addresses firearm restrictions in two methods. First, the ordinance sets forth that the City Manager is to "ensure that written notice" is posted as set forth in Sections 45-9-53(a) and (b) "in which the carrying of a concealed firearm or other deadly weapon is prohibited." The ordinance does not specify which municipal properties fit within the two subsections nor does it specify the sign and wording to be used with regard to these locations. We can offer no opinion beyond the obvious that if the requirements of Sections 45-9-53(a) and (b) are met, no violations would occur.

However, neither the ordinance nor this opinion would shield the City from liability if a sign were, in spite of the ordinance, posted in violation of the law.

The second prohibition in the ordinance is contained in Article I which states:

The open carrying of any firearm or deadly weapon by any person, except any duly authorized law enforcement officer, is strictly prohibited at: (i) public parks; (ii) public meetings of any governmental body, *including but not limited to*, council meetings, *municipal court proceedings* and planning and zoning meetings; (iii) political rallies; (iv) parades; or (v) non-firearm-related school, college, or professional athletic events. (emphasis added).

Section 45-9-53 authorizes municipalities:

To regulate the carrying of a firearm at: (i) a public park or at a public meeting of a county, municipality or other governmental body; (ii) a political rally, parade or official political meeting; or (iii) a non-firearm-related school, college or professional athletic event;

The ordinance is broader in its application than the statute granting the City firearm regulatory authority. Specifically, the ordinance purports to criminalize the open carrying of a firearm into municipal court proceedings. It is the opinion of this office that a court proceeding does not constitute a ""meeting" of a municipal body or "other governmental body." Although governmental body is not defined for purposes of Section 45-9-53, we believe the definitions given to "meeting" and "public body" used in the Open Meetings Law provide the best analogous references to draw from. Section 25-41-3 states, in relevant part:

For purposes of this chapter, the following words shall have the meaning ascribed herein, to wit:

(a) *"Public body" means any executive or administrative board, commission, authority, council, department, agency, bureau or any other policy-making entity, or committee thereof, of the State of Mississippi, or any political subdivision or municipal corporation of* the state, whether such entity be created by statute or executive order, which is supported wholly or in part by public funds or expends public funds, and any standing, interim or special committee of the Mississippi Legislature. The term "public body" includes the governing board of a charter school authorized by the Mississippi Charter School Authorizer Board.

There shall be exempted from the provisions of this chapter:

(I) The judiciary, including all jury deliberations;

*****

(b) *"Meeting" means an assemblage of members of a public body* at which official acts may be taken upon a matter over which the public body has supervision, control, jurisdiction or advisory power; "meeting" also means any such assemblage through the use of video or teleconference devices.

(Emphasis added). Applying the Open Meetings Law, its definitions and its exclusions of courts from the meaning of public body to Section 45-9-53 leads this office to conclude that when the Legislature authorized municipalities to regulate firearms "at a public meeting of a county, municipality or other governmental body," that authority was not extended to municipal courts. We believe this conclusion is supported by the manner in which the Legislature chose to restrict the rights of regular concealed permit holders in Section 45-9-101(13). There, the Legislature specifically included restrictions on "any courthouse," "any courtroom" and "any meeting place of the governing body of any governmental entity." The Legislature could have used similar words with a specific reference to courts when granting regulatory authority to municipalities and counties but did not. Accordingly, it is the opinion of this office that municipalities are not authorized to pass ordinances restricting the carrying of firearms in courtrooms.

The Legislature's restrictions on the ability of municipalities and counties to regulate carrying of firearms appear to be an express intention to reserve such regulatory authority to the Legislature and to require local governments to rely solely on State statutes in this regard. If it appeared that authority to regulate firearms in courts was a Legislative oversight or that this lack of authority was due to mistake, this office might take a different interpretive approach. However, there are numerous other sensitive areas in which the Legislature has likewise withheld regulatory authority from cities and counties. For example Section 45-9-53 does not authorize local government regulations over firearms in places of nuisance as defined in Section 95-3-1, police stations, sheriff offices, detention facilities or prisons. Given that the Legislature did not authorize local governments to regulate in these sensitive places and facilities, we believe that the lack of reference to courthouses or courtrooms in Section 45-9-53 was by design and not through any error.

Thus, with regard to restriction of firearms in courthouses and other sensitive places, it is our opinion that counties and municipalities are relegated to reliance on State statutes. We are aware that this leaves apparent gaps in the ability to regulate the carrying of firearms openly in certain places. State law restricts the rights of regular license holders to carry weapons in the specified places by virtue of Section 45-9- 101(13). However, those restrictions only apply to concealed carry by license holders. Even the signage language of this

Section applies only to the carrying of "a stun gun, concealed pistol or revolver." Both Section 97-37-7 and Section 45-9-101(13) limit the rights of license holders to carry certain firearms in "any place of nuisance as defined in Section 95-3-1, any police, sheriff or highway patrol station or any detention facility, prison or jail." However, neither of these provisions address the open carrying of firearms in these places. Section 97-37-1 is the general criminal statute (to which the licensing statutes are exceptions) regarding carrying of weapons. However, this section applies only to carrying a specified weapons "concealed on or about one's person," and thus, this section has no applicability to open carry.

Section 97-37-5 restricts the right of a felon to possess "any firearm" which would include an openly carried weapon. Section 97-37-14 provides that it shall be "an act of delinquency for any person who has not attained the age of eighteen (18) years knowingly to have any handgun in such person's possession" and would accordingly restrict such person's right of open carry. Section 97-37-17 makes it a felony for "any person to possess or carry, whether openly or concealed, any gun, rifle, pistol or other firearm of any kind ... on educational property." These appear to be the only legislative restrictions applying, in whole or part, to the open carrying of weapons. While we understand the desire of local governments to apply limitations beyond these areas, we can find no legislative grant of authority to do so.

For the reasons stated above, we believe that the proposed ordinance is beyond the authority of a municipality to enact an ordinance restricting the possession of a firearm. The ordinance includes municipal courts, which in the opinion of this office, are not included in the enumerated places listed in Section 45-9-53(f). With regard to posting of signs, the City should ensure that any locations where signs are posted are properly characterized as places identified in Sections 45-9-53 (a) and (b) and that any such signs include the proper restricting language as required in the statute.

We note for your information that the "WHEREAS" clause discussing Section 45-9-101(13) incorrectly states that the Section prohibits the carrying of "any firearm." Section 45-9-101(13) restricts the carrying of concealed stun guns, pistols and revolvers by license holders. It does not address the carrying of other firearms. Additionally, the ordinance prohibits the open carrying of deadly weapons other than firearms. It is our opinion that the part of the ordinance is facially valid. Section 45-951 restricts the right of local governments to "adopt any ordinance that restricts the possession, carrying, transportation, sale, transfer or ownership of firearms or ammunition or their components." Section 45-9-53 provides exceptions to Section 459-51. However, neither statute has any application to deadly weapons other than firearms.

Conclusion

It is the opinion of this office that the proposed ordinance violates Section 45-9-53(1)(f) in that it attempts to regulate the possession of firearms in municipal court and is beyond the scope of the City's authority. With regard to the application of the ordinance to deadly weapons other than firearms, it is generally within the regulatory authority of a municipality. Since a conclusive opinion regarding the enforceability of the ordinance would require us to interpret and apply the ordinance, such an opinion is beyond the scope of an official opinion issued pursuant to Section 7-5-25. Likewise, we cannot, by official opinion, specify how the ordinance should be drafted to comply with State law.

If this office can be of further assistance, do not hesitate to contact us.

By: Ricky G. Luke
Assistant Attorney General

Footnotes

1

The "opinion" was issued pursuant to Section 45-9-53 and is characterized by that statute as a "notice" of violations. *See* fn. 2, *infra.*

2

The statutory framework of Section 45-9-53 does not indicate that a finding by this office of a violation, *velnon*, has any binding effect on a court or the parties. Our understanding is that notice by this office is a predicate to a suit in a vein similar to a right-to-sue letter issued by the EEOC.

3

We note that we perceive this office's authority regarding official opinions issued pursuant to Section 7-5-25 and reports or notices issued in response to complaints under Section 45-9-53 to be different. Under Section 7-5-25 our opinions are offered to provide limited immunity to prospective acts and are limited to questions involving the determination solely of questions of state law. In regard to official opinions, we do not perform any factual investigations or make determinations on questions of fact, and instead we rely on the facts as represented in the request. To interpret and apply a municipal ordinance, we would be required to go beyond these limits and make determinations that were factual in nature or that involved mixed questions of law and fact. With regard to Section 45-9-53, the Legislature expressly mandated that this office conduct factual investigations regarding alleged violations of firearm laws and issue "notice" of the "findings" made based off of the evidentiary materials included with the complaint and learned through the required investigation. Thus, the report or opinion issued by this office in response to a complaint under Section 45-9-53 could, and most likely would, contain factual conclusions and findings that this office could not make in an official opinion under Section 7-5-25. Likewise, this office could be required to interpret and apply a municipal ordinance under Section 459-53 which would be improper if done pursuant to an official opinion request under Section 7-5-25.

Jackson, MS

Chapter Fifteen
Attorney General Opinions 2015

Office of the Attorney General
State of Mississippi

Opinion No. 2013-00224

February 3, 2015

Re: Municipal Authority Relating to Carrying of Weapons on Municipal Property

Colmon S. Mitchell, Esq.
Smith, Phillips, Mitchell, Scott & Nowak, LLP
Post Office Drawer 1586
Batesville, Mississippi 38606

Dear Mr. Mitchell:

Attorney General Jim Hood has received your request for an official opinion and assigned it to me for research and response.

Issues Presented

Your letter seeks the opinion of this office on the extent to which the City of Batesville (the "City") may regulate the carrying of firearms on municipal property. You note that the City has specific concerns regarding: (1) Meeting of the Mayor and Board of Aldermen; (2) Public hearings; (3) Events on public streets and public square such as parades; (4) Events at the Batesville Civic Center when the Civic Center is leased to a private promoter including such things as a dirt bike race; (5) City employees, other than law enforcement, while engaged in their duties as employees.

Response and Legal Analysis

This office discussed a municipality's authority to regulate carrying of weapons in MS AG Op. Trapp (Dec. 2, 2013)(copy attached). In Trapp, we opined that such authority is governed by Miss. Code Ann. Sections 45-9-51 and 45-9-53. Section 45-9-51 states that "[s]ubject to the provisions of Section 45-9-53, no county or municipality may adopt any ordinance that restricts ... the possession ... of firearms." Section 45-9-53 authorizes limited regulations by a municipality as follows:

(1) This section and Section 45-9-51 *do not affect the authority that a county or municipality may have under another law:*

* * * * *

(f) To regulate the carrying of a firearm at: (i) a public park or at a public meeting of a county, municipality or other governmental body; (ii) a political rally, parade or official political meeting; or (iii) a non-firearm-related school, college or professional athletic event;

Based on these statutes, we opined in Trapp as follows:

Our reading of these statutes is that a municipality may regulate, by ordinance, the carrying of any firearm, whether concealed or not, at only the locations or events identified in Section 45-9-53 if, as the statute notes, the municipality is authorized by "another law" to enact such an ordinance. Our research has found no law that expressly authorizes municipalities to regulate the carrying of a firearm. However, it is the opinion of this office that the Home Rule

Statute, Miss. Code Ann. Section 21-17-5, provides such authority and would constitute "another law" as referenced in Section 45-9-53.

Thus, it is the opinion of this office that a municipality could pass an ordinance or regulations prohibiting concealed carry under a regular carry permit or open carrying of weapons *only* at the following locations: (1) a public park or at a public meeting of the municipality or other municipal governmental body; (2) a political rally, parade or official political meeting; or (3) a non-firearm-related school, college or professional athletic event.[1]

We further opined in Trapp that:

This opinion and a municipality's authority, however, are limited with regard to enhanced permit holders because such enhanced permit holders are expressly authorized via Section 97-7-7(2) and Section 45-9-101(13) to carry concealed pistols in a "meeting place" of a governmental entity or to a "non-firearm related school, college or professional athletic event." Thus, a municipality could not prohibit enhanced permit holders from carrying in these locations by ordinance.

MS AG Op. Trapp (Dec. 2, 2013). The Trapp opinion was issued before the passage of H.B. 314 in the 2014 Regular Session. There is a long-standing and inherent conflict between Section 97-37-7(2) and Section 45-9-53(1)(f). Section 45-9-53(1)(f) gives authority to municipalities to regulate open or concealed carrying of a firearm at "a public meeting of a county, municipality or other governmental body" and a [political] parade and "a non-firearm-related school, college or professional athletic event." On the other hand, Section 97-37-7(2), by reference to Section 45-9-101(13), allows an enhanced permit holder to carry in "any meeting place of the governing body of any governmental entity," "any school, college or professional athletic event not related to firearms," and "in a parade or demonstration for which a permit is required." Thus, the two statutes are at odds with regard to where enhanced license holders can carry and where a city can regulate such carry.

When Trapp was issued, we dealt with this conflict by applying the law as most recently enacted. Section 97-37-7-(2), as it relates to enhanced carry licenses, was the most recently enacted statute and specifically granted rights to enhanced permit holders. Applying interpretive rules and guidelines, this office concluded that the specific and more recently enacted provisions of Section 97-37-7(2) should be given precedence, and this office concluded that municipalities were precluded from prohibiting concealed carry by enhanced license holders at "a public meeting of a county, municipality or other governmental body" and a [political] parade and "a non-firearm-related school, college or professional athletic event." H.B. 314, however, amended Section 45-9-53 with specific reference to the authority of municipalities (and counties as well) regarding prohibiting the carry of firearms. Generally speaking, and in this regard, H.B. 314 modified Section 45-9-53 by setting up three identified groups of places in which municipalities could prohibit weapons by signage. Under the newly amended statute, municipalities can post signs and prohibit carry of weapons in (1) places identified in Section 45-9-53(1)(f) with no limiting language; (2) places identified in Section 45-9-101(13)[2] if, in essence, the sign indicates that it is only applicable to regular concealed license holders; and (3) any place controlled by the municipality other than a place identified in Section 45-9-53(1)(f) or Section 45-9-101(13) if the sign indicates that it does not apply to regular concealed license holders, enhanced concealed license holders or a person otherwise lawfully and openly carrying a firearm. See Miss. Code Ann. Section 45-9-53(4), (4)(a) and 4(b). This office interprets the new grant of authority to municipalities to prohibit carry of weapons by signage in Section 45-9-53(1)(f) locations with no restricting language to mean that municipalities can restrict even enhanced concealed license holders from carrying in those locations. It is obvious by making distinctions between the types of signs required for (1)(f) locations and 101(13) locations, the Legislature intended for municipalities to have more authority in locations identified in (1)(f). To the extent that it is inconsistent or in conflict with this opinion, our opinion in MS AG Op. Trapp (Dec. 2, 2013) is hereby modified and withdrawn.

Thus, consistent with our discussion above and the exceptions noted therein, the City could, by ordinance or regulation, prohibit the carrying of weapons, concealed or not, in meetings of the Board and Mayor or in public meetings of the City or one of its boards, commissions or other official entities including, without limitations, such entities as a zoning board. Whether or not the City could prevent weapons from being carried at events held on the public square or public street would depend on whether such events could be properly characterized as one of the locations listed in Section 45-9-53(1)(f)(ii) or (iii).[2] Likewise, to the extent that such a function occurred on a "public park," the City could regulate the carrying of weapons under Section 45-9-53(1)(f)(i).

Your letter also asks whether the City can regulate the carrying of weapons at the City's Civic Center. We find no authority to regulate the carrying of weapons at the Civic Center unless the activity or event otherwise fits within the events described in Section 45-9-53(1)(f)(i). Your letter asks specifically regarding private events held at the Civic Center. In such cases, this office believes that the City could, as a condition of the lease agreement, require that the private lessee prohibit the carrying of weapons to the event.

Additionally, the City could take the additional step of restricting the carrying of concealed weapons by concealed permit holders by posting signage consistent with the provisions of Section 45-9-101(13) and Section 45-9-53(4), (4)(a) and 4(b).[4] The ability to post signs under Section 45-9-101(13) is, however, limited to concealed weapons. Under the newly amended Section 45-9-53(4), a municipality can prohibit, by posting signage, concealed carrying of weapons by regular or enhanced license holders in places identified in Section

45-9-53(1)(f). A municipality can prohibit, by posting signage, concealed carrying of weapons by regular license holders in places identified in Section 45-9-101(13). *See* Miss. Code Ann. Section 45-9-53(4)(a). Section 45-9-53(4)(b) provides very little authority to municipalities since it only applies to someone that is carrying a weapon illegally under another statute.[5] However, because the signage allowed under Section 45-9-101(13) on its face applies only to concealed carry,[6] a municipality wishing to restrict open carry in Section 45-9-53(1)(f) locations should pass an ordinance prohibiting open carry.

When regulations or ordinances affecting open carrying of weapons are considered constitutional issues that arise by virtue of the Second Amendment to the United States Constitution must be addressed. In Trapp, we discussed this issue as follows:

[A]ny municipal ordinance that regulates the open carry of weapons in the places enumerated in Section 45-9-53[1](f) must meet constitutional muster. While many courts have considered restrictions on concealed carry of firearms to be either presumptively valid or not involving constitutional protections granted under the Second Amendment to the United States Constitution, a ban on the open carry of firearms at least potentially impinges on rights granted under both Article 3, Section 12 of the Mississippi Constitution and the Second Amendment. In MS AG Op. Lance (June 13, 2013), this office opined on the factors that must be considered in determining whether open carry of weapons can be restricted on public property. In Lance, we noted that each individual property and restriction or regulation must be considered on a case-by-case basis in light of both Mississippi state law and federal constitutional law. With regard to this aspect of the applicable law, we refer you to the Lance opinion as our best analysis on that topic.

Conclusion

To summarize, it is the opinion of this office that a municipality may regulate either open or concealed carrying of weapons only in those places authorized under Section 45-9-53. Any regulations or ordinances on open carrying of weapons would have to meet federal constitutional muster. Additionally, a municipality is authorized to utilize the signage requirements set forth in Section 45-9-101(13) subject to the restrictions and specified limiting language as set out in Section 45-9-53(4), (4)(a) and (4)(b).

By: Ricky G. Luke
Assistant Attorney General

Footnotes

1
The City could, of course, enforce any restrictions placed on the carrying of weapons imposed by State law.

2
Section 45-9-53 is internally inconsistent, because there is some overlap between Section 45-5-53(1)(f) and Section 45-9-101(13). Thus, the statute facially places two different signage requirements on the same places that are listed in both statutes.

3
These include "(ii) a political rally, parade or official political meeting; or (iii) a non-firearm-related school, college or professional athletic event."

<u>4</u>

The Legislature in the 2014 Regular Session passed H.B. 314 which was signed into law by the Governor and became effective July 1, 2014. H.B. 314 amended Section 45-9-53 to expressly restrict municipalities and counties from using the signage provisions of Section 45-9-101(13) except as provided in the amended Section 45-9-53. Under the amended version of Section 45-9-53 and after July 1, 2014, municipalities and counties may not "use the written notice provisions of Section 45-9-101(13) to prohibit firearms on property under their control except in the locations listed in subsection (1)(f)" of Section 45-9-53. A county or municipality may post signs "[a]t a location listed in Section 45-9-101(13)" if the sign indicates that "a license issued under Section 45-9-101 does not authorize the holder to carry a firearm into that location." However, the sign must also indicate that "carrying a firearm is unauthorized only for license holders without a training endorsement or that it is a location included in Section 310 97-37-7(2) where carrying a firearm is unauthorized for all 311 license holders." A county or municipality may also post a sign "[a]t any location under the control of the county or municipality aside from a location listed in subsection (1)(f) of this section or Section 45-9-101(13) indicating that the possession of a firearm is prohibited on the premises, as long as the sign also indicates that it does not apply to a person properly licensed under Section 45-9-101 or Section 97-37-7(2) to carry a concealed firearm or to a person lawfully carrying a firearm that is not concealed." Thus, with regard to locations other than those listed in Section 45-9-53(1)(f), it appears that a county or municipality can only post signs prohibiting carrying of weapons by individuals who are otherwise illegally carrying either a concealed or openly carried weapon.

<u>5</u>

Examples would include convicted felon, minors in some instances and persons carrying concealed without a license.

6

Section 45-9-101(13) states in relevant part: "In addition to the places enumerated in this subsection, *the carrying of a* stun gun, *concealed pistol or revolver may be disallowed* in any place in the discretion of the person or entity exercising control over the physical location of such place *by the placing of a written notice clearly* readable at a distance of not less than ten (10) feet that the "carrying of a pistol or revolver is prohibited." Miss. Code Ann. Section 45-9-101 (as amended)(emphasis added).

Office of the Attorney General
State of Mississippi

Opinion No. 2014-00363

February 6, 2015

Re: County Regulation of the Carrying of Firearms in Courthouses

Haley Broom, Esq.
Dukes, Dukes, Keating & Faneca, P.A.
2209 13th Street, Sixth Floor
Gulfport, Mississippi 39501

Dear Ms. Broom:

Attorney General Jim Hood has received your request for an official opinion of this office submitted on behalf of Harrison County Sheriff Melvin Brisolara and assigned it to me for research and reply.

Issues Presented

Your letter asks four questions concerning the authority of a sheriff to regulate or control the carrying of firearms in a courthouse. To better facilitate answering your question, we believe that a general discussion of the application of Mississippi's gun laws, the distinctions between local regulation and local governmental use of State signage laws and the distinctions between open carry and concealed carry would be useful. Accordingly, your questions will be set out in their entirety below along with a brief answer after the general discussion.

Discussion and Legal Analysis

1. Open Carry in Mississippi.

Open carry of a firearm in Mississippi is not a right established by any particular statute. Section 12 of the Mississippi Constitution states:
The right of every citizen to keep and bear arms in defense of his home, person, or property, or in aid of the civil power when thereto legally summoned, shall not be called in question, but the legislature may regulate or forbid carrying concealed weapons.

MS Const. Art. 3, Sec. 12. Thus, the right to "open carry" under Mississippi law apparently derives from this constitutional provision. There are no Mississippi statutes that expressly grant the right to open carry and no statutes that address requirements, qualifications or limitations regarding open carrying of a firearm. With one exception, there are no statutes that authorize signage or that purport to set out locations where open carry of a firearm is prohibited. The one exception is Section 97-37-17(2) which states: ""It shall be a felony for any person to possess or carry, whether openly or concealed, any gun, rifle, pistol or other firearm of any kind ... on educational property." House Bill 2, which was passed in the 2013 Regular Session (H.B. 2), is commonly referred to as Mississippi's "Open Carry Law." However, the principal effect of H.B. 2 was to amend Section 97-37-1 which criminalizes the concealed carry of various weapons. The primary amendment by H.B. 2 was to change or clarify the definition of "concealed" and to remove the criminal penalties for carrying a weapon "concealed in whole or part." After H.B. 2 a weapon, in order to be concealed and subject to criminal penalties, has to be hidden from "common observation." Moreover, the provisions of H.B. 2 provide examples of what is not concealed making clear that "a loaded or unloaded pistol carried upon the person in a *sheath, belt holster or shoulder holster that is wholly or partially visible,* or *carried upon the person in a*

scabbard or case for carrying the weapon that is wholly or partially visible"
does not fall within the statute's use of the term ""concealed."

H.B. 2 did not expressly authorize the carrying of an open weapon and, instead made clear that carrying a *weapon* that was not hidden from common observation or a *pistol* in a sheath, holster or a scabbard did not violate the concealed weapon statute, Section 97-37-1. Thus, to the extent that carrying a weapon openly in this State is legal, that right must be based on the premise that (1) such carry is protected by Section 12 of the Constitution and (2) the Legislature has not, absent limited exceptions, made open carrying of a weapon a violation of the law.

2. Concealed Carry in Mississippi.

This State's regulation of concealed weapons, and in particular concealed stun guns, pistols and revolvers, is found primarily in Section 97-37-1 dealing with criminal penalties for unlicensed concealed carry, Section 97-37-7(2) authorizing enhanced endorsements to concealed carry licenses and Section 45-9-101(13) setting forth the licensing scheme for concealed carry of stun guns, pistols and revolvers. The Legislature's authority in this regard is drawn directly from Section 12 of the Mississippi Constitution which authorizes the Legislature to "regulate or forbid[1] carrying concealed weapons." These statutes are related and apply only to concealed carry of weapons by private citizens.[2] As noted above, Section 97-37-1 criminalizes unlicensed carry of a concealed weapon. Section 97-37-7(2), as it relates to carry by private citizens, authorizes license holders with an enhanced endorsement to carry concealed weapons in various places such as "in courthouses except in courtrooms during a judicial proceeding, and any location listed in subsection (13) of Section 45-9-101, except any place of nuisance as defined in Section 95-3-1, any police, sheriff or highway patrol station or any detention facility, prison or jail."

Section 45-9-101(13) applies to both the licensing requirements for concealed carry licenses and to the posting of signs to prevent concealed carry by individuals.[3]

The attempts to apply these "concealed" firearms provisions to openly carried weapons have created no small amount of confusion across the State. This is particularly true with regard to Section 45-9-101 and in particular Subsection (13). Section 45-9-101 is a concealed weapon licensing scheme. Subsection (13) lists places in which concealed weapons cannot be carried by regular license holders,[4] and the signage provisions specifically authorize signs for prohibiting *concealed* carry of stun guns, pistols and revolvers. In summary, neither the locations listed in Subsection (13) nor the authority to post signs to prohibit weapons has any applicability to open carry of weapons.

3. County and Municipality Authority when Restricting Firearm Possession.

Municipalities and counties are given their own independent regulatory authority to enact ordinances or adopt orders regulating the carrying or possession of firearms pursuant to Section 45-9-51 and Section 45-9-53. Section 45-9-51, subject to limited exceptions, prohibits municipalities from regulating the carrying of firearms as follows:

(1) Subject to the provisions of Section 45-9-53, no county or municipality may adopt any ordinance that restricts the possession, carrying, transportation, sale, transfer or ownership of firearms ...

Section 45-9-53 authorizes limited regulations by stating:

(1) This section and Section 45-9-51 do not affect the authority that a county or municipality may have under another law:

* * * * *

(f) To regulate the carrying of a firearm at: (i) a public park or at a public meeting of a county, municipality or other governmental body; (ii) a political rally, parade or official political meeting; or (iii) a non-firearm-related school, college or professional athletic event;

We have previously opined, based on these statutes, that "a municipality may regulate, by ordinance, the carrying of any firearm, whether concealed or not, at only the locations or events identified in Section 45-9-53." MS AG Op. Trapp (Dec. 2, 2013). It remains our opinion that a municipality can utilize its independent regulatory authority to prohibit the carrying of firearms only at (1) a public park or at a public meeting of the municipality or other municipal governmental body; (2) a political rally, parade or official political meeting; or (3) a non-firearm-related school, college or professional athletic event. This opinion applies equally to counties.

When a county or city regulates open carry, it must also consider federal constitutional issues, and any such regulation must meet constitutional muster. In Trapp, we opined as follows:

[A]ny municipal ordinance that regulates the open carry of weapons in the places enumerated in Section 45-9-53(f) must meet constitutional muster. While many courts have considered restrictions on concealed carry of firearms to be either presumptively valid or not involving constitutional protections granted under the Second Amendment to the United States Constitution, a ban on the open carry of firearms at least potentially impinges on rights granted under both Article 3, Section 12 of the Mississippi Constitution and the Second Amendment. In MS AG Op. Lance (June 13, 2013), this office opined on the factors that must be considered in determining whether open carry of weapons can be restricted on public property. In Lance, we noted that each individual property and restriction or regulation must be considered on a case-by-case basis in light of both Mississippi state law and federal constitutional law. With regard to this aspect of the applicable law, we refer you to the Lance opinion as our best analysis on that topic.

MS AG Op. Trapp (Dec. 2, 2013). A sensitive place analysis and determination need only be made where the right to carry involves open carry. Second Amendment concerns are not raised by concealed carry regulations and, therefore, sensitive area analysis is inapposite in the context of concealed carry regulations. *See* fn. 1, *supra*.

Thus, a municipality or county has two possible courses of action if it desires to restrict the possession or carrying of firearms. First, a county may enact ordinances regulating such possession. However, as noted, the places or events where such regulations apply must be limited to the locations set forth above and found in Section 45-9-53(1)(f). It is the opinion of this office that when a county is enacting an ordinance pursuant to Section 45-9-53, the ordinance can apply both to concealed carry[5] or open carry.

Second, a municipality or county may utilize State law authority to post signs pursuant to Section 45-9-101(13) as modified and limited by Section 45-9-53. When acting pursuant to these statutes, a county "is acting pursuant to state law and not exercising its independent regulatory authority." MS AG Op. Trapp (Dec. 2, 2013). Short of an order to have appropriate signs posted in appropriate places, a county or municipality does not need an ordinance in order to avail itself of the right to place signs under these State statutes. However, the authority for a county or municipality to post signs is not as broad as the authority of a state or private entity. When Section 45-9-53 was amended by H.B. 314, the Legislature added additional restrictions to the authority of counties and municipalities to post signs to prohibit carrying of firearms.

Under the amended version of Section 45-9-53, municipalities and counties may not "use the written notice provisions of Section 45-9-101(13) to prohibit firearms on property under their control except in the locations listed in subsection (1)(f)" of Section 45-9-53. A county or municipality may post signs "[a]t a location listed in Section 45-9-101(13)" if the sign indicates that "a license issued under Section 45-9-101 does not authorize the holder to carry a firearm into that location." However, the sign must also indicate that "carrying a firearm is unauthorized only for license holders without a training endorsement or that it is a location included in Section 97-37-7(2) where carrying a firearm is unauthorized for all license holders." A county or municipality may also post a sign "[a]t any location under the control of the county or municipality aside from a location listed in subsection (1)(f) of this section or Section 45-9-101(13) indicating that the possession of a firearm is prohibited on the premises, as long as the sign also indicates that it does not apply to a person properly licensed under Section 45-9-101 or Section 97-37-7(2) to carry a concealed firearm or to a person lawfully carrying a firearm that is not concealed." Thus, with regard to locations other than those listed in Section 45-9-53(1)(f) and Section 45-9-101(13), it appears that a county or municipality can only post signs prohibiting carrying of weapons by individuals who are otherwise illegally carrying either a concealed or openly carried weapon.

There is an apparent inconsistency in Section 45-9-53(4) which merits discussion. Section 45-9-101(13) contains a catchall provision that states:

In addition to the places enumerated in this subsection, the carrying of a stun gun, concealed pistol or revolver may be disallowed in any place in the discretion of the person or entity exercising control over the physical location of such place by the placing of a written notice clearly readable at a distance of not less than ten (10) feet that the "carrying of a pistol or revolver is prohibited."

This catchall provision of Section 45-9-101(13) allows the "entity exercising control over the physical location" to post signs prohibiting the carrying of a concealed pistol or revolver in "any place" over which the entity exercises control. This provision causes what is apparently an ambiguity in or inconsistency with Section 45-9-53(4), because subsection 45-9-53(4)(b) provides that "[a]t any location under the control of the county or municipality aside from a location listed in subsection (1)(f) of this section or Section 45-9-101(13)," the posted signage does not apply to persons licensed under Section 45-9-101 or persons with enhanced carry rights under Section 97-37-7(2) or to a person lawfully and openly carrying a firearm. If the reference in Section 45-9-53(4)(a) authorizing counties and municipalities to post signs under subsection (4)(a) is read to include the catchall in Section 45-9-101(13), then that reading has the effect of nullifying subsection (4)(b) and rendering the entirety of subsection (4)(b) meaningless. This is true because the inclusion of the catchall in Section 45-9-101(13) would make it applicable to all county or municipal property. Thus, when subsection (4)(b) makes references to places other than a location listed in subsection 45-9-53(1)(f) of this section or Section 45-9-101(13), it could have no meaning. It would be impossible for a county or municipal property to exist that was not included in the catchall of Section 45-9-101(13). Thus, subsection (4)(b) would never be applicable. Moreover, the entire legislative scheme to limit the authority of counties and municipalities to post signage prohibiting firearms would be thwarted since counties could post signage under subsection 4(a) to any property or facility controlled by the county or municipality. Accordingly, it is the opinion of this office that when counties or municipalities are using the posting provisions of Section 45-9-53(4)(a), they are not authorized to post signs unless the places or events are specifically named or listed, and they may not use subsection (4)(a) signage in places covered by the catchall provision.

4. Specific Questions Posed by the Request for Opinion.

Your request sets out four questions enumerated in the request as follows:

1. Is Sheriff Brisolara authorized, pursuant to Miss. Code Ann. § 45-9-101 and § 45-9-53, to regulate the carrying of weapons and firearms within the courthouses in Harrison County, Mississippi, based on a finding that they constitute "sensitive places"?

1(a). If the answer to Question No. 1 is in the affirmative, may Sheriff Brisolara utilize signage to provide notice of the prohibition with the following language?

Carrying of weapons and firearms is prohibited. This restriction is applicable only to license holders without a training endorsement.

2. If Sheriff Brisolara is authorized to regulate the carrying of firearms in the courthouses in Harrison County, Mississippi, is he also authorized to prohibit the open carry of weapons and firearms ... in those courthouses, based on a finding that they constitute "sensitive places"?

2(a). If the answer to Question No. 2 is in the affirmative, may Sheriff Brisolara utilize signage to provide notice of the prohibition with the following language?

Carrying of weapons and firearms is prohibited. This restriction does not apply to license holders with a training endorsement.

In response to question numbers 1 and 1(a), the Sheriff may post signs pursuant to Section 45-9-101(13) as specifically allowed by Section 45-9-53(4)(a). Those signs should follow the language as set forth in the various statutes. Section 45-9-101(13) specifies the sign requirements including the language and location of the sign as follows:

In addition to the places enumerated in this subsection, the carrying of a stun gun, concealed pistol or revolver may be disallowed in any place in the discretion of the person or entity exercising control over the physical location of such place by the placing of a *written notice clearly readable at a distance of not less than ten (10) feet that the "carrying of a pistol or revolver is prohibited."*

(Emphasis added; Quotations in original). Section 45-9-53(4)(a) further requires that "the sign also indicates that carrying a firearm is unauthorized only for license holders without a training endorsement or that it is a location included in Section 97-37-7(2) where carrying a firearm is unauthorized for all license holders." The statute states that the sign should read that the "carrying of a pistol or revolver is prohibited." The language in your request does not comply with this specified language. A court might determine that the proposed language complies or substantially complies. Our office can only state that the sign differs from the language set out in quotes within the statute.[6]

The wording regarding license holders without a training endorsement is close to the actual language of Section 45-9-53(4)(a) but not exact. The sign could easily be worded to include the language that "carrying a firearm is unauthorized only for license holders without a training endorsement" which would remove any question. Thus, we believe the Sheriff could post a sign as discussed in this opinion. We do not believe that the Sheriff has any independent authority to regulate beyond usage of the sign under State law. This is because a courthouse is not listed in Section 45-9-53(1)(f) which, as discussed above, sets forth exclusively where municipalities or counties can regulate carry of firearms under their independent regulatory authority.

In response to question number 2, we do not believe that a Sheriff has authority to regulate open carry of weapons in a courthouse. The signage authority under Section 45-9-53(4)(a) over locations listed in Section 45-9-101(13), which includes courthouses, expressly states that a sign must indicate that "carrying a firearm is unauthorized only for license holders without a training endorsement." A concealed carry license applies only to concealed carry, not open carry. *See* Miss. Code Ann. § 45-9-101(14)("***The licensing requirements*** of this section ***do not apply to the carrying by any person of a stun gun, pistol or revolver***, knife, or other deadly weapon ***that is not concealed*** as defined in Section 97-37-1."). The Legislature has specifically restricted the signage used for subsection 101(13) locations to regular concealed license holders, and this provision has no application to open carry. Moreover, as noted, the signage authority under Section 45-9-101(13) may be used to prohibit "the carrying of a ... concealed pistol or revolver ... by the placing of a written notice ..." Sections 45-9-101(13) and 45-9-53(4)(a) are clear, at least on this point, that they apply only to concealed weapons. Thus, the Sheriff has no authority to post signs regarding open carry in the courthouse. As previously noted, counties have no authority to regulate, independently of state law, firearm possession in courthouses. Accordingly, the answer to question number 2 is no. This negative response makes question number 2(a) moot.

5. This Office's Opinion in Lance was Supplanted by H.B. 314.

Your opinion cites to this office's opinion in MS AG Op. Lance (June 13, 2013). In the Lance Opinion, we note the following general proposition regarding control over public property:

Custodians or owners of public property generally have the authority and duty, express or necessarily implied, to manage that property in the public interest. This often includes the authority to deny entry to the property, to place conditions upon entry onto the publicly-owned property, and to otherwise regulate and govern that property short of enforcing the state criminal laws. For example, a municipality may prohibit smoking in the city hall, and a public library may prohibit loud speech. These activities are perfectly legal, but the municipality and the state library have the statutory authority to prohibit them and to exclude persons who do not comply. See, *Bigham v. Huffman*, 199 WL 33537149 (N.D. Miss. 1999)(Criminal trespass laws applied to public property). The authority of state or local officials to govern and manage government property may be separate and apart from any power to enact police-power ordinances or regulations having criminal or misdemeanor penalties.

After citing various general propositions regarding the authority of sheriffs within this State, we further opined:

Thus, it is our opinion that the sheriff has the state-law authority, if he determines it reasonable and necessary to the security of the courthouse, to disallow the open carry of firearms in the courthouse. As stated above, the second part of the question is whether such action by the sheriff is constitutional. Please note that an official opinion of the Attorney General does not provide immunity from liability for violations of federal law, including possible violations of individual rights under the U.S. Constitution. See Miss. Code Section 7-5-25.

MS AG Op. Lance (June 13, 2013). At the time that Lance was issued, this office assumed that the Legislature would intend this authority to be available to a sheriff or other public official charged with responsibility over a public building. At the time of Lance's issuance, counties and municipalities had full authority under Section 45-9-101(13) to use the catchall provisions of this subsection to post signs prohibiting all concealed weapons at any building owned or controlled by a county or municipality.

Moreover, numerous federal court decisions had recognized that under federal law governmental proprietors of property were justified in restricting firearm possession on governmental property. The Fourth Circuit set forth the rationale as follows:

In reaching this result, we conclude first that the government has a substantial interest in providing for the safety of individuals who visit and make use of the national parks, including Daingerfield Island. Although the government's interest need not be "compelling" under intermediate scrutiny, cases have sometimes described the government's interest in public safety in that fashion. See *Schenck v. Pro-Choice Network*, 519 U.S. 357, 376, 117 S.Ct. 855, 137 L.Ed.2d 1 (1997) (referring to the "significant governmental interest in public safety"); *United States v. Salerno*, 481 U.S. 739, 745, 107 S.Ct. 2095, 95 L.Ed.2d 697 (1987) (commenting on the "Federal Government's compelling interests in public safety"). The government, after all, is invested with "plenary power" to protect the public from danger on federal lands under the Property Clause. See U.S. Const. Art. IV, § 3, Cl. 2 (giving Congress the power to "make all needful Rules and Regulations respecting the Territory or other Property belonging to the United States"); *Utah Div. of State Lands v. United States*, 482 U.S. 193, 201, 107 S.Ct. 2318, 96 L.Ed.2d 162 (1987); *Camfield v. United States*, 167 U.S. 518, 525, 17 S.Ct. 864, 42 L.Ed. 260 (1897); see also *United States v. Dorosan*, 350 Fed.Appx. 874, 875 (5th Cir.2009) (per curiam) (noting that U.S.

Postal Service is authorized under the Property Clause to exclude firearms from its property); Volokh, *Implementing the Right for Self-Defense*, 56 U.C.L.A. L. Rev. at 1529-33. As the district court noted, Daingerfield Island is a national park area where large numbers of people, including children, congregate for recreation. See *Masciandaro*, 648 F.Supp.2d at 790. Such circumstances justify reasonable measures to secure public safety.

U.S. v. Masciandaro, 638 F.3d 458, 473 (4ᵗʰ Cir. 2011). A recent case from the Northern District of Georgia concluded that the Corps of Engineers could essentially ban guns on its recreational property by prohibiting loaded guns or ammunition. *GeorgiaCarry.Org, Inc. v. U.S. Army Corps of Engineers*, 2014 WL 4059375, 2 (N.D. Ga. Aug. 18, 2014). In *GeorgiaCarry.Org, Inc.*, the Court noted that the Supreme Court has "long held the view that there is a crucial difference, with respect to constitutional analysis, between the government exercising 'the power to regulate or license, as a lawmaker,' and the government acting 'as proprietor, to manage [its] internal operation."'D' *Id.* *(citing Engquistv.Oregon Dept. of Agr.*, 553 U.S. 591, 598, 128 S.Ct. 2146, 170 L.Ed.2d 975 (2008) *(quoting Cafeteria & Restaurant Workers v. McElroy*, 367 U.S. 886, 896, 81 S.Ct. 1743, 6 L.Ed.2d 1230 (1961)) (alterations in original); *Nordyke v. King*, 681 F.3d 1041, 1044 (9th Cir.2012). (Upholding a law that stated "[e]very person who brings onto or possesses on County property a firearm, loaded or unloaded, or ammunition for a firearm is guilty of a misdemeanor."); *United States v. Masciandaro*, 638 F.3d 458, 473 (4th Cir.2011) (upholding restrictions on firearms in national parks based, in part, on the rule that "[t]he government ... is invested with 'plenary power' to protect the public from danger on federal lands under the Property Clause").

When Lance was issued, we believe that we reasonably relied on these general notions of property owners and the governmental interest relating to safety in public buildings and on public property to conclude that a sheriff had authority to restrict open or concealed carry into a courthouse. We, however, now believe that the Legislature has rejected our reasoning in Lance. We conclude this based on several factors. First, H.B. 314 expressly removed from counties or municipalities the authority to post signs preventing carrying of weapons by enhanced license holders into courthouses. In so doing, the Legislature expressly stated that a sign at a courthouse (a place listed in Section 45-9-101(13)) must state that "carrying a firearm is unauthorized only for license holders without a training endorsement." Such a sign would not apply to enhanced concealed license holders or to open carriers. Likewise, the Legislature removed the "catchall" provision from the purview of counties and municipalities, which evidences a clear intent to limit the authority of these local governmental entities. Moreover, the Legislature authorized suits against counties and municipalities and individual damages awards against elected officials who violated either the restrictions on posting signs or enacting or failing to rescind ordinances that violate the law. The limitations placed on ordinances in Section 45-9-53(1)(f) clearly exclude courthouses from inclusion in a local ordinance.

For these reasons, we are now of the opinion that the Legislature has foreclosed any avenue under which this office could opine that a sheriff has any authority under existing State law to prevent open carry of weapons into courthouses. With regard to courthouses, the sole authority for a county or sheriff is to limit concealed license holders without a training endorsement under the provisions of Section 45-9-101(13) as limited by Section 45-9-53(4)(a). To the extent that MS AG Op. Lance (June 13, 2013) is inconsistent with this opinion, it is modified and/or withdrawn.

By: Ricky G. Luke
Assistant Attorney General

Footnotes

1

The ability to regulate or forbid the carry of concealed weapons does not present a Second Amendment problem. This is so, because a majority of courts to have considered restrictions on concealed carry of firearms have found them to be either presumptively valid or not involving constitutional protections granted under the Second Amendment to the United States Constitution. *See Peterson v. Martinez*, 707 F.3d 1197 (10th Cir.2013) (holding Second Amendment does not provide the right to carry a concealed firearm); *Kachalsky v. County of Westchester*, 701 F.3d 81 (2nd Cir. 2012)(holding New York legislation limiting concealed firearms in public does not violate the Second Amendment); *Hightower v. City of Boston*, 693 F.3d 61, 73 (1st Cir.2012) (holding revocation of license to carry concealed firearm did not violate Second Amendment); *United States v. Rene E.*, 583 F.3d 8, 12 (1st Cir.2009) ("laws prohibiting the carrying of concealed weapons" are an "example [ ] of 'longstanding' restrictions that [are] 'presumptively lawful' under the Second Amendment") (*quoting Heller*, 554 U.S. at 626); *Richards v. County of Yolo*, 821 F.Supp.2d 1169, 1174 (E.D. Cal.2011) ("[T]he Second Amendment does not create a fundamental right to carry a concealed weapon in public"); *Martinkovich v. Oregon Legislative Body*, 2011 WL 7693036, at p. 2 (D. Or. Aug. 24, 2011) ("The Second Amendment does not prohibit regulations on carrying a concealed weapon."); *Dorr v. Weber*, 741 F.Supp.2d 993, 1005 (N.D. La. 2010) ("a right to carry a concealed weapon under the Second Amendment has not been recognized to date").

02

Section 97-37-7 more broadly authorizes carrying of weapons by "bank guards, company guards, watchmen, railroad special agents or duly authorized representatives who are not sworn law enforcement officers, agents or employees of a patrol service, guard service, or a company engaged in the business of transporting money, securities or other valuables, while actually engaged in the performance of their duties." It also authorizes carrying of weapons by various state employees such as "Department of Wildlife, Fisheries and Parks law enforcement officers, railroad special agents who are sworn law enforcement officers, investigators employed by the Attorney General, criminal investigators employed by the district attorneys, all prosecutors, public defenders, investigators or probation officers employed by the Department of Corrections, employees of the State Auditor who are authorized by the State Auditor to perform investigative functions, or any deputy fire marshal or investigator employed by the State Fire Marshal, while engaged in the performance of their duties as such, or by fraud investigators with the Department of Human Services, or by judges of the Mississippi Supreme Court, Court of Appeals, circuit, chancery, county, justice and municipal courts, or by coroners."

<u>3</u>

See Miss. Code Ann. § 45-9-101(1)(a)("The Department of Public Safety is authorized to issue licenses to carry stun guns, *concealed* pistols or revolvers to persons qualified as provided in this section. Such licenses shall be valid throughout the state for a period of five (5) years from the date of issuance. Any person possessing a valid license issued pursuant to this section may carry a stun gun, *concealed* pistol or *concealed* revolver."); Miss. Code Ann. § 45-9-101(13)("In addition to the places enumerated in this subsection, *the carrying of a* stun gun, *concealed pistol or revolver may be disallowed* in any place in the discretion of the person or entity exercising control over the physical location of such place *by the placing of a written notice clearly readable at a distance of not less than ten (10) feet that the "carrying of a pistol or revolver \\is prohibited*."); Miss. Code Ann. § 45-9-101(14)("*The licensing* *requirements* of this section *do not apply to the carrying by any person of a stun gun, pistol*

or revolver, knife, or other deadly weapon *that is not concealed* as defined in Section 97-37-1."). (All emphasis added).

4

By reference from Section 97-37-7(2), it also lists places in which an enhanced license holder can carry weapons.

5

In MS AG Op. Mitchell (February 3, 2015), we modified the Trapp opinion to some degree. In Trapp, we opined that municipalities could not by ordinance restrict enhanced concealed license holders from carrying in places identified in Section 45-9-53(1)(f) if that place were also listed in Section 45-9-101(13) where enhanced license holders are authorized to carry. An example of this overlap is a meeting of a public body. After the passage of H.B. 314 in the 2014 Regular Session, our opinion now is that the Legislature has authorized municipalities, both through signs or ordinance, to restrict even enhanced license holders from carrying in places identified in (1)(f) locations. See the Mitchell opinion for a full discussion.

6

The proposed language apparently applies to weapons other than firearms. The restrictions on counties and municipalities by Section 45-9-51 and Section 45-9-53 relate to firearms. Our office is of the opinion that counties or municipalities can ban carry of weapons other than firearms. *See* MS AG Op. Tindell (September 18, 2014).

Municipal/County Gun Ordinance and Sign Complaint Form

Complainant's Name:
    Address
    Phone Number
    Email

Name of municipality/county _____

Is your complaint about a **sign** on county or municipal property?   Yes___ No____

If yes, please give the date, address, location and name of the building or property where you saw the sign:

Do you have a cell phone or other digital photo of the sign? If so, please provide your email address and we will contact you so that you may email us the photo: _____

Is your complaint about a city or county **ordinance**? Yes ___ No ___
If you have a copy of the ordinance, or news article or other information about it, please attach. Otherwise, please give as much information as you have concerning the ordinance:

_____

_____

_____

Names, addresses and contact information for any witnesses

_____

_____

Do you believe your rights as a concealed-carry license holder have been violated? If so, provide a copy of any license(s) to carry a concealed weapon (include copy of front and back of license).

I certify that the above and foregoing is true and accurate to the best of my knowledge.

Signature: _____

                Sworn to this the ____ day of _____, 20___
(Affix seal here)

_____
           Notary Public

Submit form to: Mississippi Attorney General's Office
                  Attention: State Regulatory Division
                  Post Office Box 220
                  Jackson, MS 39205

Chapter Sixteen
Attorney General Opinions 2016

Office of the Attorney General
State of Mississippi

Opinion No. 2016-00325

July 22, 2016

Re: Municipal Law Enforcement Questions

Shannon Gallagher
Municipal Court Clerk
City of Durant
Post Office Box 272
Durant, Mississippi 39063-0272

Dear Ms. Gallagher:

Attorney General Jim Hood has received your request and has assigned it to me for research and reply.

Your letter provides that the Durant Police Department is in need of assistance, and you pose the following questions:

1. Can the Department petition the Municipal Judge to confiscate any

firearm in the case of a misdemeanor charge? If the defendant cannot provide proof of ownership of the weapon, can we confiscate? What if they can show proof? What are the grounds in that circumstance? What is the proper procedure?

RESPONSE: A firearm may be confiscated if the weapon was used in the commission of a crime pursuant to Section 97-37-3 of the Mississippi Code and may be disposed of pursuant to that section:

(1) Any weapon used in violation of Section 97-37-1, or used in the commission of any other crime, shall be seized by the arresting officer, may be introduced in evidence, and in the event of a conviction, shall be ordered to be forfeited, and shall be disposed of as ordered by the court having jurisdiction of such offense. In the event of dismissal or acquittal of charges, such weapon shall be returned to the accused from whom it was seized.

(2)(a) If the weapon to be forfeited is merchantable, the court may order the weapon forfeited to the seizing law enforcement agency.

(b) A weapon so forfeited to a law enforcement agency may be sold at auction as provided by Sections 19-3-85 and 21-39-21 to a federally-licensed firearms dealer, with the proceeds from such sale at auction to be used to buy bulletproof vests for the seizing law enforcement agency.

2. Can a municipal police officer write traffic violations on a state highway that happens to be located within the city limits of Durant? This particular highway is North or South Jackson Street within the city limits, and Highway 51 outside the city limits.

RESPONSE: It is noted at the outset that even though U.S. Highway 51 is given a street name within the city limits, it remains a U.S. highway. However, municipal police officers may make traffic stops on both state and U.S. highways for all traffic violations occurring within the city limits. It is noted that speeding captured by radar on a U.S. highway, within the municipality, may only be used by municipalities having a population in excess of fifteen thousand according to the latest federal census. See MS AG Op., Carona (July 20, 2007). See also *Moore v. Louisville*, 716 So. 2d 1136 (Miss. 1998), which authorizes the use of radar on a state highway located within a municipality having a population of two thousand or more.

3. If a person charged with a misdemeanor charge posts a cash bond and is found not guilty in court, can the city prosecutor request the cash bond forfeited to the City? If so, how do I account for this money within my law enforcement data base? Receipts are certainly given out when payment is received, but the data base will not allow me to 'post' it if they aren't guilty.

RESPONSE: If the individual is found not guilty, the cash bond must be returned to the individual. The purpose of a bond is to require the defendant's appearance in court.

Permit(s) Honored In:
Alabama, Alaska, Arizona, Arkansas, Colorado, Florida, Georgia, Idaho, Indiana, Iowa, Kansas, Kentucky, Louisiana, Maine, Michigan, Mississippi, Missouri, Montana, Nevada, New Hampshire, New Mexico, North Carolina, North Dakota, Ohio, Oklahoma, Pennsylvania, South Dakota, Tennessee, Texas, Utah, Vermont, Virginia, West Virginia, Wisconsin, Wyoming

Permit(s) Not Honored In:
California, Connecticut, Delaware, District of Columbia, Guam, Hawaii, Illinois, Maryland, Massachusetts, Minnesota, Nebraska, New Jersey, New York, New York City, Oregon, Puerto Rico, Rhode Island, South Carolina, Virgin Islands, Washington, American Samoa, N. Mariana Islands

NOTE: South Carolina now honors Enhanced Permits (only) from MS.

Office of the Attorney General
State of Mississippi

Opinion No. 2016-00336

August 5, 2016

Re: Possession of Firearms by Employees of Regional Housing Authority

J. Tyler McCaughn
Monroe &McCaughn, PLLC
Post Office Box 28
Newton, MS 39345

Dear Mr. McCaughn:

Attorney General Jim Hood is in receipt of your request for an official opinion of this office and has assigned it to me for research and response:

Facts and Issues Presented

Your letter states:

I represent the Mississippi Regional Housing Authority No. V. I have been directed to receive clarification on the carry of weapons on Housing Authority property. In particular, the Housing Authority has a strict no firearms policy in place through the employee handbook. Once an employee accepts employment with the Housing Authority, the employee is issued a handbook and required to sign a notice stating that they received a copy of the employee handbook. This policy has been in place for many years and continues to be in place now.

In light of the recent state laws and opinions issued, the Housing Authority has concerns about there being a conflict between the employee handbook and the laws that have been implemented. The Housing Authority asks the following questions:

1. May an employee of the Housing Authority legally carry a firearm on Housing Authority Property even though the employee handbook prohibits firearms?

2. Do any of the laws regarding carry of firearms prevail over the policies of the employee handbook?

3. May the Board of Commissioners for the Housing Authority ban all firearms from the Housing Authority Property regardless of employee/visitor status?

Legal Analysis and Discussion

As your letter notes, the Housing Authority's firearms policy has been in place for years in the form of an employee handbook. As such, the policy constitutes a past act on which we cannot issue a formal opinion. We have repeatedly stated that opinions of this office cannot be used to either validate or invalidate past actions. Moreover, whether a firearms policy was properly promulgated and the effect of inclusion of such a purported policy in a handbook are matters that must be determined based on factual matters. *See e.g., Lee v. Golden Triangle Planning & Dev. Dist., Inc.*, 797 So. 2d 845, 848 (Miss. 2001); *Bobbitt v. Orchard, Ltd.*, 603 So.2d 356, 361 (Miss. 1992). Because of the factual nature of your inquiry and the fact that it is based on prior acts, we are required to decline to issue a formal opinion on the specific facts stated in your letter. However, we understand your inquiry to generally be whether the Housing Authority can adopt policies preventing employees from possessing firearms on Housing Authority property. This office has opined that public employers may restrict the right of employees to possess weapons under the contract of employment. For example, this office opined:

The school board may establish employment policies and enter employment contracts which prohibit the carrying of concealed weapons by employees, even with enhanced carry certification.

MS AG Op., Cantrell (Oct. 1, 2013). Additionally, we have opined that:

Although the carrying of a weapon on school facilities is authorized for an individual with an enhanced permit, the school board or, if applicable, the conservator under the direction of the State Board of Education could under the terms of its contract with the school employee disallow the school employee from carrying a weapon on the school facility or in certain areas or buildings. MS AG Op., Bounds (January 5, 2012). A school employee violating the terms of the contract would not be criminally liable but would be subject to penalties as provided by contract.

MS AG Op., Pennington (Mar. 1, 2013). Thus, in response to your first question, it is the opinion of this office that the Housing Authority may restrict employees from possessing weapons on Housing Authority property if done pursuant to a duly adopted, lawful employment policy. Although our prior opinions applied to concealed carry with a permit, we believe the same rationale would apply to prohibiting open carry by employees.

Your second question asks whether "any laws" prevail over the "policies" of the employee handbook. We have not reviewed the employee handbook nor the policies of the Housing Authority. Aside from relating to prior actions, this question is too broad and lacks the specificity needed with regard to either the subject laws or subject policies[1] for this office to respond. As a general matter, we believe this question to be directed at whether there is any law that authorizes an employee to carry a weapon at work even when the employer has adopted a policy prohibiting such possession. We are unaware of any such law.

Your third question asks whether the Housing Authority can ban "all firearms ... regardless of the employee/visitor status[.]" This question is not limited to employees and presumably would apply to anyone on the property other than a tenant. Likewise, your request does not identify any specific place, nor does it differentiate between concealed carry or open carry. This question is too broad and the facts too undelineated for us to offer a dispositive opinion. The gun laws in Mississippi are complicated and complex and do not lend themselves to broad generalizations. Different issues arise depending on the type of carry, whether the individual is licensed and the nature of the place or places where carry rights are to be restricted. If, for example, a ban on open carry rights is proposed, the Housing Authority would be required to comply with federal constitutional requirements. *See* MS AG Op., Lance (June 13, 2013)(discussing sensitive places analysis under federal constitution). Accordingly, we must decline to respond to your question as written.

However, we note that recent amendments to Mississippi Code Ann. Sec. 45-9-51 do appear to provide, or at least acknowledge, regulatory authority of housing authorities in the firearm arena. Section 45-9-51 together with Section 45-9-53 operate to limit the authority that counties and municipalities have to regulate the possession of firearms. The effect of these statutes is that a county or municipality can only regulate possession of firearms in those places listed in Section 45-9-53(1)(f).[2] Regional housing authorities are created by counties, and this office has opined that such authorities are political subdivisions, as opposed to state agencies. MS AG Op., Rhodes (May 5, 2006).

Absent express reference to housing authorities, we would likely find that the provisions of Sections 45-9-51 and 45-9-53 applied to housing authorities as local political subdivisions. *See* MS AG Op., Cartlidge (Sept. 18, 2014)(analogizing a local rails-to-trails recreational district to a local political subdivision and applying provisions of Section 45-9-53).

Section 45-9-51, however, was amended by House Bill No. 314 in the 2014 Regular Session. The language in paragraph (2) was specifically added regarding housing authorities as follows:
(2) No public housing authority operating in this state may adopt any rule or regulation restricting a lessee or tenant of a dwelling owned and operated by such public housing authority from lawfully possessing firearms or ammunition or their components within individual dwelling units or the transportation of such firearms or ammunition or their components to and from such dwelling.

If the broader prohibitions of Sections 45-9-51 and 45-9-53 were applicable to housing authorities, then paragraph (2) would have been unnecessary. Accordingly, we understand this restriction found in paragraph (2) to be a legislative acknowledgment of a general authority of housing authorities to promulgate rules and regulations relating to firearm possession on property controlled by such authorities. Thus, our opinion is that regional housing authorities have general authority to regulate firearm possession. However, this authority is not absolute and must be exercised consistent with federal constitutional requirements. Like regulations by other local political subdivisions, any regulations adopted cannot directly conflict with applicable state law.

If our office can be of further assistance, do not hesitate to contact us.

By: Ricky G. Luke
Assistant Attorney General

Footnotes

1

Our office generally does not interpret policies or regulations of agencies or political subdivisions. Accordingly, we typically decline to respond to any request that requires such interpretation.

2

These places are "(i) a public park or at a public meeting of a county, municipality or other governmental body; (ii) a political rally, parade or official political meeting; or (iii) a non-firearm-related school, college or professional athletic event[.]"

Office of the Attorney General
State of Mississippi

Opinion No. 2016-00299

August 12, 2016

Re: Request for Official Opinion Regarding Firearms Possession in Courthouses

Honorable Gary A. Chism
State Representative
P.O. Box 1018
Jackson, MS 39215-1018

Dear Representative Chism:

Attorney General Jim Hood has received your request for an official opinion of this office and assigned it to me for research and reply.

Issues Presented and Analysis and Discussion

A. Question No. 1

Your letter states as follows:

Section 97-37-7(2) of the Mississippi Code authorizes firearms permit holders who have received training described therein approved by the

Mississippi Department of Public Safety to access all areas under state control except law enforcement facilities, courtrooms during judicial proceedings and places of nuisance while armed.

1. Is there any provision in this law or any other Mississippi law or ruling that would give any public official either elected or appointed from any of the three branches of government the authority to circumvent this law or deny anyone with proper credentials access to the common area of any courthouse while armed?

Unfortunately, Section 97-37-7(2) and its interaction with other gun carry laws is not as clear in its meaning and interaction with other laws as is set forth in your letter. Instead of having one code section that addresses open carry, concealed carry with a regular permit, concealed carry with an enhanced permit and unlicensed concealed carry, there are numerous sections which been amended over several years that have created a labyrinth that is difficult for both lawyers and lay-people to navigate. Section 97-37-7 does not expressly state the premise of your letter that an enhanced license authorizes concealed carry in "all areas under state control except law enforcement facilities, courtrooms during judicial proceedings and places of nuisance while armed." In relevant part, this section states:

A person licensed under Section 45-9-101 to carry a concealed pistol, who (a) has voluntarily completed an instructional course in the safe handling and use of firearms offered by an instructor certified by a nationally recognized organization that customarily offers firearms training, or by any other organization approved by the Department of Public Safety, (b) is a member or veteran of any active or reserve component branch of the United States of America Armed Forces having completed law enforcement or combat training with pistols or other handguns as recognized by such branch after submitting an affidavit attesting to have read, understand and agree to comply with all provisions of the , or (c) is an honorably retired law enforcement officer or honorably retired member or veteran of any active or reserve component branch of the United States of America Armed Forces having completed law enforcement or combat training with pistols or other handguns, after submitting an affidavit attesting to have read, understand and agree to comply with all provisions of Mississippi *shall also be authorized to carry weapons in courthouses except in courtrooms during a judicial proceeding, and any location listed in subsection (13) of Section 45-9-101*, except any place of nuisance as defined in Section 95-3-1, any police, sheriff or highway patrol station or any detention facility, prison or jail.

Miss. Code. Ann. Section 97-37-7 (as amended)(emphasis added). This section does identify certain places where concealed weapons may *also be* carried, but neither Section 97-37-7 nor Section 45-9-101 identifies the places in which weapons can be carried in the first instance.

As your letter notes in regard to courthouses, enhanced carriers are specifically authorized to carry into courthouses and even courtrooms when a judicial proceeding is not ongoing. Based on this fact, this office has opined regarding an enhanced carrier's right to carry into courthouses and courtrooms as follows:

Reading Section 97-37-7(2) in conjunction with Section 45-9-101(13), it is the opinion of this office that an enhanced permit holder can carry a stun gun or a concealed pistol or revolver (even where governmental entities have posted signage) in the following locations found in Section 45-9-101(13):

13. In courthouses except in courtrooms during a judicial proceeding. -- (The right to carry in courthouses except in courtrooms during judicial proceedings is granted to enhanced permit holders expressly by Section 97-37-7 without reference to Section 45-9-101(13). Section 45-9-101(13) states that regular permit holders may not carry in "courthouses" or "courtrooms" with the caveat that nothing contained therein precludes a judge from determining who "will" carry a weapon "in his courtroom." Presumably under this authority, a judge has authority to determine who will, who can and who cannot carry a weapon in his courtroom. However, the governing authority of the jurisdiction, whether municipal or county could restrict a regular permit holder from initial entry into the courthouse, as opposed to the courtroom, by posting a sign. However, such signage could not prevent an enhanced permit holder from entry into the courthouse. Under no interpretation of the law would either a regular or enhanced permit holder be authorized to carry a firearm into a courtroom during a judicial proceeding unless authorized by the judge. Likewise, as noted above, an individual would not have unfettered gun carrying access to

places within the building that are not generally open to the general public. See MS AG Op. Cantrell (Oct. 1, 2013)).
MS AG Op., Trapp (Dec. 2, 2013).[1]

Thus, as a general matter, the law allows an enhanced license holder to carry into courthouses. Unfortunately, the application of this general provision is confused by Section 45-9-101(13). This section specifically authorizes owners/controllers of buildings to restrict the carry of weapons as follows:

In addition to the places enumerated in this subsection, the carrying of a stun gun, concealed pistol or revolver may be disallowed in any place in the discretion of the person or entity exercising control over the physical location of such place by the placing of a written notice clearly readable at a distance of not less than ten (10) feet that the "carrying of a pistol or revolver is prohibited."

Miss. Code. Ann. Section 45-9-101(13)(as amended). Thus, on its face, Section 45-9-101(13) gives a person or entity controlling a building the right to exclude the carrying of a "concealed" weapon in "any place" under his/her/its control. There are at least two interpretations that could reasonably be reached. Our office chose to interpret these statutes to mean that an enhanced license holder could carry into a *public building* that is specifically listed in Section 45-9-101(13) even if the controlling entity posted a sign.

With regard to county courthouses, Section 45-9-53 limits the authority of a county to use the signage provisions of Section 45-9-101(13). In Section 45-9-53(4), a county is allowed to post a sign at a location listed in Section 45-9-101(13) only if the sign (in essence) expressly states that it does not apply to enhanced license holders. Thus, it does not appear that a county or a county officer[2] has any authority to restrict an enhanced license holder from entering a county courthouse.

One issue that we believe may be in part the basis for your opinion request involves state judges, such as a chancellor or circuit judge. We have been informed anecdotally and through complaints filed with our office that some judges in the state have issued orders either prohibiting weapons based on inherent judicial powers or stating that the courthouse is an extension of the courtroom and entering orders prohibiting firearms. Section 97-37-7 states: "This section shall in no way interfere with the right of a trial judge to restrict the carrying of firearms in the courtroom." Our office has always taken the position in formal opinions that court orders are to be followed until modified or reversed by an appellate court. To the extent your opinion request encompasses court orders we do not opine on such orders and Section 7-5-25 prohibits the Office of Attorney General from opining on matters in litigation or past conduct.

Whether the statutes on firearm regulations can be read to preclude a judge from ordering a ban on weapons throughout a courthouse in conjunction with the inherent authority the judicial branch has over administration of justice is a matter involving constitutional separation of powers. We do not opine on the constitutional issues that may be raised by your opinion which could implicate the inherent authority of the judicial branch to protect witnesses, jurors, and officers of the court from coercion or danger by methods taken both inside or outside the courtroom. We do note that the Supreme Court has apparently taken a broad view of judicial authority when it comes to matters affecting the courts and administration of justice. *See Hosford v. State*, 525 So. 2d 789, 798 (Miss. 1988)(Court has "inherent authority as part of a separate and co-equal branch to make such orders to insure [its] independence and integrity."). In *Hosford* the Mississippi Supreme Court held that the Circuit Court should have entered an order requiring the board of supervisors to abate a noise nuisance outside the courtroom. Whether under these circumstances here and given the statutes that authorize or fail to prohibit guns in courthouses and courtrooms the Court would find authority in trial courts to prohibit weapons throughout a courthouse is an issue beyond the scope of an official opinion.

B. Question No. 2

Your letter states as follows:

Section 19-25-69 of the Mississippi Code says, "The sheriff shall have charge of the courthouse and jail of his county."

2. Is there any section of the law or any power granted to any other official through statutory or case law that would allow them to usurp

the sheriff's authority or assume his power, imposing restrictions that violate the rights granted to citizens under 97-37-7(2)?

It is the opinion of this office that the Legislature has negated any authority of local sheriffs regarding regulation of firearms in courthouses. However, as noted above a sheriff would be bound by a court order until the order is modified or reversed on appeal. The authority and limited scope of counties with regard to regulating firearms in courthouses are governed, in our opinion, under Section 45-9-51 and Section 45-9-53. Thus, the only places that a county may regulate, under its own authority, the carrying of firearms are at "(i) a public park or at a public meeting of a county, municipality or other governmental body; (ii) a political rally, parade or official political meeting; or (iii) a non-firearm-related school, college or professional athletic event." Miss. Code. Ann. Section 45-9-53(1)(f) (as amended). Counties, pursuant to Section 45-9-53(4), may only post signs at courthouses if, as noted above, the signs state that firearms restrictions apply only to regular, as opposed to enhanced, license holders. Thus, with regard to firearms in courthouses, we are of the opinion that the Legislature, through Sections 45-9-51 and 53, has completely occupied this area of law. Thus, any general authority a sheriff might have had under Section 19-25-69 as it relates to guns is supplanted by the more specific restrictions under Section 45-9-53 that relate specifically to firearms and apply to counties and county officers such as a sheriff.

If this office can be of further assistance, do not hesitate to contact us.

By: Ricky G. Luke
Special Assistant Attorney General

Footnotes

1

The Trapp Opinion has been modified and/or supplanted by legislative amendments to Section 45-9-53, which now significantly limit, if not abolish, a local government's right to use the signage provisions of Section 45-9-101(13). *See* Laws 2014, Ch. 443 (H.B. No. 314), Section 4, eff. July 1, 2014; Laws 2015, Ch. 433 (S.B. No. 2619), Section 4, eff. from and after passage.

2

Sections 45-9-51 and 45-9-53 do not make it clear whether the prohibitions against counties and municipalities regulating the carry of firearms apply only to boards of supervisors and governing bodies of municipalities. We have assumed for opinion purposes that a county officer such as a sheriff is limited in the same manner as a "county" is by these statutes.

Office of the Attorney General
State of Mississippi

Opinion No. 2016-00384

August 26, 2016

Re: Storage and Citizen Access to Public Records

Honorable Dana Criswell
Post Office Box 1321
Olive Branch, MS 38654

Dear Representative Criswell

Attorney General Jim Hood has received your request for an official opinion of this office and assigned it to me for research and response.

Facts and Issues Presented

Your letter states as follows:

I am trying to determine what rights a citizen has to public information when the information is stored in digital format and not designated for a stand-alone computer. For now, I am particularly interested in the Docket of Seized Deadly Weapons (formerly a large bound book) required by MCA 45-9-151.

I have located an opinion that addresses this issue (2003-0664) affirming to Michael Acey of the State Auditor's Office that the docket could be maintained on a computer. But, I also noted that the law enforcement agency would still have to make it available to the public and comply with the Public Records Act.

1. Since that is a 2003 opinion, has anything changed regarding privacy issues, etc. that would preclude the public from having access (including the ability to inspect the records personally) to the Docket of Seized Deadly Weapons?

2. The second question is based on MCA 25-61-10(1). If the agency stores the Docket of Seized Deadly Weapons on a computer where nonpublic records may also be stored, must they use sensitive software that password protects the data but still grants access for the public to "inspect" public records?

3. The third question is based on a review, but not clear understanding of MCA 25-61-7(1). While inspecting records, can the agency assign a senior person (over-watch) and force you to pay a higher cost than that of the lowest grade employee (who may just show you how to use the system and leave you to yourself)?

4. Lastly, can the law enforcement agency physically place the computer hardware that has the Docket of Seized Deadly Weapons and/or other public data in a restricted room not accessible to the public?

Discussion and Legal Analysis

As an initial matter, we must note various restrictions on the formal opinion authority of this office. Our formal opinions are generally limited to the duties and prospective actions of the public official or body requesting the opinion. We do not provide opinions to one entity regarding duties of another nor do we provide opinions that purport to limit or define the rights of private citizens. We do not opine on past actions, and our opinions cannot be used to either validate or invalidate the past actions of a public official or entity. Your questions, although not naming a public body, do appear very specific in nature and presumably could relate to events that either have already transpired or are actions that are currently being undertaken by a public body. This opinion does not adjudicate, validate or invalidate any prior actions or actions by some public entity not requesting a formal opinion of this office.

Additionally and from the nature of your questions, it appears that there may be some confusion regarding the mechanics of how the Mississippi Public Records Act applies (the "Act"). The Act does not create an unfettered right of the public to review or inspect public records on demand. Instead, the Act gives the public the right to inspect documents in accordance with procedures adopted by the agency or after a "written request" has been received by the public entity. The applicable code section states:

(1)(a) Except as otherwise provided by Sections 25-61-9 and 25-61-11, all public records are hereby declared to be public property, and *any person shall have the right to inspect, copy or mechanically reproduce or obtain a reproduction of any public record* of a public body *in accordance with reasonable written procedures adopted by the public body concerning the cost, time, place and method of access*, and public notice of the procedures shall be given by the public body, or, if a public body has not adopted written procedures, *the right to inspect, copy or mechanically reproduce or obtain a reproduction of a public record of the public body shall be provided within one (1) working day after a written request for a public record is made. No public body shall adopt procedures which will authorize the public body to produce or deny production of a public record later than seven (7) working days from the date of the receipt of the request for the production of the record.*

Miss. Code. Ann. Section 25-61-5 (as amended). Thus, if no procedures are adopted, a public body must provide access within one day of a written request. If procedures have been adopted, those procedures may address reasonable procedures on "cost, time, pace and method of access" and access must be allowed within seven days.

There is no general requirement that public records be maintained so that they are instantly available for inspection. Likewise, there are no general prohibitions on where a public body can maintain the records or, with regard to the specific scenario in your letter, where the computers which house the public records must be maintained. The document your letter concerns is the Docket of Seized Deadly Weapons (the "Docket"") which is required by Section 45-9-151. This code section, however, does not mandate that the Docket be made public nor does it mandate any particular access to the Docket. The Docket is a public record by virtue of the definition of Section 25-61-3(b) and access is governed by Section 26-61-5.[1] So long as the public body complies with the Act, there are no specific restrictions on where electronic documents must be maintained, what software must be used or where the computer must be located. Parts of your letter and questions appear to presuppose that there must be some type of public access computer terminal in order to comply with the Act. This is not a necessarily required condition under the Act.

Your first question asks if since our opinion in MS AG Op., Acey (Dec. 19, 2003) was issued, anything has changed to affect the public's ability to access to the Docket. In the Acey opinion, we opined that the Docket is a public record. This remains our opinion, and access to the Docket is still allowed under the provisions and in accordance with the Act.

Your second question asks if an agency stores a Docket "on a computer where nonpublic records may also be stored, must they use sensitive software that password protects the data but still grants access for the public to 'inspect' public records." Sensitive software is a type of data processing software. Section 25-61-9 defines "sensitive" to mean those portions of data processing software, including the specifications and documentation, used to: (a) Collect, process, store, and retrieve information which is exempt under this chapter. (b) Control and direct access authorizations and security measures for automated systems.

(c) Collect, process, store, and retrieve information, disclosure of which would require a significant intrusion into the business of the public body.

Miss. Code. Ann. Section 25-61-9. In our understanding, the use of sensitive software has nothing to do with the use of passwords or whether public records are stored on computers which, likewise, contain documents that are exempt and not subject to disclosure. Section 25-61-10 does not require the use of sensitive software but instead states that if sensitive software is used, such use "will not be deemed to have diminished the right of the public" to inspect and copy a public record so long as the public body either

(a) if legally obtainable, makes a copy of the software available to the public for application to the public records stored, manipulated, or retrieved by the software; or (b) ensures that the software has the capacity to create an electronic copy of each public record stored, manipulated, or retrieved by the software in some common format such as, but not limited to, the American Standard Code for Information Interchange.

Miss. Code. Ann. Section 25-61-10 (as amended).

If sensitive software is used, the public body can assure compliance with the Act by taking either one of the actions listed in subsection (a) or (b). Whether the computer has exempt and nonexempt documents located on it is not relevant. Likewise, the use of passwords is not a relevant consideration. The agency can either provide the software presumably on a computer where the public can inspect the record or provide and electronic copy in a common format such as ASCII.

Your third question asks "can the agency assign a senior person (over-watch) and force you to pay a higher cost than that of the lowest grade employee (who may just show you how to use the system and leave you to yourself)" Section 21-65-7 provides with regard to fees incidental to providing the records, "[a]ny staff time or contractual services included in actual cost shall be at the pay scale of the lowest level employee or contractor competent to respond to the request. What constitutes the lowest level employee competent to provide the needed access is a question of fact which would be dependent on the specific facts related to the individual request. Our office only opines on questions of law, and we cannot answer this specific question other than to say, the law requires the "lowest level employee" that is competent with regard to the request.

Your final question asks "can the law enforcement agency physically place the computer hardware that has the Docket ... and/or other public data in a restricted room not accessible to the public." A public body has no general duty to make a computer available to the public to review public records. A public body could make records available in this manner or as stated above could make records available by providing an electronic copy in ASCII or other common format. Additionally, a public body could make documents such as the Docket available on its website. Thus, there is no law that would prohibit an agency from placing the Docket on a computer which is in a restricted area. The agency has to make public records available on the time line provided in the Act and in the manner specified therein.

Conclusion

In conclusion, there is no general requirement that an agency make a computer available to the public for inspections of public records. The Docket of Seized Deadly Weapons is a public record and must be made available for inspection in accordance with the Public Records Act. The time frame for such inspection could be as little as one or as many as seven days from the request to inspect under the Public Records Act. The document can be made available for inspection on a computer of a public body or can be provided in electronic format or could be posted on the public body's website. There is no requirement that a public body use "sensitive software" only a requirement that if such software is used, certain steps must be taken to ensure public access to public documents is not diminished.

If this office can be of further assistance, do not hesitate to contact us.

By: Ricky G. Luke
Assistant Attorney General

Footnotes

1

The Docket is in contrast to minutes of meetings of public bodies. Minutes are made public by virtue of the Open Meetings Act and under that act, the minutes must be available at any time for inspection during regular business hours. *See* Miss. Code. Ann. § 25-41-11 (as amended)("[M]inutes ... shall be open to public inspection during regular business hours."). There is not similar requirement for the Docket to be made continuously available during business hours.

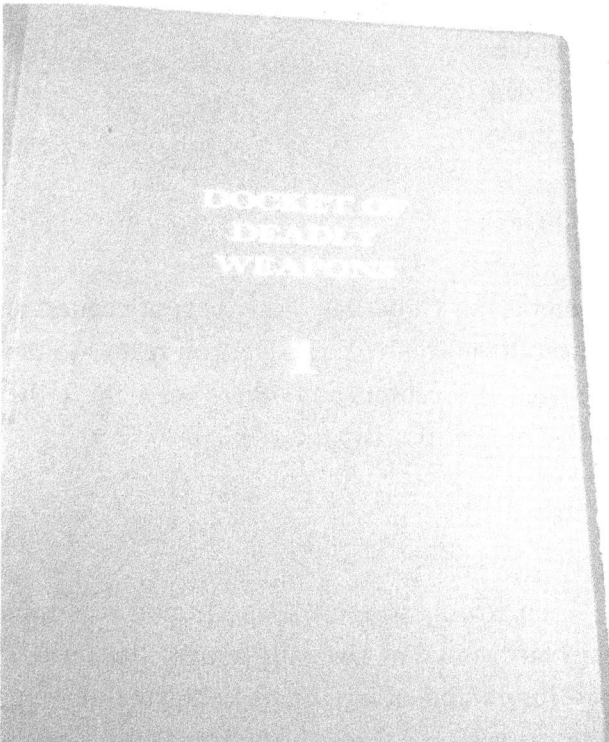

Office of the Attorney General
State of Mississippi

Opinion No. 2016-00415

September 30, 2016

Re: Section 97-37-7 of the Mississippi Code

John Mark Mitchell
Justice Court Judge
75 Timberline Road
Picayune, MS 39466

Dear Judge Mitchell:

Attorney General Jim Hood has received your request and assigned it to me for research and reply. Your question relates to the carrying of a firearm by Judges, Prosecutors and others pursuant to the provisions of Section 97-37-7 of the Mississippi Code.

ISSUE

You state: "I am writing to request an opinion regarding the firearms authorization card issued by law enforcement standards and training to Judges, Prosecutors and others listed in the statute. Question, is this card equal to cards issued through the Department of Public Safety to citizens?

RESPONSE

Section 97-37-7 (2) and (3) provides:

(2) It shall not be a violation of this or any other statute for pistols, firearms or other suitable and appropriate weapons to be carried by Department of Wildlife, Fisheries and Parks law enforcement officers, railroad special agents who are sworn law enforcement officers, investigators employed by the Attorney General, criminal investigators employed by the district attorneys, all prosecutors, public defenders, investigators or probation officers employed by the Department of Corrections, employees of the State Auditor who are authorized by the State Auditor to perform investigative functions, or any deputy fire marshal or investigator employed by the State Fire Marshal, while engaged in the performance of their duties as such, or by fraud investigators with the Department of Human Services, or by judges of the Mississippi Supreme Court, Court of Appeals, circuit, chancery, county, justice and municipal courts, or by coroners. Before any person shall be authorized under this subsection to carry a weapon, he shall complete a weapons training course approved by the Board of Law Enforcement Officer Standards and Training. Before any criminal investigator employed by a district attorney shall be authorized under this section to carry a pistol, firearm or other weapon, he shall have complied with Section 45-6-11 or any training program required for employment as an agent of the Federal Bureau of Investigation. A law enforcement officer, as defined in Section 45-6-3, shall be

authorized to carry weapons in courthouses in performance of his official duties.

A person licensed under Section 45-9-101 to carry a concealed pistol, who (a) has voluntarily completed an instructional course in the safe handling and use of firearms offered by an instructor certified by a nationally recognized organization that customarily offers firearms training, or by any other organization approved by the Department of Public Safety, (b) is a member or veteran of any active or reserve component branch of the United States of America Armed Forces having completed law enforcement or combat training with pistols or other handguns as recognized by such branch after submitting an affidavit attesting to have read, understand and agree to comply with all provisions of the , or (c) is an honorably retired law enforcement officer or honorably retired member or veteran of any active or reserve component branch of the United States of America Armed Forces having completed law enforcement or combat training with pistols or other handguns, after submitting an affidavit attesting to have read, understand and agree to comply with all provisions of Mississippi shall also be authorized to carry weapons in courthouses except in courtrooms during a judicial proceeding, and any location listed in subsection (13) of Section 45-9-101, except any place of nuisance as defined in Section 95-3-1, any police, sheriff or highway patrol station or any detention facility, prison or jail. For the purposes of this subsection (2), component branch of the United States Armed Forces includes the Army, Navy, Air Force, Coast Guard or Marine Corps, or the Army National Guard, the Army National Guard of the United

States, the Air National Guard or the Air National Guard of the United States, as those terms are defined in Section 101, Title 10, United States Code, and any other reserve component of the United States Armed Forces enumerated in Section 10101, Title 10, United States Code. The department shall promulgate rules and regulations allowing concealed pistol permit holders to obtain an endorsement on their permit indicating that they have completed the aforementioned course and have the authority to carry in these locations. This section shall in no way interfere with the right of a trial judge to restrict the carrying of firearms in the courtroom.

(3) It shall not be a violation of this or any other statute for pistols, firearms or other suitable and appropriate weapons, to be carried by any out-of-state, full-time commissioned law enforcement officer who holds a valid commission card from the appropriate out-of-state law enforcement agency and a photo identification. The provisions of this subsection shall only apply if the state where the out-of-state officer is employed has entered into a reciprocity agreement with the state that allows full-time commissioned law enforcement officers in Mississippi to lawfully carry or possess a weapon in such other states. The Commissioner of Public Safety is authorized to enter into reciprocal agreements with other states to carry out the provisions of this subsection.

Section 97-37-7 (2) authorizes the carrying of weapons by the listed individuals and provides that it is "not a violation of this or any other statute for pistols, firearms or other suitable and appropriate weapons to be carried" by the listed individuals. The Board of Law Enforcement Officer Standards and Training provides a "firearms authorization card" for qualified individuals. This is not the same authorization as provided in Section 45-9-101, which provides a license to be issued for the carrying of concealed weapons. Section 97-37-7 (2) authorizes the carrying of the firearm in the State of Mississippi. It does not reference or authorize the carrying of a firearm by the listed individuals out of the State of Mississippi. Whether or not another state would recognize this card would be entirely up to that state.

It is noted that Section 97-37-7 (3), which pertains to full-time commissioned law enforcement officers, authorizes the Department of Public Safety to enter into reciprocal agreements with other states to carry out the provisions of Subsection (3). This language is not contained in Subsection (2). Furthermore, Section 45-9-101(19) authorizes the Department of Public Safety to enter into reciprocal agreements with other states related to the license issued under Section 45-9-101.

The provisions of the authorization card under Section 97-37-7 (2) and the license under Section 49-5-101 are not related, are not the same, and are not equal.

By: James Y. Dale
Special Assistant Attorney General

Office of the Attorney General
State of Mississippi

Opinion No. 2016-00498

December 5, 2016

Re: Gun Possession on Leased Governmental Property

Honorable Dana Criswell
Mississippi House of Representatives
Post Office Box 1018
Jackson, MS 39215-1018

Dear Representative Criswell:

Attorney General Jim Hood has received your request for an official opinion and assigned it to me for research and response.

Background and Issue Presented

Your letter sets out various facts concerning the operation and leasing of a coliseum and convention center in Desoto County known as the Lander's Center. The Lander's Center is owned by Desoto County and under the management of the Desoto County Convention and Visitors Bureau ("Visitors Bureau"). You note a recent email exchange in which the Executive Director of the Visitors Bureau stated:

We follow Sections 45-9-101 and 97-37-7 to carry a concealed firearm, or to a person lawfully carrying a firearm that is not concealed as defined by Section 97-37-1. However, because private entities lease the facility those entities may choose to follow the law as stated or they may choose to prohibit weapons of any kind from entering into their private event. This is established at contract negotiations.

Your question posed is:

[D]oes a private entity who leases a county owned and managed property have the authority to prohibit weapons of any kind from entering into their event? Is there a difference if an entity enters a long-term lease as opposed to a short contract for a single event? If they do have that authority what is considered a "private event"? Is an event that invites public attendance such [as] a concert, hockey game, or county fair considered a "private event"?

Response and Legal Discussion

As an initial matter, we cannot answer your question as posed to us. The question asks us to opine as to the legal rights of private individuals and, specifically, as to rights that may be granted to them by a contract/lease/rental agreement with a governmental entity. As a general matter, our opinions are limited to advising public officials regarding questions of state law concerning prospective actions those officials propose to take. We do not, by official opinion, opine on contractual matters, nor can we adjudicate the rights of any party to a contract. More broadly, we read your question to ask about the authority of a governmental entity to contract for the lease or rental of governmental property wherein the agreement gives the right to control possession of weapons to the private lessor or renter.

As a general matter, a lessor and lessee can agree, unless otherwise prohibited by law, as to the terms and conditions on which a lease agreement is entered. A lease is generally defined to mean a "contract by which one owning such property grants to another the right to possess, use, and enjoy it for specified period of time in exchange for periodic payment of a stipulated price, referred to as rent." *Facilities, Inc. v. Rogers-Usry Chevrolet, Inc.*, 907 So. 2d 960, 964 (Miss. Ct. App. 2004), *rev'd*, 908 So. 2d 107 (Miss. 2005)(*citing* Black's Law Dictionary, Abridged Sixth Edition, 1991, Page 615). Similarly, Black's Law Dictionary, Fifth Edition, defines "lease" as a "contract for exclusive possession of lands or tenements for [a] determinate period." The essence of a lease is that a leasehold interest in real estate is granted, and during the period of the lease, the real estate is under the control of the lessee. We generally discussed this in a prior opinion as follows:

A private property owner or manager of a retail store, grocery store or restaurant may exercise his property rights and deny entry to persons carrying weapons on his property (verbally, by posting a sign or by other means). A private property owner may even prohibit enhanced concealed permit holders from their property. As stated by the Mississippi Supreme Court in *Biglane v. Under the Hill Corporation*, 949 So.2d 9, at 16 (Miss. 2007):

It is a basic tenet of property law that a landowner or **tenant may use the premises they control in whatever fashion they desire, so long as the law is obeyed.** This leads to the logical conclusion that **a** landowner or **valid tenant may forbid any other persons from using their property.** This ideal is protected in our law to the point that there are both civil and criminal prohibitions against trespassing.

See also, GeorgiaCarry.Org v. Georgia, 687 F.3d 1244 (11th Cir. 2012)(2nd amendment **right to bear arms is limited by equally fundamental rights of private property owners to control their property**).

MS AG Op., Lance (June 13, 2013)(emphasis added).

Thus, it is our opinion that, as a general matter, a lease of public property to a private entity can and, in the absence of either a contract provision or provision of law to the contrary, would grant the lessee the right to control the possession of weapons on the property[1] during the term of the lease/rental. We are aware of no law that would prohibit our conclusion or this right of a lessee. We note that there are no legislative pronouncements on point in this area of the gun laws. However, the only legislative action we have found tends to support our conclusion. Section 45-9-101(13), which relates to concealed carry prohibitions, states that the "**person or entity exercising control** over the physical location" of property **can prohibit the carrying** of concealed **firearms** by posting a sign that the "carrying of a pistol or revolver is prohibited."

Section 45-9-53 prohibits a county or municipality from using this provision except in limited circumstances. However, once a county or municipality leases property, that entity is no longer in its control unless such right is reserved under the agreement. Absent such a reservation, it is the lessee who is in control of the premises, and Section 45-9-53 does not prevent a private lessee from posting signs. These statutes are limited in their application, because they apply to concealed weapons; but, as a general matter, they support the premise that a tenant has control over how his or her leased property is used.

Thus, our general opinion is that a private party leasing a facility, as a general matter, has the right to restrict the possession of weapons on the property during the period of the agreement. However, we cannot anticipate each situation that may arise, so we can only opine in the most general manner and caveat our opinion with the warning that any number of facts could change our opinion. Likewise, applicable statutes, ordinances and contractual provisions could affect our opinion.

Your letter also asks us to opine whether a long-term versus short-term lease and whether an event is considered a public versus private event would determine the answer. These types of fact-dependent questions are beyond the purview of an official opinion. Indeed, it would be virtually impossible to account for and identify every potential situation and then discuss it. Moreover, the determinative legal issue appears to be who is in control of the premises and not necessarily the nature of the event. As demonstrated above, a typical lease transfers this type of control to a lessee. However, even the question of control could and likely would turn on either a factual determination or an interpretation of a lease agreement. Both contract and factual issues are beyond the scope of our official opinions.

If this office can be of further assistance, do not hesitate to contact us.

By: Ricky G. Luke
Assistant Attorney General

Footnotes

<u>1</u>
Care must always be taken when we are asked to opine on a broad and undeterminable set of factual circumstances. Thus, we cannot by opinion speak as to all occasions and scenarios. However, by way of example, buildings at the Ag Museum were in the past routinely rented for weddings and similar affairs. It would seem anomalous to reach a conclusion that the leasing party could not prohibit guests at the wedding from bringing firearms.

Chapter Seventeen
Attorney General Opinions 2017
(through March 2017)

Office of the Attorney General
State of Mississippi

Opinion No. 2017-00009

February 3, 2017

Re: Sale of Firearms Pursuant to Section 97-37-3

Nicholas H. Manley, Esq.
Butler Snow
Post Office Box 171443
Memphis, Tennessee 38187-1443

Dear Mr. Manley:

Attorney General Jim Hood is in receipt of your opinion request and has assigned it to me for research and response.

Facts, Issues Presented and Analysis

Your letter states:

Pursuant to Mississippi Code Section 97-37-3, certain firearms were forfeited to the City Police Department. Upon receipt of the firearms and assuming the City Police inventory the firearms, may the City Police then dispose of the firearms pursuant to Section 17-25-25.

In response, Section 97-37-3(1) provides:

(1) **Any weapon** used in violation of Section 97-37-1, or used in the commission of any other crime, shall be seized by the arresting officer, may be introduced in evidence, and in the event of a conviction, shall be ordered to be **forfeited**, and **shall be disposed of as ordered by the court** having jurisdiction of such offense. In the event of dismissal or acquittal of charges, such weapon shall be returned to the accused from whom it was seized.

This office has previously opined that the language in Section 97-37-3(1) grants the court broad discretion in the disposition of weapons, including but not limited to destruction, sale at public auction, and placement on the governmental entity's property rolls, i.e., municipal or county property rolls. MS AG Ops., Jenkins (June 28, 1985); Price (January 31, 1990); Ringer (May 16, 1991); Aldridge (October 9, 1998); and Donald (April 10, 1998).

The legislature amended Section 97-37-3 in 2003 by adding subsection (2) which reads:

(2)   (a) If the weapon to be forfeited is merchantable, the court may order the weapon forfeited to the seizing law enforcement agency.

(b) A weapon so forfeited to a law enforcement agency **may be sold at auction as provided by Sections 19-3-85 and 21-39-21 to a federally-licensed firearms dealer**, with the proceeds from such sale at auction to be used to buy bulletproof vests for the seizing law enforcement agency.

(Emphasis added.)

Subsection (2) provides that once the weapons are forfeited[1] by the court to the seizing law enforcement agency, the seizing law enforcement agency may retain the forfeited weapons or sell them in the manner prescribed in Section 97-37-3(2)(b), absent an order of the court authorizing a different method of disposal.

Section 17-25-25 is a statute of general application and provides other methods of sale/disposal that are not available under Section 97-37-3(2). A court has the discretion under Section 97-37-3(1) to order a disposition of the forfeited weapons in accordance with the provisions of Section 17-25-25 or otherwise. However, in the absence of such an order, the seizing law enforcement agency receiving forfeited weapons must follow the statutory provisions of Section 97-37-3(2).

If this office can be of further assistance, do not hesitate to contact us.

By: Ricky G. Luke
Assistant Attorney General

Footnotes

1

We assume for purposes of this opinion that the provisions of Section 97-37-3 were followed and that the weapons were properly seized and forfeited after conviction pursuant to a court order.

Office of the Attorney General
State of Mississippi

Opinion No. 2016-00475

February 16, 2017

Re: Concealed Weapons on Desoto County School District ("District") Property

Keith Treadway, Esq.
General Counsel
Desoto County Schools
5 East South Street
Hernando, MS 38632

Dear Mr. Treadway:

Attorney General Jim Hood is in receipt of your opinion request and has assigned it to me for research and response.

Facts and Issues Presented

Your letter states:

The District has posted signs outside of both of its school buildings and other buildings stating that pistols or revolvers are prohibited.

The District posted said signs pursuant to Mississippi Code Annotated Section 45-9-101. The District would request opinions on the following:

1. Is the District required to post said notice pursuant to Mississippi Code Annotated Section 45-9-101 in order to prevent holders of a concealed carry permit from carrying a concealed weapon on school or other district property?

2. If the District is required to post a notice or chooses to post the notice should it post additional language making it clear that said notice does not apply to holders of an enhanced permit?

Discussion

As your letter notes, the District has already posted signs, and this opinion does not validate nor invalidate that past action. With regard to prospective signage and postings, we offer the following concerning concealed carry and prohibitive signs under Section 45-9-101(13). In MS AG Op., Cantrell (Oct. 1, 2013), we discussed the rights of individuals with enhanced concealed carry licenses as follows:

Section 97-37-7 (2) was amended in 2011 to create a second category of concealed carry license, commonly called an "enhanced license." This authorizes the enhanced licensee to carry a concealed pistol or revolver even in the places named in Section 45-9-101 (13). In other words, the person holding an enhanced license may carry concealed handguns in the listed locations without violating the concealed weapons law

(Section 97-37-1), whereas the carrying of a concealed handgun in those locations with a standard license does violate that law.

Two of the listed locations are "any elementary or secondary school facility" as well as "any school, college or professional athletic event not related to firearms." Therefore, the holder of an enhanced license does not violate the concealed weapon statute, 97-37-1, by carrying a firearm into a public school facility or non-firearm related athletic event. Further, as we stated in our opinion to Bounds, dated January 5, 2012, it is our opinion that the enhanced permit law is an exception to Section 97-37-17, which otherwise makes it a felony to possess a firearm on educational property.

Noting that "the legislature has expressly stated in Section 97-37-7 (2) that an enhanced permit holder 'shall also be authorized to carry weapons in ... any location listed in subsection (13) of Section 45-9-101,' including 'any elementary or secondary school facility' and 'any school ... athletic event ....'"D', we opined in Cantrell that a school district may not prohibit an enhanced license holder from possessing a concealed weapon on school property. We did, however, opine that a school district could deny even an enhanced license holder from access "to non-public area[s] of the school."

Thus, as a general matter, a school district may not prohibit an enhanced concealed license holder from carrying on school property by virtue of a sign posted pursuant to Section 45-9-101(13). With regard to your question number 1, we answer it with respect to a regular concealed license holder. A school district is not required to post a sign under Section 45-9-101(13) in order to prohibit a regular license holder from possessing a concealed weapon. Section 97-37-1 makes it unlawful for a person to carry concealed any "deadly weapon" except as provided for in Section 45-9-101. Section 45-9-101(13), in turn, states that "[n]o license issued pursuant to this section shall authorize any person to carry a stun gun, concealed pistol or revolver into ... any elementary or secondary school facility." Thus, it is a violation of state law for a regular concealed license holder to carry a weapon onto school property, and this violation is not dependent on the posting or presence of any sign.

Your last question is if the District, in fact, posts a sign, must it contain language that it does not apply to enhanced license holders. The District's schools are locations listed in Section 45-9-101(13). Section 45-9-53(4)(a) states that a county may post signs "[a]t a location listed in Section 45-9-101(13) ... as long as the sign also indicates that carrying a firearm is unauthorized only for license holders without a training endorsement ..." Thus, because the District's schools are listed in Section 45-9-101(13), the signs must give notice that the carry prohibitions do not apply to holders of enhanced concealed licenses.

If this office can be of further assistance, do not hesitate to contact us.

By: Ricky G. Luke
Assistant Attorney General

Chapter Eighteen
Federal Gun Laws

I get asked all the time in enhanced classes about federal laws. They want to know if they can carry in federal buildings like post offices, etc. They want to know about carrying into Federal Gun Free School Zones. Some want to know about military bases or Indian Reservation and others are curious about the Natchez Trace and other Federal Park Facilities. Lastly, they want to know about carrying their weapons through those states that don't reciprocate, in accordance with federal law.

I won't try to address all federal laws but I will include the laws that apply to the above questions. Anybody unsure of what the law really says should consult an attorney. I may comment on what I think it means but that is not carved in stone, nor is it legal advice or intended to be.

First I would like to say, I lived in Brandon for several years and the post office I used had no signage. I often go to the main post office downtown where my niece has worked for years. The only signs they have posted are No Smoking and a small red decal that says robbing the facility would be a federal crime.

The first law I will address is the federal law that prohibits guns in federal buildings. If you intend to scan over it, at least read the last paragraph highlighted in bold and underlined. It makes all the difference.

18 U.S.C. § 930: US Code - Section 930: Possession of firearms and dangerous weapons in Federal facilities

(a)   Except as provided in subsection (d), whoever knowingly possesses or causes to be present a firearm or other dangerous weapon in a Federal facility (other than a Federal court facility), or attempts to do so, shall be fined under this title or imprisoned not more than 1 year, or both.

(b)   Whoever, with intent that a firearm or other dangerous weapon be used in the commission of a crime, knowingly possesses or causes to be present such firearm or dangerous weapon in a Federal facility, or attempts to do so, shall be fined under this title or imprisoned not more than 5 years, or both.

(c)   A person who kills any person in the course of a violation of subsection (a) or (b), or in the course of an attack on a Federal facility involving the use of a firearm or other dangerous weapon, or attempts or conspires to do such an act, shall be punished as provided in sections 1111, 1112, 1113, and 1117.

(d)   Subsection (a) shall not apply to - (1) the lawful performance of official duties by an officer, agent, or employee of the United States, a

(e)   State, or a political subdivision thereof, who is authorized by law to engage in or supervise the prevention, detection, investigation, or prosecution of any violation of law; (2) the possession of a firearm or other dangerous weapon by a Federal official or a member of the Armed Forces if such possession is authorized by law; or (3) the lawful carrying of firearms or other dangerous weapons in a Federal facility incident to hunting or other lawful purposes.

(e)(1) Except as provided in paragraph (2), whoever knowingly possesses or causes to be present a firearm or other dangerous weapon in a Federal court facility, or attempts to do so, shall be fined under this title, imprisoned not more than 2 years, or both. (2) Paragraph (1) shall not apply to conduct which is described in paragraph (1) or (2) of subsection (d).

(f) Nothing in this section limits the power of a court of the United States to punish for contempt or to promulgate rules or orders regulating, restricting, or prohibiting the possession of weapons within any building housing such court or any of its proceedings, or upon any grounds appurtenant to such building. (

g) As used in this section: (1) The term "Federal facility" means a building or part thereof owned or leased by the Federal Government, where Federal employees are regularly present for the purpose of performing their official duties. (2) The term "dangerous weapon" means a weapon, device, instrument, material, or substance, animate or inanimate, that is used for, or is readily capable of, causing death or serious bodily injury, except that such term does not include a pocket knife with a blade of less than 2 1/2 inches in length. (3) The term "Federal court facility" means the courtroom, judges' chambers, witness rooms, jury deliberation rooms, attorney conference rooms, prisoner holding cells, offices of the court clerks, the United States attorney, and the United States marshal, probation and parole offices, and adjoining corridors of any court of the United States.

(h) Notice of the provisions of subsections (a) and (b) shall be posted conspicuously at each public entrance to each Federal facility, and notice of subsection (e) shall be posted conspicuously at each public entrance to each Federal court facility, and no person shall be convicted of an offense under subsection (a) or (e) with respect to a Federal facility if such notice is not so posted at such facility, unless such person had actual notice of subsection (a) or (e), as the case may be.

18 USC 922(q)(1) Federal Gun-Free School Zones

(2) (A) It shall be unlawful for any individual knowingly to possess a firearm that has moved in or that otherwise affects interstate or foreign commerce at a place that the individual knows, or has reasonable cause to believe, is a school zone.

(B) Subparagraph (A) does not apply to the possession of a firearm--

(i) on private property not part of school grounds;

(ii) *if the individual possessing the firearm is licensed to do so by the State in which the school zone is located or a political subdivision of the State, and the law of the State or political subdivision requires that, before an individual obtains such a license, the law enforcement authorities of the State or political subdivision verify that the individual is qualified under law to receive the license;*

(iii) *that is--*

(I) not loaded; and

(II) in a locked container, or a locked firearms rack that is on a motor vehicle;

(iv) by an individual for use in a program approved by a school in the school zone;

by an individual in accordance with a contract entered into between a school in the school zone and the individual or an employer of the individual; by a law enforcement officer acting in his or her official capacity; or

that is unloaded and is possessed by an individual while traversing school premises for the purpose of gaining access to public or private lands open to hunting, if the entry on school premises is authorized by school authorities.

(3) (A) Except as provided in subparagraph (B), it shall be unlawful for any person, knowingly or with reckless disregard for the safety of another, to discharge or attempt to discharge a firearm that has moved in or that otherwise affects interstate or foreign commerce at a place that the person knows is a school zone.

(B) Subparagraph (A) does not apply to the discharge of a firearm--

on private property not part of school grounds;

as part of a program approved by a school in the school zone, by an individual who is participating in the program;

by an individual in accordance with a contract entered into between a school in a school zone and the individual or an employer of the individual; or by a law enforcement officer acting in his or her official capacity.

(4) Nothing in this subsection shall be construed as preempting or preventing a State or local government from enacting a statute establishing gun free school zones as provided in this subsection.

Regulation 90-114

Regulation 90-114 regulates firearms on military bases.

It was implemented by President Bill Clinton in 1993. This regulation made military installations gun free-zones. Military and civilian personnel are prohibited from possessing weapons without special authorization. This policy includes those living on military bases who are not allowed to keep personal weapons in their domiciles.

Individuals authorized to carry firearms may be involved in law enforcement or base security, including the protection of military or civilian personnel, protection of classified documents or military equipment, and guarding prisoners. Generally, authority is implied when ammunition is issued with the weapon.

Military or civilian personnel prohibited from carrying weapons on military bases include those who are medically disqualified, have had a security clearance revoked or denied, or those who are taking medication which may impair judgment. Additionally, anyone who has consumed alcohol within the past 8 hours is denied access to firearms.

The Pentagon expounded on this Presidential Order as it applies to military personnel in 2010. Law enforcement and security personnel are authorized to carry weapons consistent with their duties by field grade officers-- or the civilian equivalent--of GS-12 or higher. Authorization for carrying a weapon for personal protection is based on case-by-case basis. The Secretary of the Army reserves the right to authorize the carrying of weapons for personal protection within the United States. The carrying of weapons on military installations outside of United States is authorized by the base commanders.

<u>Carrying of Firearms on the Natchez Trace (from their website)</u>

Any firearm that is prohibited by State or Federal law is prohibited on the Parkway.

As of February 22, 2010, a new federal law allows people who can legally possess firearms under applicable federal, state, and local laws, to legally possess firearms in this park. It is the responsibility of visitors to understand and comply with all applicable state, local, and federal firearms laws before entering this park.

In addition, Federal law prohibits firearms in certain facilities in this park. Those facilities are posted at public entrances to identify them and notify the public that firearms are not allowed in those areas.

Mississippi State Law Synopsis (Mile Post 1-310)

Any Firearm that is legal to possess under state law may be carried in your personal vehicle while traveling the Natchez Trace Parkway.

Effective July 1, 2010 in Mississippi, the possession of a handgun permit is required when in possession of a concealed handgun outside your vehicle.

NOTE: Even though Mississippi authorized non-permit concealed carry in 2016, as of yet the Natchez Trace has not indicated that it will allow a person outside a vehicle on the Trace with a concealed handgun.

https://www.nps.gov/natr/learn/management/firearms-policy.htm

FIREARMS IN NATIONAL PARKS (National Park Service website)

As of February 2010 concealed handguns are for the first time legal in all but 3 of the nation's 391 national parks and wildlife refuges so long as all applicable federal, state, and local regulations are adhered to. Hawaii is a notable exception. Concealed and open carry are both illegal in Hawaii for all except retired military or law enforcement personnel. Previously firearms were allowed in parks non-concealed and unloaded.

That means people can openly carry legal handguns, rifles, shotguns and other firearms and also may carry concealed guns as allowed by state statute. While this law changes gun regulations in national parks, there are still many important restrictions on the transportation and use of guns under state and federal laws:

(8) The Federal laws should make it clear that the second amendment rights of an individual at a unit of the National Park System or the National Wildlife Refuge System should not be infringed.

PROTECTING THE RIGHT OF INDIVIDUALS TO BEAR ARMS

IN UNITS OF THE NATIONAL PARK SYSTEM AND THE NATIONAL

WILDLIFE REFUGE SYSTEM.—The Secretary of the Interior shall not promulgate or enforce any regulation that prohibits an individual from possessing a firearm including an assembled or functional firearm in any unit of the National Park System or the National Wildlife Refuge System if—(1) the individual is not otherwise prohibited by law from possessing the firearm; and (2) the possession of the firearm is in compliance with the law of the State in which the unit of the National Park System or the National Wildlife Refuge System is located. (SEE COMMON QUESTIONS/ANSWERS NEXT PAGE)

https://www.nps.gov/appa/learn/management/questions-and-answers.htm

COMMON QUESTIONS AND ANSWERS

Q. Can I have a firearm in every park after February 22, 2010?

A. If you can legally possess a firearm outside of a national park, you can possess it in that park on and after February 22, 2010. It is up to visitors to understand the requirements of federal law and the laws of the states/localities they live in or are travelling to (or through). Park websites have been updated to offer basic information about the applicable state law(s) and will generally include a link to a state website with more information.

Q. How do I know where I can take a firearm?

A. *It is the responsibility of each individual to know and understand applicable federal, state, and local firearms laws.*

Q. Can I openly carry my firearm in a national park?

A. *If it is allowed by applicable federal, state, and local firearms laws.*

Q. Can I carry a concealed firearm in a national park?

A. *If it is allowed by applicable federal, state, and local firearms laws.00*

Q. Can I have a firearm in my car or tent?

A. *If it is allowed by applicable federal, state, and local firearms laws.*

Q. Can I take a firearm anywhere I go in the park?

A. *No. Federal law prohibits firearms in "federal facilities," which are generally defined as federally-owned or -leased buildings where federal employees work on a regular basis. Buildings that meet this definition will have signs posted at public entrances noting the prohibition on firearms.*

Q. I've got my firearm, can I hunt while I'm here?

A. *Only a limited number of national parks allow hunting. You must adhere to the park's hunting rules and regulations.*

Q. I have a permit to carry a concealed firearm from my home state, does that allow me to carry a firearm here?

A. Some permits are recognized in multiple states, many are not. It is up to the individual to know which states accept their concealed carry permit.

Q. How do I know when I'm in a national park?

A: National parks will generally have posted signs indicating that you are entering a national park. In backcountry areas or large expanses such as those in Great Smoky Mountains National Park or Yellowstone National Park, it is up to the individual to know where they are and what the laws of that state are.

Q. Where can I find the firearms laws for each state?

A: Go to the following link for individual state websites. http://www.usa.gov/Agencies/State_and_Territories.shtml

Q. What kinds of firearms are allowed?

A: Any firearm that is not prohibited by applicable federal, state, or local law.

Q. My family and I come here to enjoy the peacefulness of the park – why is the National Park Service allowing people to bring firearms?

A. Firearms are allowed – consistent with applicable federal, state, and local firearms laws – as a result of a new federal law enacted in May 2009.

Q. What should I do if I feel threatened by someone with a firearm?

A. Contact the nearest park ranger or contact the park office and let them know why you feel threatened.

Q. What should I do if I see someone drinking alcohol who has a firearm?

A. *Contact the nearest park ranger or contact the park office and report what you have seen*

THIS INFORMATION IS ACCURATE AS OF APRIL 1, 2017.

FEDERAL LAW ON "TRANSPORTING (NOT CARRYING ON PERSON) IN STATES WHERE RECIPROCITY IS NOT AN OPTION

18 USC § 926A - INTERSTATE TRANSPORTATION OF FIREARMS

Notwithstanding any other provision of any law or any rule or regulation of a State or any political subdivision thereof, any person who is not otherwise prohibited by this chapter from transporting, shipping, or receiving a firearm shall be entitled to transport a firearm for any lawful purpose from any place where he may lawfully possess and carry such firearm to any other place where he may lawfully possess and carry such firearm if, during such transportation the firearm is unloaded, and neither the firearm nor any ammunition being transported is readily accessible or is directly accessible from the passenger compartment of such transporting vehicle: Provided, That in the case of a vehicle without a compartment separate from the driver's compartment the firearm or ammunition shall be contained in a locked container other than the glove compartment or console.

NOTE:

Until you pass into the TSA area of an airport in Mississippi you are not on federal property. Although the Jackson Airport has a "no gun" sign upon entry I would personally carry a gun onto their premises if I were there only to pick up somebody or take somebody to buy a ticket. I would not cross the protected area under TSA control though. If you want legal advice on this subject, ask a lawyer.

MISSISSIPPI BAND OF CHOCTAW INDIAN RESERVATION LANDS

§3-6-17   Carrying a Concealed Deadly Weapon

Any person who shall go about in public places with a deadly weapon concealed in whole or in part upon his person or in his possession shall be deemed guilty of this offense. For purposes of this title, a "deadly weapon" is defined as any firearm, whether loaded or unloaded; or any weapon which is capable of producing death or great bodily harm, including but not restricted to any type of daggers, brass knuckles, switchblade knives, Bowie knives, poniards, butcher knives, dirk knives and all such weapons with which dangerous cuts can be given, or with which dangerous thrusts can be inflicted, including swordcanes, and any kind of sharp pointed canes, also slingshots, slung shots, bludgeons; or any other weapons with which dangerous wounds can be inflicted.

Any person found in violation of subsection 1 of this section shall have said weapon seized by the arresting officer and such weapon upon conviction of the person charged shall be disposed of as ordered by the court.

Carrying a concealed weapon is a Class B offense.

There is no indication in their law that they honor Mississippi law concerning concealed or open carry. However a Class B offense only requires a $250 cash or surety bond and does not require a personal appearance before a judge if the defendant chooses to pay a fine, or forfeit the cash bond.

Mississippi Band of Choctaw Indians
Office of the Tribal Chief

P.O. Box 6010
Choctaw, Mississippi 39350
601.656.5251

18 U.S. Code § 926B - Carrying of concealed firearms by qualified law enforcement officers

(a)   Notwithstanding any other provision of the law of any State or any political subdivision thereof, an individual who is a qualified law enforcement officer and who is carrying the identification required by subsection (d) may carry a concealed firearm that has been shipped or transported in interstate or foreign commerce, subject to subsection (b).

(b)   This section shall not be construed to supersede or limit the laws of any State that—

(1)   permit private persons or entities to prohibit or restrict the possession of concealed firearms on their property; or

(2)   prohibit or restrict the possession of firearms on any State or local government property, installation, building, base, or park.

(c) As used in this section, the term "qualified law enforcement officer" means an employee of a governmental agency who—

(1) is authorized by law to engage in or supervise the prevention, detection, investigation, or prosecution of, or the incarceration of any person for, any violation of law, and has statutory powers of arrest or apprehension under section 807 (b) of title 10, United States Code (article 7(b) of the Uniform Code of Military Justice);

(2) is authorized by the agency to carry a firearm;

(3) is not the subject of any disciplinary action by the agency which could result in suspension or loss of police powers;

(4) meets standards, if any, established by the agency which require the employee to regularly qualify in the use of a firearm;

(5) is not under the influence of alcohol or another intoxicating or hallucinatory drug or substance; and

(6) is not prohibited by Federal law from receiving a firearm.

(d) The identification required by this subsection is the photographic identification issued by the governmental agency for which the individual is employed that identifies the employee as a police officer or law enforcement officer of the agency.

(e) As used in this section, the term "firearm"—

(1) except as provided in this subsection, has the same meaning as in section 921 of this title;

(2) includes ammunition not expressly prohibited by Federal law or subject to the provisions of the National Firearms Act; and

(3) does not include—

(A) any machinegun (as defined in section 5845 of the National Firearms Act);

(B) any firearm silencer (as defined in section 921 of this title); and

(C) any destructive device (as defined in section 921 of this title).

(f) For the purposes of this section, a law enforcement officer of the Amtrak Police Department, a law enforcement officer of the Federal Reserve, or a law enforcement or police officer of the executive branch of the Federal Government qualifies as an employee of a governmental agency who is authorized by law to engage in or supervise the prevention, detection, investigation, or prosecution of, or the incarceration of any person for, any violation of law, and has statutory powers of arrest or apprehension under section 807 (b) of title 10, United States Code (article 7(b) of the Uniform Code of Military Justice).

(a)   Notwithstanding any other provision of the law of any State or any political subdivision thereof, an individual who is a qualified retired law enforcement officer and who is carrying the identification required by subsection (d) may carry a concealed firearm that has been shipped or transported in interstate or foreign commerce, subject to subsection (b).

(b)   This section shall not be construed to supersede or limit the laws of any State that—

(1)   permit private persons or entities to prohibit or restrict the possession of concealed firearms on their property; or

(2)   prohibit or restrict the possession of firearms on any State or local government property, installation, building, base, or park.

(c) As used in this section, the term "qualified retired law enforcement officer" means an individual who—

(1)　　separated from service in good standing from service with a public agency as a law enforcement officer;

(2)　　before such separation, was authorized by law to engage in or super-vise the prevention, detection, investigation, or prosecution of, or the incarceration of any person for, any violation of law, and had statutory powers of arrest or apprehension under section 807 (b) of title 10, United States Code (article 7(b) of the Uniform Code of Military Justice);

(3)　　(A) before such separation, served as a law enforcement officer for an aggregate of 10 years or more; or

(B) separated from service with such agency, after completing any applicable probationary period of such service, due to a service-connected disability, as determined by such agency;

(4)　　during the most recent 12-month period, has met, at the expense of the individual, the standards for qualification in firearms training for active law enforcement officers, as determined by the former agency of the individual, the State in which the individual resides or, if the State has not established such standards, either a law enforcement agency within the State in which the individual resides or the standards used by a certified firearms instructor that is qualified to conduct a firearms qualification test for active duty officers within that State;

(5)   (A) has not been officially found by a qualified medical professional employed by the agency to be unqualified for reasons relating to mental health and as a result of this finding will not be issued the photographic identification as described in subsection (d)(1); or

(B) has not entered into an agreement with the agency from which the individual is separating from service in which that individual acknowledges he or she is not qualified under this section for reasons relating to mental health and for those reasons will not receive or accept the photographic identification as described in subsection (d)(1);

(6) is not under the influence of alcohol or another intoxicating or   hallucinatory drug or substance; and

(7) is not prohibited by Federal law from receiving a firearm.

(d) The identification required by this subsection is—
(1)   a photographic identification issued by the agency from which the individual separated from service as a law enforcement officer that identifies the person as having been employed as a police officer or law enforcement officer and indicates that the individual has, not less recently than one year before the date the individual is carrying the concealed firearm, been tested or otherwise found by the agency to meet the active duty standards for qualification in firearms training as established by the agency to carry a firearm of the same type as the concealed firearm; or

(2)   (A) a photographic identification issued by the agency from which the individual separated from service as a law enforcement officer that

(3)   *identifies the person as having been employed as a police officer or law enforcement officer; and*

(B) a certification issued by the State in which the individual resides or by a certified firearms instructor that is qualified to conduct a firearms qualification test for active duty officers within that State that indicates that the individual has, not less than 1 year before the date the individual is carrying the concealed firearm, been tested or otherwise found by the State or a certified firearms instructor that is qualified to conduct a firearms qualification test for active duty officers within that State to have met—

(I)   *the active duty standards for qualification in firearms training, as established by the State, to carry a firearm of the same type as the concealed firearm; or*

(II)   *if the State has not established such standards, standards set by any law enforcement agency within that State to carry a firearm of the same type as the concealed firearm.*

(e) As used in this section—

(1) the term "firearm"—

(A) except as provided in this paragraph, has the same meaning as in section 921 of this title;

(B) includes ammunition not expressly prohibited by Federal law or subject to the provisions of the National Firearms Act; and

(C) does not include—

(i) any machinegun (as defined in section 5845 of the National Firearms Act);

(ii) any firearm silencer (as defined in section 921 of this title); and

(iii) any destructive device (as defined in section 921 of this title); and

(4)   the term "service with a public agency as a law enforcement officer" includes service as a law enforcement officer of the Amtrak Police Department, service as a law enforcement officer of the Federal Reserve, or service as a law enforcement or police officer of the executive branch of the Federal Government.

I hope you enjoyed reading this book as much as I enjoyed writing it !!!

If you have any questions or comments anytime you are welcome to call me at

601-665-6088 or email me at rickward47@hotmail.com Thank you very much.

About the Author

I began my law enforcement career in 1975. I joined the pistol team that next year and also got shot in the line of duty the following year. I lost interest quickly in competition shooting and always thought of shooting after that as a very serious matter, not a sport. Over the next several years with the Mississippi Bureau of Narcotics and landing at the Desoto County Sheriff's Department, I built a range on county property using county asphalt equipment to build lanes up to 50 yards from the target.

I went back into the Navy Law Enforcement Program in 1983 and became a Navy Small Arms Instructor after 2 weeks intense training at the Naval Amphibious Base in Little Creek, VA. I continued to instruct and began to specialize in Close-In Protection as Officer in Charge of the Dignitary Protection Unit. I began to realize that long range shooting for self-protection was not only unnecessary, but improper. I began training with the FBI SWAT Team in San Juan, Puerto Rico and most of the firearms training involved close-in shooting after breaching houses.

I later became Security Officer in Charge of Military Police Operations at Pearl Harbor, HI and then a base hidden in Pineapple fields on the North side of the island where NSA operations were run. I made sure all my military police personnel were trained in Close Quarter Combat Shooting.

I left active duty in 1995 for 5 more years, remaining in the reserves and worked as an Attorney General Investigator and then Gaming Commission Division Director. I continued to push the need for close-in shooting.

I went back on active duty in 2000 and took charge of the Counter Drug Operations, pilot/crew protection in El Salvador and personally conducted all firearms training of protection personnel with embassy weapons.

My last 5 years were spent as Navy Region Northeast Officer in Charge of all security, ending with my assignment to NCIS in Washington, DC. and Commander, Navy Installations Command, Washington, D.C.

After retiring from the Navy officially on February 6, 2006 after 20 total active years service, I went back to work for the Navy as a Defense Contractor for one year before becoming a sub-contractor for the company I worked for another 4 years. I r eitred in late 2011.

On April 21, 2012, I became the 53rd instructor approved by the Mississippi Department of Public Safety to teach the Enhanced Concealed Firearms Course. At that time most of the other instructors saw it as a part-time job serving as a weekend warrior in the general vicinity of where they lived. There were many instructors in the same counties and many of our 82 counties without instructors. I developed a model to teach all over the state, any day of the week and would take the training to the customer. All I asked was that they provide the land to shoot on and a place to have the classroom portion. I gave a free seat if they set up the class and got the students, another one for providing the land and other one for providing a classroom.

I wrote my own book on the training and laws and provided them as textbooks for the classes. I purchased land in Covington County and set up a range and classroom to teach classes at home as well teaching hundreds from the Hattiesburg area. I quit counting the classes in 2016 after my student roster exceeded 3,000.

Now I am in semi-retirement still doing classes for friends, forcing public

officials to do their jobs every chance I get and challenging court rulings.

Lieutenant Commander Rick Ward
Staff Photo, USN
2004 Naval Criminal Investigative Command (NCIS) Washington, DC
(Retired 2 years later)

www.ingramcontent.com/pod-product-compliance
Lightning Source LLC
Chambersburg PA
CBHW020603270326
41927CB00005B/148